Social Work with Older People

Second Edition

Social Work
with
Older People

Betsy Ledbetter Hancock, ACSW

BELMONT COLLEGE

PRENTICE HALL, ENGLEWOOD CLIFFS, NEW JERSEY 07632

Library of Congress Cataloging-in-Publication Data

HANCOCK, BETSY LEDBETTER.
Social work with older people/Betsy Ledbetter Hancock.—2nd
  ed.
    p. cm.
    Includes bibliographical references.
    ISBN 0-13-816968-3
    1. Social work with the aged—United States. 2. Aged—Health and
hygiene—United States. 3. Medical social work—United States—Case
studies. 4. Social work with the aged—United States—Case studies.
I. Title
HV1461.H33   1990   89-25585
362.6'0973--dc20

Editorial/production supervision: *Edith Riker/Chris Nassauer*
Cover design: *Bruce Kenselaar*
Manufacturing buyer: *Ed O'Dougherty*

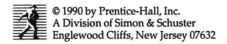
Printed in the United States of America

10 9 8 7 6 5 4 3 2 1

ISBN   0-13-816968-3

Prentice-Hall International (UK) Limited, *London*
Prentice-Hall of Australia Pty. Limited, *Sydney*
Prentice-Hall Canada Inc., *Toronto*
Prentice-Hall Hispanoamericana, S.A., *Mexico*
Prentice-Hall of India Private Limited, *New Delhi*
Prentice-Hall of Japan, Inc., *Tokyo*
Simon & Schuster Asia Pte. Ltd., *Singapore*
Editora Prentice-Hall do Brasil, Ltda. *Rio de Janeiro*

In memory of my parents

MYRTLE ALLEN
and
JOHN HENRY LEDBETTER, M.D.

CONTENTS

PREFACE

The most striking demographic change to occur in this country has been the aging of the nation's population. There are now 25 million Americans over 65 years old—a figure that is expected to increase to nearly 32 million by the year 2000. The implications of this large number of individuals, in terms of assessing and meeting economic, health, and social needs, are prodigious.

Social work educators are aware of the need for social work input in planning policy, preparing new programs, and delivering services to the older population. Many books pertaining to these issues have been published, as well as books on social work practice with older people. However, there has been less focus on health aspects, except in relation to residents in hospitals and long-term-care facilities. The majority of older people who come to the attention of social workers in the community, as well as in health-care settings, are coping with physiological changes and chronic disease in addition to emotional and other problems. Some understanding of health problems of the elderly is a vital basic component in the knowledge base required for working with older clients.

A major purpose of this book is to promote awareness of the preventive aspects of social work intervention in relation to working with older people. Some health conditions, such as hypothermia, are preventable, just as some family problems, such as abuse of the older person, may be prevented by being alert to the signs and symptoms of a developing crisis.

An important objective of *Social Work with Older People* is to help those who work with this population to overcome stereotypes associated with old age. Repeated emphasis is placed on the *diversity* of the aging population, the complexity of older individuals, and the fact that they have many of the needs of people in any age group.

This textbook is intended primarily for those graduate and undergraduate social work students and practitioners who are interested in providing services to the older population. However, the information and suggested methods of service provision should also be of interest to members of other disciplines involved in providing services for older people. Case examples are presented throughout the book to demonstrate possible methods that may be used. They are not extensive, in-depth studies, but contain as many variables as needed for a comprehensive illustration. The need for case management skills, knowledge and use of community resources, and the advocacy role are emphasized. One specific method is not singled out for use. Task-oriented, problem-solving approaches, behavior modification, insight and supportive therapy are used in the case examples. The importance of the environment in relation to the older individual and consideration of the systems with which older people interact are stressed.

Social Work with Older People consists of four parts. Part One introduces the reader to the older population, identifying some of the myths associated with old age and the aging process. A number of the changes in cultural attitudes and events that have taken place in the past hundred years are discussed in order to provide some idea of the cultural context of men and women who are now in their sixties, seventies, and older. Members of the older population are presented as strong men and women, survivors who have managed to live to old age in spite of the effects of physical and mental trauma. Part Two deals with mental and physical conditions that may impair physical and mental function and the ways that social workers may assist the older person to cope with these conditions and continue functioning. Chapters 2 and 3 are concerned with helping older clients to deal with physical problems: stroke, cancer, heart attacks, hypertension, arthritis, impaired hearing, and other chronic conditions that plague the older population. Chapters 4 and 5 focus on brain disorders that can be reversed or prevented and the progressive, deteriorating effects of the irreversible Alzheimer's disease. The role of the social worker in helping to identify reversible disorders is described; ways of working with patient and family to reduce stress and keep the older person functioning are explored. In Chapter 6 the major psychiatric problem of old age, depression, and other psychiatric problems that are predominant among older people are discussed.

Throughout the section on physical and mental conditions, the reader is repeatedly reminded that the *majority* of older people are able to cope with the physiological changes and the chronic conditions that occur with aging, but that the *minority* are probably most likely to come to social work attention. Social workers can be effective with both groups. They can be instrumental in improving the quality of life of the coping elderly and can work toward maintaining function in the more disabled elderly. Attention is also called to the fact that the family may be the major client, as in the case of Alzheimer's disease, and frequently needs help in dealing with their own stresses and losses in relation to the aging spouse or relative.

Emphasis is placed on the social worker's responsibility to acquire a good understanding of the older individual's specific health condition in order to counsel and plan effectively with the client.

Part Three describes the kinds of social work services that are provided in hospitals and nursing homes. Problems that are indigenous to each setting are described, and social work methods for intervening to resolve or ameliorate the problems are presented. Part Four is involved with measures that help keep older men and women in the mainstream of life. The focus in this part of the book is on providing services to more able-bodied older individuals. Preventing bodily deterioration and preserving function are emphasized. Chapter 9 deals with the role of nutrition and exercise in maintaining health, and Chapter 10 discusses the physiological changes in relation to sexual activity and attitudes toward sex. The need for consideration of sexuality as a human component in old age as well as youth is treated. The identification and prevention of potential problems arising from bereavement, retirement, and stresses associated with home care of the aged, which may result in abuse, are discussed in Chapter 11. Chapter 12 presents community supports and services that social workers may use to maintain older people in the community. Legal questions in relation to common marriage, willing property, and the like are also briefly discussed with the reminder that advice from a qualified attorney should be obtained before decisions are made and carried out.

CHANGES IN THE SECOND EDITION

Data in each of the chapters have been updated wherever possible. Additional resources to assist older people are provided in various chapters, and an appendix has been added which lists all of the resources mentioned in the book. Chapter Three includes an addition related to policies on energy. In Chapter Five, the suggestions on helping families of Alzheimer's patients have been reorganized and are more inclusive. A section on case management has been added to Chapter Six. Discussions of new legislation that affects the health needs of the elderly, the Medicare Catastrophic Coverage Act and the Omnibus Budget Reconciliation Act of 1987 (OBRA 87), have been added to Chapter Seven. Information on AIDS is included in Chapter 10.

ACKNOWLEDGMENTS

There are a great many people, besides the author, involved in the output of a book. There must also be a patient family, such as mine, who exercises an inordinate forbearance for the duration of the project.

Many social workers in the field, as well as administrators and educators, contributed suggestions. For their observations on topics related to their areas of expertise, I owe thanks to social workers Stephanie Doehring, Joe Eades, Paula Fogelburg, Dorothy Gager, Adelaide Hohannes, Debbie Martin, David Moulder, Joe Moore, Betty Neiswender, Virginia Patterson, and Sam Tomlin.

Several obliging physicians provided helpful comments on various chapters. I am very much indebted to Roy Elam, M.D., Teresa Huggins, M.D., Georgia Montouris, M.D., and A. Dixon Weatherhead, M.D. for their time and suggestions.

Special mention must be made of my niece and nephew, Barbara Heflin, M.S.S.W. and B.B. Ledbetter, Jr., M.D., for their enthusiasm and interest, in addition to their thoughtful observations throughout the preparation of the manuscript.

An overall attempt has been made in this revision to make *Social Work with Older People* a more useful practice manual to help the elderly. I would like to express once more my sincere and grateful thanks to all of those individuals who assisted with the first edition of the book and those who were called upon again and responded so helpfully.

1

THE SURVIVORS

The literature on aging in general can be overwhelming, for much of it is dedicated to the recounting of losses that can occur: loss of family and friends through absence or death, loss of health, and loss of income. The unfortunate implications often seem to be that advanced age is synonymous with grief, senility, disability, and poverty. Popular misconceptions add to the generally negative attitudes toward aging.

The fact that older people have lived through times of cultural, economic, and technological change unmatched by any other century is sometimes overlooked. Some understanding of the general events and changes of the past 100 years may contribute toward a better appreciation of the kinds of experiences that shaped the attitudes, values, and beliefs of today's aged.

The purpose of Chapter 1 is to provide a general background, a frame of reference for the remainder of the book. A brief review of some of the myths associated with older people and a description of the physical challenges and cultural changes that have occurred during the twentieth century are included. Much of the material presented may be familiar. However, attempting to relate the past to the present may provide another perspective when considering the needs of older men and women of today.

MYTHS

The majority of older people are disabled by poor health. Fortunately, aging occurs hour by hour, day by day, instead of overnight. The transitions are gradual. Physical and emotional adaptation are part of the process, so there is time to become accustomed to change as it occurs gradually.

Looking closely at those who are the oldest—in their sixties, seventies, eighties, nineties, and beyond—we find that the great majority of older people make adaptations to these changes; for example, hearing and eyesight losses occur slowly. Many adaptations are usually made unconsciously before the individual even realizes that new eyeglasses or a hearing aid may be needed. Most older people seem able to dismiss normal changes in aging as little more than aggravations.

The majority of older men and women generally view themselves as enjoying good health. In a 1986 survey by the National Center for Health Statistics, 70 percent of older adults 65 and over rated their health as good or excellent. Differences existed in relation to income. About 24 percent of older men and women with incomes over $20,000 reported their health as excellent for people their age, whereas only 11 percent with incomes less than $10,000 described their health as excellent. Although the institutionalized elderly were excluded from this survey, the results are a good indicator of overall health status of the elderly in the community.[1]

Older people are abandoned by their children.   Using data from nationwide probability surveys of noninstitutionalized persons aged 65 and older, Shanas reported that about four out of five persons who were not in institutions had one or more surviving children and three out of four lived in the same household or within a travel time of half an hour. Although the proportion of parents and children living in the same household has decreased, the proportion of older individuals living within ten minutes' distance of a child has increased. This living arrangement is in keeping with the desire for independence and privacy for both generations.[2]

According to analyses of data from the Health Care Financing Administration's 1982 Long Term Care Survey, children of aging parents provided care to about one-quarter of elderly disabled males in 1982 and to slightly more than one-third of elderly women. Other relatives, such as siblings or nieces, also provided substantial care to older disabled family members, representing 23 percent of all community caregivers for men and 35 percent for women.[3]

Older people inevitably withdraw from the mainstream of society as they grow older.   The theory of disengagement, the process whereby older individuals gradually withdraw from society and become increasingly occupied with self, has been challenged by a number of theorists. The term *disengagement* was first applied to this process in 1961 by Cummings and Henry.[4] Since that time, the results of a great deal of research do not support the idea that disengagement is an inevitable process. Some older men and women do withdraw from the outside world. They may prefer to do so, or they may not be able to adjust to the changing world, or they may be forced to disengage because society desires their withdrawal. The main point to remember about disengagement is that both society and the individual are involved in the process. The situation may be created by the attitudes and values of a society which may provide few opportunities for continued involvement. Older individuals respond to the situation according to their personal resources.

Most older people live in nursing homes. Of people aged 65 and over, 5 percent are in nursing homes on a given day.[5] However, statistics can be misleading, for it is also true that many more than 5 percent of older people spend some time of their lives in long-term-care facilities.

In 1985 it was estimated that only 1 percent of the age group from 65 to 74 were in nursing homes compared to about 6 percent of people aged 75 to 84 and about 22 percent of those aged 85 and over.[6]

The increased use of nursing homes by individuals over 85 may reflect not only their increased fragility but the results of longevity in terms of outliving close relatives and friends who ordinarily provide support systems. Some or many of the very old may be able to continue to live in the community with the provision of supportive resources.

Senility is an accompaniment of old age. It is estimated that only 5 percent of those 65 and older suffer from serious intellectual impairment.[7] Research is being conducted to learn more about the causes of reversible and irreversible mental disorders. When these causes can be determined, treatment and preventive measures can be provided to reduce the instances of these disorders.

Poverty accompanies old age. It is true that large numbers of older people are poor or are in the "near poor" classification, but this is certainly not the fate of the *majority*. In 1986, 12.4 percent of those 65 or older had incomes below the poverty level compared to 10.8 percent of those from 18 to 64 and 13.7 percent of all people under 65 years of age.[8] There has been a relative improvement in the economic conditions of older adults in the last 20 years. This is largely due to Social Security benefits, annuities, and expanded private pensions.

Older adults are also likely to own their own homes. Of the 18.2 million households headed by older people in 1985, 75 percent were owner-occupied and 25 percent were rental units. Of the owner-occupied homes, 83 percent in 1983 were owned free and clear.[9] Many of these homes are in need of repair. There are some resources to help pay for repairs, but more are needed.

Older adults are poorly educated and spend most of their time looking at television. In 1986, only about 49 percent of those 65 and older were high school graduates.[10] This is a reflection of the limited educational opportunities in the early 1900s and the lack of emphasis on education at that time. Future older populations will tend to have more skills and knowledge that can be additional resources for the country. In addition, adult educational opportunities are expanding. Most colleges are offering special programs for older people. Private and community organizations, voluntary organizations, government agencies, business, and industry are also offering educational activities. In the year ending May 1984, the U.S. Department of Education reported that 900,000

(4 percent of the total taking courses) were 65 or older and 2.7 million (12 percent) were 55 or older.[11]

Older people do not spend most of their time looking at television. Many are active volunteers providing a wide range of services. A survey in 1974 conducted by the Bureau of the Census for ACTION found about 7 million people 55 and older engaged in volunteer work at that time. A companion study estimated the total value of these services at more than $11.6 billion.[12] A survey conducted by Louis Harris Associates also revealed that Americans 65 and older are involved in a wide variety of creative and cultural activities.[13]

Older individuals do enjoy a variety of television programs, just as do people of any age. However, the over-55 population has a much higher preference for news and public affairs programming than the younger population. A recent national survey reported daily news viewing by 74 percent of adults 55 to 64 and 80 percent by those over 65 compared to only 48 percent of those 18 to 24 and 55 percent of viewers 25 to 29. In addition, men and women 65 and older are the heaviest subscribers to daily newspapers of any age group.[14] As education of our older population increases, these impressive figures are likely to become even higher.

These and other misconceptions have served to increase our negative attitudes about aged individuals and about age itself. Yet, as the title of this chapter suggests, the aged of today had to be the strongest and most able of their generations in some ways in order to survive into old age. Many of them may also have had better health care and more socioeconomic advantages than some of their contemporaries, but older people of today are representative of every socioeconomic group.

SURVIVORS OF DISEASE

In this day of heart and kidney transplants and immunizations, it is a strain on the imagination to recall that people in their sixties and over began life in a very different medical world. It is difficult to realize that it was not until the 1890s and the early 1900s that surgery became a viable medical method as a result of improvements in diagnostic tools, especially the X-ray in 1895. The Mayo brothers, William and Charles, had performed only 54 abdominal operations between 1889 and 1892 but recorded 612 in 1900 and 2,157 five years later.[15]

In the early 1900s, the death of women in childbirth and the death of infants and children were accepted as part of life. Most people died at home with family members looking after the dying person. The extraordinary measures now taken with the dying did not exist. Family members often bathed the bodies of their relatives before burial and funerals were held in the home. These experiences with death must still be a part of the memories of many older people.

Except for influenza and, recently, the onslaught of AIDS, epidemics of infectious diseases are now virtually non-existent in the United States. Older men and women of today have lived through times in which inoculations and antitoxins were practically unknown.

The three leading causes of death in 1900 were influenza and pneumonia, tuberculosis, and gastroenteritis.[16] Children and adults in the first 40 or so years of this century also died as a result of yellow fever, diphtheria, scarlet fever, typhoid fever, poliomyelitis, complications from measles, and other infectious diseases as well as from chronic disease and infections of various kinds.

Influenza was the cause of the worst epidemic in this century. In 1918, during World War I, three successive waves of influenza occurred throughout the world, killing between 15 and 25 million people. Deaths from this disease exceeded all the casualties of all the wars of the twentieth century. The flu virus was later identified as the swine influenza virus.[17] A great many older people of today recall the feelings of fear and helplessness that were experienced as loved ones became stricken and died.

During the nineteenth century it was understood that bacteria could be carried from insects and animals to people and could cause illness. Developments in medicine and in public hygiene began to reduce infectious disease and lower mortality rates. Public health measures such as the pasteurization of milk, the purification of water, treatment and disposal of sewage in ways that prevent infection, and draining swamps to destroy the breeding place of mosquitoes were carried out on a massive basis. These procedures, along with the development of immunization against diphtheria, yellow fever, whooping cough, tetanus, typhoid fever, poliomyelitis, and many other diseases, have produced dramatic results in reducing disease.[18]

These changes did not take place all at once in the early part of this century; for example, only in the 1940s did the discovery of chloromycetin put an end to typhoid fever as a life-threatening disease.[19] Measles continued to be a threat until 1944 when gamma globulin was discovered to be effective in its prevention. However, an inoculation against measles was not developed until about twenty years later.[20] Poliomyelitis caused much suffering throughout the first 60 years of this century. Adults as well as children were victims. The Salk vaccine in 1955 and the Sabin vaccine in 1961 put an end to epidemics of this disease. There remain a number of older men and women who are partially disabled as a result of poliomyelitis.

Tuberculosis was greatly dreaded by the adult population. As recently as 1950, tuberculosis was the sixth leading cause of death. From 1950 to 1977 the age-adjusted death rate from tuberculosis declined 95 percent.[21] The treatment of tuberculosis consisted of isolating the tuberculin patient in a community (sanatorium) with other tuberculin patients for months and even years. They were taught to live with their disease. The effects of these long separations on the patient and family can only be conjectured. Although tuberculosis has not been eradicated, a schema of antibiotic drugs has been developed which has completely changed its treatment. In a short period of time the disease can be made incommunicable, making long-term separation from the family and community unnecessary.

Pellagra, a disease caused by nutritional deficits, rarely occurs nowadays, but was the cause of many deaths in the United States in the early part of this century, particularly in the South. Tenant farmers, poorly paid factory workers, and other poor and ill-fed people were felled by pellagra. In 1917 over 170,000 cases were reported in the United States. As late as 1930, 7,000 deaths from pellagra were recorded.[22]

Victims of pellagra were ostracized, as they had severe dermatitis. Their skin erupted with large sores; insanity often followed. The cause of the disease was unknown. They were even turned away from hospitals, so great was the fear of infection. The nutritional cause for pellagra was discovered in 1915 by Dr. Joseph Goldberger,[23] but the disease continued to exist until the 1940s.

Some, perhaps most, of today's older adults must have been affected deeply by experiences associated with illnesses during the first half of this century. Some must have been stricken and yet lived through the disease, and others must have nursed loved ones who died while under their care. Older men and women may yet harbor feelings of guilt, anger over losses, or lingering fears of infectious disease as a result of such experiences.

Skolnick and Skolnick summarize it well:

> Death and birth, essentially uncontrollable and unpredictable, hovered constantly over every household only about seventy years ago....Although infant and child mortality rates had begun to decline a century earlier, the average family could not assume it would see all its infants survive to middle or old age. Death struck most often at children.[24]

In addition to knowing the personal story of the older client, it may be helpful to know about the general life experiences and the background of history and social change against which this particular client's life has been played. Failure to do so may result in a breakdown in communication due to inability of the younger person to understand behavior that is a vestige of times long past. An example of this kind of problem is the irritation experienced by a social worker who cannot understand why an elderly couple carefully saves every extra cent although it would be possible for them to purchase a few pleasurable extras. The social worker may not even take into consideration the possibility that both of them still suffer from the financial insecurity of the Great Depression and cannot break old habits. The following section deals with some of the events and cultural changes that have occurred in an attempt to provide, at the very least, the flavor of the times.

THE WARS

War was a personal experience for a substantial number of our older population. The number of United States veterans of war aged 65 or over was estimated at 5.3 million (19 percent of the total veteran population) in 1986. This number of aged veterans is expected to increase to 8.9 million in 1999, a 69 percent increase.[25]

Those who are 90 or over were young children during the Spanish-American War in 1898. Some may have actual memories of this event or may remember the emotional temper of the times from stories they heard as children. Hostile American feelings toward Spain were aroused largely as a result of exaggerated reports by the American press of Spanish oppression and misrule of Cuba. Many Americans demanded U.S. intervention in order to help Cuba attain independence. The sinking of the battleship Maine ("Remember the Maine!"), the battle of San Juan Hill (led by Colonel Leonard Wood and Lieutenant Colonel Theodore Roosevelt) are events that made indelible impressions on many Americans.

The fighting was over within ten weeks of the declaration of war. With a dazzling naval victory less than a week after the onset of fighting, it was one of the most popular wars America has fought. As it was such a brief war there was not enough time for disillusionment to take place.[26]

Some very old people of today may recall hearing about the fierce criticism of the treaty when the war was over. The treaty required Spain to relinquish Cuba and cede Puerto Rico and Guam to the United States. The treaty was denounced by many Americans, as they believed the annexation of the Philippines amounted to a repudiation of America's moral position in the war. However, the treaty was ratified in 1899. America had now become a colonial empire.[27] To many Americans these signs of power were a source of great pride.

The period between the Spanish-American War and World War I is a part of history well known to social workers, for it was a time of vigorous social reform. Some older people of today who were immigrants or children of immigrants around the turn of the century may have known or heard about the pioneering social reformers of that period: Jane Addams, Mary Richmond, and Lillian Wald.

The beginning of World War I, only 16 years after the Spanish-American War, may be vividly remembered by many older adults in their seventies and eighties. Selective Service was initiated in 1917, and every young man between the ages of 21 and 30 had to register for the draft (men born between 1887 and 1896). There are about 278,000 still surviving veterans of World War I.[28] Machine guns and armed tanks were new and frightening inventions. Submarines were used on a large scale for the first time. There was a great fear of being gassed. Soldiers who suffered from the emotional effects of war were termed "shell-shocked."

The slogan for World War I, "The world must be made safe for democracy," was taken from a speech made in 1917 by Woodrow Wilson. Public opinion was deeply divided as to whether to become involved in the war that had been waged for two-and-a-half years. Many older people may have vivid recollections of the propaganda of the time which became, as the war progressed, crude and savage with movies bearing such titles as *The Prussian Cur*. Altogether 75 million pieces of prowar literature were distributed. There was also repression of those who were against the war. Legislation was passed to make public expression of opposition to the war illegal. Some older people, particularly Irish-American and Jewish immigrants and members of German-American communities, may remember the vigilante groups that formed and targeted them for abuse.[29]

The period immediately following the war was marked by economic instability. There was an increase in labor unrest, which resulted in a large number of strikes in 1919, and racial unrest. Prohibition of manufacture and sale of alcoholic beverages, which lasted 13 years, began in 1920, but violations were rampant. Then, from 1921 to 1929, the economy grew without precedent until it collapsed dramatically. The Great Depression was underway; the economic slump continued until the outbreak of World War II.

People of all ages and classes found themselves unable to meet even the daily basic needs of food, shelter, and clothing. Many middle-aged and older people lost their life savings in the banks that folded. Aged relatives had traditionally been cared for by their families, but unemployment was so high that home care was now impossible for many family members.

The effects of the Depression may still be expressed in terms of the insecure feelings of many of those who lived through the Depression years. Unemployment figures of the time now sound almost unbelievable. In 1932 unemployment was at 50 percent in Cleveland, Ohio; 60 percent in Akron; and 80 percent in Toledo.[30]

Life was no better in many rural areas. A great drought which persisted throughout the thirties swept a large area of the Southwest and Midwest. Farm income declined by more than 60 percent, and an estimated one-third of all American farmers lost their land. Added to this disaster were swarms of grasshoppers that swept through the affected regions, devouring the little that was left, even to the extent of consuming "fenceposts or clothes hanging out to dry."[31]

The Social Security Act of 1935 established a federal old-age pension program and a federal-state system of unemployment insurance. Other social programs were begun during Franklin D. Roosevelt's administration to remedy the effects of the downward financial spiral. Public housing to replace substandard housing of the poor, Aid to Families with Dependent Children, Old Age Assistance, and Aid to the Blind were among them. Many people rejected the programs, for they had been imbued with the belief that individuals relied on themselves and that failure to find employment was shameful, as it was due to personal failure. Many of those who accepted assistance from the relief agencies that existed at the time felt humiliated, but chose humiliation above starvation.

America began to pull out of the Depression by the end of the thirties, and preparation for fighting in World War II brought new prosperity to this country. The attack on Pearl Harbor had produced national unity. The aggressive actions of Japan and of Adolf Hitler were clearly a threat to England and the United States, and the American people were ready and willing to fight for their country. There was a reshuffling of a large part of the population as the nation rapidly mobilized a large fighting force. Soldier, sailor, marine, and air force bases were established throughout the country; wives and families often followed. "Battle fatigue" replaced "shell shock" to describe the emotional aftermath for many young soldiers in battles of World War II. There was once again a push by industry to supply the weapons for war, and many housewives became factory workers. Men and women over the age of 45 or 50 have memories of food rationing, gasoline rationing, even fears of invasion. There are memories of civilian activities, such as folding bandages for the Red Cross, "knittin' for Britain" before the United States entered the war, practicing air raid procedures, and reading slogans like, "Loose talk costs lives" and "A slip of the lip may sink a ship."

Propaganda again played its part by whipping up prejudices and fears, this time directed toward those of German ancestry and toward Japanese Americans. Approximately 116,000 Japanese Americans were placed under the supervision of the War Relocation Authority and moved to relocation camps in California, Colorado, Utah, Idaho, Arizona, Wyoming, and Arkansas.[32] Japanese Americans and German-born Americans who recall that period must have many bitter memories of that time.

Today's older men and women remember victory celebrations when the war was won. However, the awesome ending of the war with the atomic bomb signaled a new era. Only the middle-aged and older people of today can recall the feelings that accompanied the dawning realization that every person on earth would live with the possibility or threat of nuclear devastation.

The world had not finished its clean-up of World War II before the Korean conflict began in 1950. This war was different from the three previous wars, for it was a "limited war." The United States was trying to avoid a direct conflict with China. The war reached a stalemate. Although negotiations began in 1951, the war continued until 1953. This period was frustrating for the military and for a country that had grown accustomed to victories in war. The older members of today's population were in their forties, fifties, and sixties during that war. Some fought or had children who fought in both World War II and the Korean conflict.

There was now only a short breather before the beginning of the undeclared war with Vietnam. The American involvement with Vietnam began very slowly and began to escalate in 1964 until it became a war. A withdrawal of troops began in 1969 so that relatively few remained by 1972, and the following year an agreement on ending the war was signed. The fighting had been savage and demoralizing.

In addition to the Vietnam War and the Korean conflict, there has been the cold war between Russia and the United States. In the sixties, the situation became extremely tense. About the time that today's college students were toddlers, many of their parents were building bomb shelters, enlarging their basements for use as shelters, or stocking parts of their houses with canned or dehydrated food in the event of a nuclear war.

Effects of War

The effects of living through two major world wars, a major conflict, a limited war, and the ongoing cold war vary according to the experiences and coping mechanisms of each individual. However, there are some general effects that may contribute to the lack of communication between generations.

Those who were alive early in this century or during the end of the last century witnessed the emerging of the United States as a world power. Although many Americans were ambivalent or negative about America's colonialism at the end of the Spanish-American War, many felt a great deal of pride in the fact that the victory over Spain had been swift and with little cost to the United States.

The increasing industrialism during the early last half of the nineteenth century, continuing into the twentieth century, the rapid change from peacetime to wartime industry when America entered World War I, and vastly increasing technology were additional reasons for pride. Both world wars seemed justified. The belief that they were fighting for a worthy cause enabled many young soldiers and their families to accept casualties of war with the feeling that the sacrifices had meaning and were not in vain.

The Korean conflict and the Vietnam War were more difficult for many people in this country to accept. The reasons for the hostilities were harder to define and to understand. Many were bitterly disappointed by the failure to win the Korean War, by the prolonged battles of Vietnam, and by the suffering on both sides. The fighting in those countries perhaps was more real to Americans than earlier wars, for television brought the fighting into the living room and vividly portrayed the brutality of war.

In addition, many older people were probably greatly disappointed that their hopes had never been realized for the League of Nations and the United Nations Organization as measures to put an end to aggression.

Two world wars within two-and-a-half decades, and the quick onset of the Korean conflict, followed only a decade later by the Vietnam War, not only raised the question as to whether fighting wars actually would end wars, but seemed to answer it. Younger people made their feelings known during the protests of the sixties when draft cards were burned, and some young men found refuge from the draft by going to Canada. However, for many of the older population who fought in World War II and for those who had fought in both world wars, it was extremely difficult to accept the refusal of any young Americans to go to war for their country, regardless of the reason for the war. It has also been troubling to some older people to see the flag of the United States being desecrated, in their eyes, by being attached to the pockets of blue jeans or emblazoned on T-shirts.

RACIAL AND ETHNIC PREJUDICE AND DISCRIMINATION

To most of us under 70 or 80, the Civil War seems a remote period in history and slavery an archaic institution. The Emancipation Proclamation, which proclaimed the freedom of approximately 4 million slaves, was issued in 1863. In 1900 there were a great many black men and women still alive who had been born slaves and who had memories of actually living in slavery. As late as the 1960s, a few hardy individuals born as slaves were still living. Older adults of today in their sixties and seventies may have known former slaves or had relatives who were born slaves. The ties of older men and women with events in a past that seems so distant today are closer to them than we often realize.

Black people throughout the United States had had their hopes and expectations raised immediately after the Civil War, only to have them dashed by the end of the century. In 1896, the Plessy vs. Ferguson case resulted in the "separate but equal" ruling which established segregation as the practice throughout the country.

Many older black people and white people were taught as children in the 1890s and early 1900s about Booker T. Washington, the founder of the Tuskegee Institute in 1881, who had been born a slave in 1856. His book, *Up From Slavery*, was published in 1901. Washington emphasized vocational education for black youngsters. Although Washington spoke out against lynching, criticized the extremely unequal educational facilities for black people, and argued against segregation laws, he did not make the active pursuit of full civil and political rights a major part of his policy and attempted to turn black people's minds to other directions.[33]

Washington was harshly criticized by some of his black contemporaries, particularly W.E.B. Du Bois, but his policy of accommodation to the white majority was readily accepted by many people of both races. Du Bois and a group of his supporters joined with white progressives to form the National Association for the Advancement of Colored People in 1909.

The young of that time grew up in a world of sharply segregated races. Race relations were extremely poor in many areas. Lynchings and riots were common occurrences from the turn of the century until about 1920. There was a mass migration of black men and women to northern cities, partly in response to mob violence. They found the same segregationalist practices wherever they went, but some were able to locate jobs and to better their conditions.

These segregationist racist attitudes persisted, but, in spite of those attitudes, by 1940 a middle class of black Americans emerged, as many became teachers, doctors, lawyers, government employees, and businessmen. However, this middle class consisted of a minority of blacks. About 80 percent of the black population were estimated to be in the lowest socioeconomic class, as opposed to 20 percent of the white population during the same period.[34]

An indicator of the prejudice of the times is the fact that no civil rights legislation was passed from the time of the Reconstruction period after the Civil War until the middle of the twentieth century. Segregation continued throughout World War II. Although black soldiers volunteered and were drafted into the armed services in both World War I and II, they lived on segregated military posts. Post theaters, clubs, mess halls, and living areas were segregated. It was only in 1949, after World War II was over, that segregation in the armed forces and in the government was ended by President Truman through executive action.[35]

Following the Supreme Court's 1954 decision which directed the integration of public schools, civil rights groups were organized. During the 1950s when our present-day 80-year-olds were in their fifties, there were many clashes between white segregationists and these groups.

Martin Luther King rose to national prominence when he led a nonviolent boycott of segregated buses. It now seems preposterous that a boycott was necessary at the time to obtain the demands which were as follows:

> ...that Negroes be seated on a first-come, first-serve basis without having to vacate their places for white passengers; that white bus drivers show more courtesy toward Negro passengers; that Negro drivers be employed on buses traveling mostly through Negro districts.[36]

Nonviolent sit-ins and marches occurred throughout the sixties, but there were also episodes of violence and riots. Most of today's older adults lived in or near areas in which some violence occurred.

Only in 1964 did the Civil Rights Act come into being. The act contained 11 titles which addressed many issues, including the guarantee of protection against applying different standards to black voters and outlawing the exclusion of black individuals from public accommodations such as restaurants and hotels and from use of public facilities such as swimming pools and parks. This act also provided financial aid to all schools that were in the process of desegregation.

The Voting Rights Act of 1965, which outlawed literacy tests, was another needed legislation. The percentage of black voters rose from 27 to 53 percent in Georgia in less than two years. In Mississippi the rise was from less than 7 to 60 percent.[37]

In addition to racial prejudice in the last hundred years, there has been prejudice toward ethnic groups. American Indians, Italians, Irish, Polish, and Jews were targets, much as Hispanic Americans and Asians sometimes are today. Strong feelings developed against the great influx of immigrants from Europe from the 1840s until after 1920, when quotas were established.

Although ethnic prejudice did not disappear, it did diminish. Some of the reasons were the restricted number of immigrants coming into the country; the Americanization and more complete assimilation of earlier immigrants; and the popularity of certain Jews in entertainment, sports, and politics.[38]

Parents of many older people of today immigrated to this country in the 1880s and 1890s and are primarily from southern and eastern Europe. Most of them settled in industrial cities where jobs could be found most easily and where communities of their own nationalities were established. The majority of them took whatever work they could obtain at whatever wages were offered. Many Americans viewed them as presenting threats to their jobs. As noted earlier, prejudicial feelings toward immigrants were particularly intense during wartime, when they were shunned or accused of sympathizing with the enemy.

Many of the working-class Jewish immigrants lived in the East Side ghetto, in Brooklyn, or the Bronx. As they moved upward into the middle class, many residential restrictions were placed against them. Gentile resort areas were closed to them, as were apartments, homes in suburban areas, golf clubs, and city clubs. Consequently, middle-class Jews began to build their own vacation areas in the Catskills and other areas, as well as apartment buildings and equivalent suburban housing.

Some older people may continue to harbor prejudices against ethnic groups. Social workers need to be aware of the possibility of prejudicial feelings and discriminatory acts that may occur in the institutions in which they work, as well as the possibility that those who have been victimized may have accepted and internalized the negative attitudes held by the dominant class. Attitudes can be changed and self-concepts can be improved. This is an area that bears examination, and one for which social workers in institutions may need to try innovative solutions.

CHANGES IN FAMILY LIFE

We tend to think of the "good old days" in family life as the extended family with three generations living together in the same household. There has never been a time in American society that this was a commonplace living arrangement, if for no other reason than that the life span would not accommodate this life-style.

Throughout the nineteenth and early twentieth centuries, households did not consist of two or three generations of kin, but they did consist of the nuclear family and strangers. Families were not isolated from relatives, as they frequently lived nearby. Taking in lodgers or boarders was a common practice. Many of these lodgers were young people who migrated to a new community and lived with older people whose children had left home, and some were immigrants. Studies of census data at the turn of the century show that boarding was not primarily a foreign immigrant practice, but a migrant practice.[39] More available housing and a greater value placed on privacy in family life have caused the decline of this practice, although it persists to some extent in black families.

Hareven points out that this loss of flexibility of the family, which once allowed households to expand when necessary to include other people, is a great loss. If this flexibility still existed, solitary living could be avoided and surrogate family living could be offered to lonely individuals such as widows.[40]

When industrialization separated the home and the workplace, the home became glorified as a retreat from the outside world. Middle-class families became child-centered and private. Childhood was viewed as a distinct stage of development, and children were perceived as needing protection and nurturance. One of the central assumptions of the "cult of domesticity" was "the role of women as custodians of the domestic retreat and as full-time mothers."[41]

Most rural and factory-employed mothers were far too busy attending to household chores, working long hours in garment factories or on farms to spend much time playing, conversing with, or entertaining their children. However, the middle-class ideology slowly evolved into the larger society, becoming a part of the ideology of the second and third generation of immigrants and the working class. The women who worked did so out of necessity, not from choice. Their appropriate, accepted role was that of homemaker and mother.

The changes in thinking in regard to women's role in the home, particularly in the last 20 years, are so well-known that a review of this aspect of domestic change is not needed here. However, it should be noted that some older people have difficulty in accepting a departure from that earlier concept of women's role, particularly if it involves role reversal. Social workers frequently encounter older men who have never performed house-keeping or cooking chores and are at a loss when their wives become ill or die. They may be unable or unwilling to maintain their homes, grocery shop, or prepare meals.

CHANGES IN SEXUAL ATTITUDES

There is a marked difference in today's frank and open examination of all things sexual as opposed to the sexual climate of the nineteenth century and the first 30 or 40 years of this century. The hushed secrecy of the Victorian era surrounded the childhood and early adulthood of most of our oldest men and women.

From around 1900 to 1912 there was great emphasis on the restraint of passion and desires. Chastity was a key not only to salvation but to success. Some of the reasons for the extremely heavy emphasis on continence may have been the later age of marriage; more employment of women outside the home, with possibly more sexual temptation; the possibility of illegitimate or un-wanted pregnancies; and the fear of venereal disease.[42]

In the middle and upper classes, men and women were expected to keep both their bodies and their minds pure. Words like *sex, pregnant,* and *menstruation* were not spoken aloud in mixed company. Children were told absolutely nothing about sex. Young pregnant women were not expected to appear in public, except perhaps at church, once their pregnancy was obvious. They were referred to as "expecting" or "in the family way." Unwed mothers were considered a family disgrace and were sent in great secrecy to distant relatives or maternity homes to deliver. The babies were then put up for adoption. There are many older women of today who still bear the scars of such early experiences.

Physicians disagreed as to what should be the desirable frequency of sexual intercourse, some arguing that it should take place infrequently and only for the sake of procreation. Physicians also warned against "marital excesses" and emphasized their belief that there were negative moral and psychological effects of masturbation.[43]

This atmosphere of sexual repression prevailed in America when Sigmund Freud visited this country in 1909. As a result of psychoanalytical theory and the study and discussions of American physicians, sociologists, and psychologists during the late nineteenth and early twentieth centuries, a more open attitude developed toward sexuality. Pamphlets on sexual hygiene were prepared and distributed. There was much less reticence in reference to writing about sex and about the controversial psychoanalytical theories in newspaper and journal articles.

Changes in the sexual behavior of both men and women also occurred. Alfred Kinsey's interviews document a number of changes.[44] Surveys of American magazines during the twenties also revealed a marked change in American attitudes and behavior toward sex.[45]

Along with the more open expression of ideas about sex, the whole subject of contraception was brought into open discussion, largely through Margaret Sanger's efforts. Sanger coined the term "birth control" in 1913, three years before she opened the first birth control clinic in the United States. Shortly after opening the first birth control clinic in 1916, only a little over six decades ago, Margaret Sanger was arrested and jailed.[46]

As with any other change, the dissemination of new ideas and the adoption of new attitudes and behavior moved slowly. In rural areas and small towns, and probably in many communities in urban areas, earlier conventions held sway. The sexual freedom that exists today took several decades to develop. It is probably safe to generalize that many or most people over 50 years old received little or no sex education in their childhood, very little during adolescence, and had far different attitudes toward sexuality than young people of today. The effects of early teachings on attitudes toward sexuality are discussed in more detail in Chapter 10.

The new ideas presented by the expanding fields of psychology and psychoanalysis impacted areas other than sex. There was more emphasis on the expression of feelings, examination of motivations, awareness of defense mechanisms, and general interest in dynamics of behavior. These concerns continued to gather momentum until, by the beginning of the 1950s, many children and teenagers had parents, school social workers, guidance counselors, psychologists, and school nurses who were attentive to their emotions and feelings. It may be difficult for generations born in more emotion-sensitive times to understand the reticence that may be displayed by many older men and women whose youth was spent in a much more restricted environment. Less verbal access to feelings may require social workers to place more emphasis on interpretation of the client's actions and nonverbal messages than with younger clients.

The events of the last hundred years and the changes in attitudes that have been briefly discussed were experienced in different ways and at different ages by the older individuals of today. The "over 65" population is constantly changing and, as the newer members enter, their past experiences and characteristics will also differ. Consider the "baby boom" generation after World War II, a very large group that is expected to cause a great increase in the older population. There will be overall differences related to education, career involvement of women, and attitudes toward divorce, child rearing, and other aspects of domestic life.

FUTURE PROSPECTS OF OLDER MEN AND WOMEN

When looking toward future groups of older adults, it is reassuring to find that current data indicate that concern is increasing with regard to the plight of older people. There seems to be more willingness to provide better living conditions for the older population. This is indicated by the Harris study, *The Myth and Reality of Aging in America.* A representative survey of a cross section of Americans 18 years and older was made to determine the public's attitudes toward aging and its perceptions of what it is like to be old in the United States. The findings show that the general population supports improved conditions for our aged. Older adults are viewed as deprived people who have a right to a better life. Those who were polled approved of government intervention to bring this about.[47]

It is exciting to observe the developing interest in gerontology. The growing number of books and studies is an indication of the increased interest and portends the continued appearance of new knowledge and theories from a variety of professions. One message that can be found in the literature on aging is that old age may not be "mastered" within the next few decades, and maybe never, but there are many ways in which old age may be made more productive, more rewarding, more comfortable, and more satisfying.

NOTES

1. *Aging America: Trends and Projections,* 1987–88 Edition. Prepared by the U.S. Senate Special Committee on Aging in conjunction with the American Association of Retired Persons, the Federal Council on the Aging, and the U.S. Administration on Aging, p 96.
2. Ethel Shanas, "Social Myth as Hypothesis: The Case of the Family Relations of Old People," *The Gerontologist* 19, no. 1 (February 1979), 6.
3. *Aging America,* 122.
4. Elaine Cummings and William E. Henry, *Growing Old: The Process of Disengagement* (New York: Basic Books, 1961).
5. *Aging America,* 118.
6. Ibid.
7. Robin Marantz Henig, *The Myth of Senility.* Reprinted by permission of Scott, Foresman and Company (Glenview, IL) and American Assoc. of Retired Persons and the author. Copyright ©1981, 1985 by Robin Marantz Henig.
8. *Aging America,* 42
9. Ibid., 145.
10. Ibid., 142.
11. Ibid., 143.
12. Carole Allan and Herman Brotman, comps., *Chartbook on Aging in America: The 1981 White House Conference on Aging* (Washington, D.C. Superintendent of Documents n.d.), 132.
13. Ibid., 138.
14. Ibid., 134.

15. Paul Starr, *The Social Transformation of American Medicine* (New York: Basic Books, Inc., Publishers, 1982), 156, 157.

16. William R. Rosengren, *Sociology of Medicine: Diversity, Conflict and Change* (New York: Harper & Row, Publishers, 1980), 35.

17. Arthur M. Silverstein, *Pure Politics and Impure Science: The Swine Flu Affair* (Baltimore: The John Hopkins University Press, 1981), 16.

18. Saxon Graham and Leo G. Reeder, "Social Factors in the Chronic Diseases," in *Handbook of Medical Sociology*, eds. Howard E. Freeman, Sol Levine, and Leo G. Reeder (Englewood Cliffs, N.J.: Prentice-Hall, Inc., 1972), 65.

19. Geoffrey Marks and William K. Beatty, *The Story of Medicine in America* (New York: Charles Scribner & Sons, 1973), 24.

20. Ibid., 251.

21. Dept. of Health, Education and Welfare, *Health in the United States*, Pub. No. 80-1233, (Washington, D.C.: Superintendent of Documents, 1980).

22. Harriette Chick, Margaret Hume, and Marjorie Macfarlane, *War on Disease: A History of the Lister Institute* (Great Britain: The Trinity Press, 1971), 150.

23. Marks and Beatty, *The Story of Medicine...*, 260.

24. Arlene S. Skolnick and Jerome H. Skolnick, *Family in Transition*, 4th ed., (Boston: Little, Brown and Co., 1983), 13.

25. "Masters of A Serious Number Count," *The Vanguard*, Veterans Administration, October, 1986, 6.

26. John M. Blum et al., *The National Experience: A History of the United States*, 6th ed. (San Diego: Harcourt Brace Jovanovich, Publishers, 1985), 533, 534.

27. *American History: A Survey Since 1865*, 6th ed., Richard N. Current et al., eds. (New York: Alfred A. Knopf, 1983), 11, 608, 609.

28. "Masters of a Serious Number Count," 7.

29. *American History: A Survey Since 1865*, 682.

30. Ibid., 735.

31. Ibid., 737.

32. Thomas Parrish, ed., *The Simon and Schuster Encyclopedia of World War II* (New York: Simon and Schuster, 1978), 181.

33. Herbert J. Storing, "The School of Slavery: A Reconsideration of Booker T. Washington," in *100 Years of Emancipation*, ed. Robert A. Goldwin (Chicago: Rand-McNally & Co., 1963), 54.

34. W. Augustus Low and Virgil A. Clift, eds., *Encyclopedia of Black America*, (New York: McGraw Hill Book Co., 1981), 801.

35. Blum et al., *The National Experience: A History of the United States*, 774.

36. Henry R. Luce, ed., *Time Capsule/1956* (New York: Time, Inc., 1968), 29.

37. Low and Clift, eds., *Encyclopedia of Black America*, 248.

38. *American History: A Survey Since 1865*, 772.

39. John Modell and Tamara K. Hareven, "Urbanization and the Malleable Household: An Examination of Boarding and Lodging in American Families," *Journal of Marriage and the Family*, 35, no. 3 (August 1973), 471.

40. Tamara K. Hareven, "American Families in Transition: Historical Perspectives of Change," in *Family in Transition*, eds. Arlene S. Skolnick and Jerome H. Skolnick, (Boston: Little, Brown and Co., 1983), 76.

41. Ibid., 81.

42. Nathan G. Hale, Jr., *Freud and the Americans* (New York: Oxford University Press, 1971), 33.

43. Ibid., 38, 39.

44. Alfred Kinsey et al., *Sexual Behavior of the Human Female* (Philadelphia: W.B. Saunders Co., 1953).

45. Hale, "Freud and the Americans", 476.

46. Linda Gordon, "Birth Control and Social Revolution," in *A Heritage of Her Own*, eds. Nancy F. Cott and Elizabeth H. Pleck (New York: Simon and Schuster, 1979), 467, 468.

47. Louis Harris and Associates, *The Myth and Reality of Aging in America* (Washington, D.C.: National Council on Aging, 1975), 211...242.

2

COPING WITH HEART DISEASE, CANCER, AND STROKE

Chapters 2 through 6 are concerned with physiological changes that occur with age; some of the major chronic conditions that are associated with older people; and illnesses or conditions that may occur suddenly and be short-lived, but have disastrous effects. Mental disorders that predominate among the aged and their effects on the patient and family are described. The information that is presented here is discussed in relation to social work intervention.

RESEARCH ON THE PHYSIOLOGICAL PROCESSES OF AGING

In the past 25 to 30 years, a number of longitudinal studies have been done in relation to physiological changes that occur with age. These studies have resulted in the acceptance of several general concepts of aging, as follows: Physiological changes are gradual, resulting most often in slow loss of function; the losses that occur in older adults are greater in more complex functions, such as those involved in the performance of coordinated activities; individuals age at different rates, and the systems and tissues within an individual also age at different rates; vulnerability to disease increases with age, and both physical disability and hospitalization are twice as likely to occur in older than in younger people; there is a decrease in homeostatic capacity (ability to respond to physical and emotional stress and return to prestress level).[1]

In spite of these negative effects, the majority of older adults function independently in their daily living. As noted in Chapter 1, most older men and women manage to compensate for physical changes as they gradually appear, and there is adequate time to make appropriate adjustments. Many chronic conditions associated with old age have their beginnings in the middle years or earlier, so that a sudden adjustment is not required but takes place over time.

NEED FOR SOCIAL WORK INTERVENTION

When a health crisis does occur, the older person may be hospitalized. While hospitalized for an acute condition, medical care and attention are provided, but eventually the person must return home or to some other living arrangement. If the individual returns to the community, care that is needed to prevent further complications may not be provided. In the case of chronic illness, such as high blood pressure and congestive heart failure, the person must make permanent changes in life-style that may be very difficult. If needed care is not provided or the patient cannot make necessary adaptations, illness is likely to recur and necessitate a return to the hospital. This cycle may continue until the individual becomes too dysfunctional to continue living independently. Social work intervention may be a deciding factor in disrupting this cycle.

Those individuals who experience difficulty in adjusting to change or who are coping with a health crisis often come to the attention of social workers and others in service professions. The result is sometimes a distorted view of the older population as a whole. It is important for those who work with ill, dependent, and needy older adults to remember that their clients are not representative of the majority of older people.

LEADING CAUSES OF DEATH

This chapter is concerned with the three leading causes of death among people 65 and over: heart disease, malignant neoplasms (cancer), and stroke. In 1986, heart and blood vessel diseases were responsible for almost as many deaths of Americans as cancer, accidents, pneumonia, influenza, and all other causes of death combined.[2] Since both heart disease and stroke are associated with the cardiovascular system and atherosclerosis, they will be discussed in the first two sections of this chapter, with a discussion of cancer presented in the third section.

HEART DISEASE

Arteriosclerosis and *atherosclerosis* are two cardiovascular terms that lay people often confuse. *Arteriosclerosis* refers to any type of vascular deterioration resulting in loss of elasticity, thickening, and hardening of the arteries.[3]

Atherosclerosis is a type of arteriosclerosis that is characterized by deposits of fatty substances in the walls of arteries which take the form of knobs or plaques. As these deposits form and grow larger, they may narrow the arterial lumen (passageway), which results in slower circulation. The inadequate blood supply to the tissues is called *ischemia*. Blood clots may form around these deposits which may further narrow the arteries. Coronary arteries are frequently involved in atherosclerosis and have serious consequences for the heart. This condition is known by the general term *ischemic heart disease*. It is manifested by angina of effort, myocardial infarction (heart attack), or sudden death.[4]

Angina

Anginal pain occurs when there is an inadequate supply of oxygen to the heart muscle. It is characterized by thoracic (chest) pain which may extend into the neck, jaw, and shoulders. The pain may be intense, crushing pain or mild pain. Although it is usually associated with exertion, it may also occur at rest.[5] In older individuals angina pectoris is often associated with much less severe pain than middle-aged patients experience.[6] Exertion, emotional stress, isometric exercise, and stressful dream states may bring on anginal pain. Angina is especially likely to occur when the patient is cold or digesting a meal.[7]

Angina can be treated medically or surgically. Nitroglycerin is a drug used for patients who suffer from angina caused when too little oxygen is conveyed to the heart muscle. It relaxes the arteries so that more blood can flow with less pressure required to deliver it. Nitroglycerin is not habit forming. In surgery for anginal pain, a coronary artery bypass graft allows the blood to bypass the block and flow into the heart muscle.[8]

Sudden Death

In the phenomenon known as *sudden death*, the individual suddenly collapses and dies before medical help can be obtained. Witnesses to the event frequently report that the person does not display symptoms, such as anxiety or angina, that would indicate a myocardial infarction. Ventricular fibrillation is the generally accepted explanation for these deaths. (Ventricular fibrillation is "very rapid, uncoordinated contractions of the ventricles of the heart resulting in loss of synchronization between heartbeat and pulse beat.")[9] It has become apparent in recent years that there is a significant relationship between coronary atherosclerotic heart disease and primary ventricular fibrillation.[10]

Myocardial Infarction (Heart Attack)

A myocardial infarction means that an area of the myocardium (heart muscle) was damaged or has died because of reduced blood supply. The presenting symptoms of elderly individuals are usually dizziness, breathlessness, and some confusion. This is unlike the symptomatology of middle-aged individuals: pain and shock.[11]

Although deaths from heart disease have been decreasing for many years, heart disease remains the major cause of death among the total population as well as among the older population. Three of every four deaths from heart attack occur after age 65.[12]

There is probably no incident as frightening to anyone as a heart attack. The most vital organ in the body has failed. The patient and the patient's family are alarmed and anxious during and after the occurrence. Social workers often find that both patient and family are too anxious to ask questions and do not fully comprehend the information they are given. Education about heart attacks must usually be repeated at intervals following the attack and again after hospitalization.

There are multiple factors that influence an individual's chance of experiencing a myocardial infarction. Uncontrollable factors are age, sex, race, and heredity; controllable factors are diabetes, hypertension, hyperlipidemia (related to cholesterol), sedentary life-style, cigarette smoking, and stress.[13]

In recent years attention has been focused on the last factor, stress, in producing heart attacks and in affecting the course of other diseases as well. Much has been written also about the propensity of individuals with Type A personality for heart attacks. Individuals with this type of personality experience a constant, aggressive struggle against time, ceaselessly striving to accomplish more and more in less time. Type A behavior is characterized by covert insecurity in regard to status, or hyperaggressiveness, or both. There is also a free-floating, but well-rationalized, hostility. It may be possible over time for some Type A individuals to develop a tendency toward self-destruction.[14] Recognition of this type of behavior and pointing it out as part of the social history may be of assistance to the interdisciplinary team in planning treatment.

A change in the patient's life-style is frequently required to avoid stress. The patient may be able to bring about the change with the guidance of social workers and other health care professionals. Many mental health clinics, outpatient hospital clinics, and even businesses offer stress management courses which may be very helpful.

Exercise is often recommended to strengthen the heart, but the amount and kind varies with each patient. Isometric exercises are not recommended. They tend to increase blood pressure and the need for oxygen, as they set the force of one muscle against another. These exercises may also cause arrhythmias.[15]

Social workers can help patients who deny their condition to recognize the reality of the situation. Being supportive and enlisting support from family members, the employer, and friends often is the greatest help. Most patients need time to accept the fact that they must make some adaptations in their life-style. In fact, studies indicate that full psychological adaptation to a heart attack may take as long as three years.[16] During that time, patients need reassurances and accurate information about what has happened and why it has happened.

Some men and women in their sixties or seventies who have myocardial infarctions want to return to employment. Many of them place high value on employment and find convalescence very trying. They may not discuss their financial need with the physician and may not fully understand the limitations imposed by their health, as in the brief example below.

> Mr. Jones is a 60-year-old man who has worked in a factory for years and has made good wages. After experiencing a myocardial infarction, he is told by his physician that the job is far too strenuous as it involves heavy lifting, but that he can work in a less demanding job. He is advised to start with only a few hours a day and build up to no more than twenty hours a week.
>
> When Jones returns to the outpatient clinic a week later, he does not mention employment to the physician. In response to questions, he tells the social worker that he "moonlighted" as a barber when his children were small and that he has arranged to start part-time as a barber the following week. The social worker congratulates him on his plan. She thinks that barbering is acceptable, as Jones will not be lifting heavy items or exerting himself physically. However, she suggests the patient discuss his plan with the physician. To her surprise, the physician immediately vetoes the idea, saying that barbering is stressful. The physician explains that barbering requires keeping the arms lifted and standing for long periods, both of which are stressful on the heart.

In this example, the social worker has a relationship with the client that results in his sharing information he has not given the physician. This social worker may be very knowledgeable about the kind of work cardiac patients should avoid, but she has a gap in her knowledge. As a social worker, she cannot sanction employment as being safe for the patient and fortunately does not presume to do so.

Some other effects of cardiovascular disease are common causes of concern to older adults. The symptoms of some of these conditions are not always recognized by the older client. Being alert to their symptoms and explaining the need for medical attention may be helpful in preventing the occurrence of a more serious condition.

Congestive Heart Failure (CHF)

Congestive heart failure is one of the most prevalent chronic cardiac conditions in adults.[17] When the heart is unable to pump a sufficient amount of blood to meet the body's demand for oxygen, heart failure occurs. This may be the result of cardiac disease or due to an excessive demand placed on the heart. When the blood supply to the body is inadequate, the cardiovascular system uses various compensatory mechanisms to maintain an adequate blood supply. The conditions causing the problem may exist for long periods before the heart and circulatory system exhaust their ability to compensate and failure occurs.[18]

Symptoms of heart failure include the following: *dyspnea* (breathlessness), *orthopnea* (breathlessness exhibited when the patient assumes the recumbent position), *paroxysmal (nocturnal) dyspnea* (attacks of breathlessness which generally occur at night and awaken the patient from sleep), fatigue, weakness, and edema. In severe heart failure, older people with certain other accompanying problems are especially apt to experience mental alterations, such as confusion, difficulty in concentration, poor memory, headaches, insomnia, and anxiety.[19]

Congestive heart failure can be effectively treated in most cases. It is treated initially with rest and sodium restriction. A diuretic is usually given to reduce fluid so that the load on the heart is decreased.

The management of patients with CHF depends to a great deal on the underlying cause. There are a number of diseases which lead to heart failure, including the following: myocardial infarction or angina, hypertension, valvular dysfunction, pericarditis, rheumatic fever, alcoholism, lung disease, endocrine disorders, and systemic infections.[20]

Practice Applications

Although the patient usually can lead an active life, help may be needed. It is important for patients with congestive heart failure to understand the underlying disease or diseases that cause their symptoms. They should be well acquainted with changes that are necessary in their life-style, the medication regime prescribed, and dietary restrictions.

Karch observes that patients with CHF need to think of work as anything that takes energy, such as standing up, eating, making the bed, and ironing. Patients are taught to space their activities and think of ways to conserve energy, such as sitting while ironing. She warns against trying to do too much in the morning and being worn out the rest of the day. Keeping cool is important, as temperature also affects the way the person feels.[21]

Signs of trouble which should be reported to the nurse or physician are edema (swelling), which commonly occurs in the lower leg or ankle and is symptomatic of fluid retention; the need for more pillows in order to sleep at night; shortness of breath during exercise or just walking; lightheadedness; fatigue; and waking up at night due to inability to breathe.[22]

Social workers need to be alert to sleep complaints of older people in terms of their relation to physical health. Most social workers quickly recognize sleep complaints that indicate depression but are not as accustomed to considering them in relation to disease. Questions about sleep may be included in the history. Social workers are not trained to make diagnoses, but they need to suggest a medical evaluation if the person complains of symptoms that indicate the possibility of illness.

CEREBROVASCULAR ACCIDENTS (STROKES or CVAs)

Six out of seven deaths from stroke occur after age 65. Although stroke remains the third leading cause of death in the United States, rates of death from stroke have fallen consistently over the past fifteen years.[23]

Of the conditions that usually account for strokes in the aged, partial or complete cerebral thrombosis is most often the cause.[24] A thrombus (clot) forms in one of the atherosclerotic arteries of the neck or brain and cuts off the blood supply to some part of the brain.

Warning signals of stroke include a sudden, temporary weakness or numbness of face, arm, or leg; sudden or temporary vision loss, particularly in one eye; double vision; headaches or a change in the pattern of headaches; temporary dizziness or unsteadiness; and a recent change in personality or mental ability.[25]

Hypertension

Hypertension is considered a major risk factor in cerebrovascular accidents in the aged. Hypertension, a condition more common in women than in men, denotes an unstable or persistent rise in blood pressure above the accepted norm.[26]

Essential hypertension has no identifiable cause. In *secondary* hypertension a specific cause can be identified, such as renal disease, endocrine disease, or a more recently discovered cause, the use of oral contraceptives. Hypertension damages body arteries, for it thickens arterial walls, thereby predisposing them to atherosclerosis. It causes injury to the interior arterial walls so that clots are more likely to form which may break loose and travel to other parts of the body (embolization). By placing increased pressure on the weakened walls of aneurysms, hypertension may cause an aneurysm to burst. Hypertension is an insidious disease, for there are no easily recognizable symptoms in the early stages.

Although there is no known cure for hypertension, the disease can be controlled through medication. As there is no pain associated with hypertension, it is often very difficult for patients to realize that they have a lifelong illness that must be controlled. It is important for the nurse or physician to discuss the importance of weight control, diet, and minimizing stress.

Transient Ischemic Attacks (TIAs)

Transient ischemic attacks are reversible episodes of decreased blood flow to a part of the brain; they can be warning signs of an impending major stroke. These episodes are resolved within 24 hours.[27]

In a TIA there may be no more than a momentary blackout, a brief feeling of numbness or tingling in an arm or leg, or a muscle weakness. If a TIA is suspected, the patient should receive immediate medical care. A TIA should be treated with as much seriousness as a major stroke, for it often serves as a predictor of a major stroke.

The following is a brief example of the social worker's use of medical knowledge which could occur in any social work setting.

The social worker from the Department of Human Services visits a 78-year-old woman who has been referred by another client as needing assistance as she "isn't acting right." She finds the woman in a slightly confused state. The social worker closely observes her and notices a large bruise on her arm. The client explains the bruise as a result of a fall a few days earlier when one knee "just buckled under." She also mentions tingling and numbness which occurred several times in one arm a few hours earlier. The social worker recognizes the symptoms as possible indicators of a TIA and immediately, with the client's agreement, makes arrangements for a medical evaluation.

Rehabilitation of Stroke Patients

Since the mid-sixties, great advances have been made in the treatment of the effects of stroke. Stroke victims have a far greater rate of recovery: 90 percent of stroke patients learn to walk again, and 30 percent can return to gainful employment.[28]

When evaluating a patient for rehabilitation, the following factors are usually considered:

1. The patient's functional ability before the stroke.
2. The patient's social situation and options for returning to the community.
3. The patient's ability to cooperate with nurses and therapists.
4. The patient's capability to learn new material.
5. Age of the patient.
6. Bowel and bladder (incontinence).[29]

Each of these factors is readily understandable. Williams observes that no patient is too old for rehabilitation but that age cannot be ignored because of its impact on the patient's motivation and ability to participate in rehabilitation.[30]

The goals of rehabilitation include helping the patient to return as much as possible to independent function in the tasks of everyday living, to be able to resume social and familial relationships, and to regain usefulness as a member of the community. Rehabilitation after stroke may involve the patient, the patient's family, the physician, social worker, physical therapist, speech therapist, and possibly other specialists. In some settings, a *physiatrist* (a physician specializing in physical medicine and rehabilitation) is available to plan treatment.

The patient usually needs to relearn lost movements, such as walking and writing. Some degree of *aphasia* (the impairment or loss of the ability to comprehend or express language) occurs in about half of all stroke cases.[31] This is a very distressing and frightening condition for both patient and family. Aphasia can be so severe that all speech function is seriously affected, it may only be evident when complicated understanding is required, or it may range somewhere between those extremes.

Speech therapists evaluate the patient, using a wide variety of methods to restore skills, but the therapy program must be designed for each individual;

for example, patients with *dysarthia* (poor articulation) are more easily understood when they speak slowly, so therapy may be aimed primarily at reducing the rate of speech. Other patients may require extensive rote repetition.[32]

Right or left *hemiplegia* (loss of ability to move and loss of feeling in one side of the body) often occurs and may be slight or severe. Damage to one side of the brain affects the opposite side of the body; for example, a CVA on the left side of the brain affects the right side of the body. On the affected side, the patient's head, eyelid, and mouth may droop, the arm may be bent and hugging the chest, with the wrist, fingers, and thumb also bent.[33]

Although visual field loss on the right occurs frequently, these field losses are not seen as often as those accompanying left hemiplegia. Loss of the visual field on the affected side may result in problems with dressing, making up one side of the face, bumping into obstacles on the left when walking, and so on.[34]

Damage to any area of the brain produces changes in behavior. There may be a reduction of the attention span, which is most likely in the first few weeks, and impairment of recent memory, to some degree, which may interfere with new learning. Patients may experience lethargy or the opposite: rapid, impulsive shifts in attention. Although lethargy usually decreases as the patient's condition becomes more stable, impulsivity may persist.[35]

Emotional lability occurs. Stroke patients are usually depressed; however, they can also be euphoric. The patient may display uncharacteristic sensitivity to remarks made by others. A comment or incident that would have elicited a mild response prior to the stroke may now be received with overpowering emotion. This reaction is very distressing to family members and may be a cause of great concern.

Practice Applications

In addition to the usual social history, it is vital to obtain a detailed pretraumatic history of the patient in regard to the demands of everyday living. This should include the physical demands made by the patient's life-style and environment. Work, recreational activities, interests, and hobbies should be carefully explored, for many adjustments may be necessary.

Information should be obtained as to the structure of the patient's house and the entries. The location of the patient's bedroom in relation to the bathroom and living areas in the home should be ascertained.

If there are steps to the entryways or a staircase inside, or if the doorways are narrow, use of a wheelchair may be impractical. Assisting the patient into and out of a vehicle may be very difficult. The location of a bedroom or other sleeping arrangement downstairs and an upstairs bathroom poses another problem. These are considerations to which family members may give little thought until questions are asked. Although physical therapists usually obtain these kinds of information, social workers are also interested in the patient's physical environment. They are often expected to locate resources for changing or overcoming environmental obstacles.

Social workers find that they can help the patient and family during rehabilitation by reinforcing education in regard to stroke. During a medical emergency so much happens so quickly that the older person and family members may experience confusion as to what has happened and what they are to do. Although aphasia or other effects may have been explained in detail in the hospital, it is often difficult for patient and family to remember explanations given them while they were under a great amount of stress.

The individual with a visual field loss, usually the person with left-sided hemiplegia, needs to be reminded again and again to remember the "missing" side. Family members must also learn to remember to approach the patient from the "good" side.

The patient's family must be made aware of the need for reinforcement while the patient eats, dresses, reads, writes, and walks, for the patient cannot help repeating the same errors. Emphasizing short-term goals is important, for motivation is difficult to maintain during long-term rehabilitation.

Changes in behavior, such as emotional lability, should be explained to the family. As the behavior may be "transient, treatable, or permanent," the prognosis should be shared with the family as soon as possible.[36]

The social worker may try to locate a patient group for the family to attend. Some hospitals have outpatient or inpatient groups composed of patients and/or family members. There may also be patient education groups for stroke victims which are sponsored by the Y, the Red Cross, or mental health agencies. The names and meeting times of groups such as these can usually be obtained from the local branch of the Heart Association.

If the patient is discharged home instead of to a rehabilitative facility, rehabilitation services must be coordinated. Transportation often must be arranged for the patient to be able to receive the physical or speech therapy that is needed. Responsibility for case management services must be assumed by the outpatient social worker, or a social worker who may be affiliated with the public health department, home health agency, or other agency in the community.

Psychotherapy and supportive social work services may be needed to help family members deal with emotional problems arising from the heavy physical and emotional demands incurred when providing care to an individual with massive loss. Sibling rivalries and family conflicts may surface under the pressure of the event. Discomfort in the role reversal of child caring for parent which often occurs may interfere with the caregiver's ability to provide care.

The caregiver, usually a spouse or daughter of the older stroke victim, may have feelings of hostility toward the patient that are being denied. Leaving the patient may arouse feelings of guilt and anxiety to the extent that the family member rarely leaves the patient's side. Caregivers often have unrealistic expectations as to the amount of care they can provide without respite.

A defense mechanism often used by patient and family is that of denial of the extent of loss from the CVA. The question, "Why did this happen to me?" is also raised by patient and family. Their world has gone awry and time is needed for them to sort out their emotions and to try to make sense out of the distressing and frightening change in their lives.

Depression frequently occurs in both patient and family, for rehabilitation may be slow and tedious. There are often unrealistic expectations in regard to goals that can be accomplished through speech and physical therapy.

Social workers can respond to these problem areas by helping relatives resolve their feelings and come to a realistic understanding of what they can expect from the patient in terms of recovery and of themselves in regard to providing care. Realistic goals need to be set and the family encouraged to be patient as they take care to note each small gain that is made.

Locating respite care is vital. Fortunately, some communities are providing resources for caregivers who need respite from their responsibilities, but these are not always available. Family conferences may be necessary in order to call on other family members to remove some of the burden from the primary caregiver. Sometimes relatives and friends are willing to be of assistance if they can be reasonably certain that they will not be expected to assume more than they offer. Reluctance to help may also stem from a lack of understanding as to the kind of care needed.

If there cannot be a full return to the patient's past activities, new ones must be explored. A loving, supportive family and the support of friends appear to be the greatest aids to recovery.

Resources

Most local Heart Associations have developed a directory of services in their communities for victims of heart disease and stroke. They also are usually able to provide information on resources for specific cases. The Heart Association also provides a number of pamphlets on prevention and rehabilitation in relation to heart disease and stroke that are helpful to many patients and their families.

In many situations the social worker finds that the patient's family is the major client. The following case example may be helpful in demonstrating the social worker as case manager with the patient's family as the major client.

CASE EXAMPLE: REHABILITATION AFTER A CVA

Mr. Harley is a 75-year-old retired plumber who has had a cerebrovascular accident resulting in expressive aphasia and extreme weakness of the right arm and right leg. Both physician and family have been encouraged by the patient's obvious efforts to respond to the speech and physical therapists. He has learned to transfer from the wheelchair to the bed and to the toilet. He appears to understand speech but initially could not speak. He is slowly learning to speak again. The physician prefers to discharge Mr. Harley to a nursing home for a few weeks of carefully regimented physical and speech therapy. The patient, as much as he is able, is involved in making the discharge plan, and the family members appear to want this plan. Then, the day before the discharge is to take place, the patient's 68-year-old wife and two married daughters insist on taking him home, as they believe he will become depressed after being placed in a nursing facility. As Mrs. Harley is in very good health and both daughters live within a 20-minute drive, the physician reluctantly agrees to the home discharge.

The altered plan is hurriedly made. A home health agency is utilized, with the social worker at the agency assuming case management responsibilities. Shortly after discharge, a social worker from the home health care agency which is providing the physical and speech therapy visits the home.

The social worker explains to the patient and his wife that a registered nurse and physical and speech therapists will be visiting the following day. She is there to try to learn the kinds of needs they have and the ways that the home health agency may be of assistance to them. Although she has a social history from the hospital, she reviews the pertinent information. Mr. Harley is included in the discussion that takes place, although he does not appear to comprehend everything that is being said. He seems to become tired after about 15 minutes and indicates that he wishes to rest but that they should continue talking.

As soon as Mrs. Harley is alone with the social worker, she begins to tell in a distressed voice about purchasing a very expensive motorized wheelchair for Mr. Harley only a few days after the CVA occurred. Mrs. Harley explains that she had not realized her husband would not require a wheelchair permanently, and she had wanted him to have the best wheelchair available. She had tried two weeks later to return it, but the salesman had said it was too late. She does not know what else to do, and she really needs the money she spent, as it is her household allowance for the month. Her daughters believe the wheelchair is rented, and she does not want to tell them.

The social worker wonders whether she should try to persuade Mrs. Harley to be more assertive and to call the salesman again, but she appears so tired and worn that she decides to intervene. The social worker promises Mrs. Harley that she will telephone the manager of the hospital appliance store and explain the situation.

Mrs. Harley insists that except for the need for speech and physical therapists and the telephone call to the wheelchair company, there is nothing else that is needed. She has her two daughters to call upon and does not require a "welfare worker." She reluctantly agrees to the social worker's returning in a few days.

The social worker makes the telephone call in regard to the purchase of the wheelchair. After some discussion, including references to consumer organizations and the Better Business Bureau, the manager agrees to refund the money. The social worker then meets with the registered nurse and physical and speech therapists to review the needs of the patient. The social worker comments on Mrs. Harley's reluctance to ask for assistance and suggests that the team be alert to unexpressed needs.

A second visit is made by the social worker to the home a short time later. The visit occurs at the time the speech therapist works with Mr. Harley. The patient is able to speak in fragmented speech and is beginning to learn to print with his left hand. The weakness in his left side is improving and he is now on a walker. He appears to be in good spirits; however, Mrs. Harley appears agitated and anxious.

She declares that "everything is fine" and she needs no help, but stands in the front doorway with the social worker, out of hearing of the patient, and comments on the cessation of the constant flow of visitors and well-wishers. Only a very few close friends continue to drop by occasionally. She is now faced with many everyday difficulties. One of the main problems is the inability to do errands that require driving. She stopped driving when Mr. Harley retired 15 years earlier, for he liked to do the driving. She has kept her license renewed, but she is now afraid to drive. She is fearful of interstate driving, as the medium-sized city in which they live had few freeways when she did drive. She cannot do any shopping due to the distance of their home from a shopping center, or take her husband anywhere, even if someone could help her assist him into the car.

In addition to the driving problems, there are banking and insurance problems. She has paid little attention to their finances and has never paid the bills or balanced a checkbook. Her husband has always given her a household allowance and she managed it well. There has never been a surplus of money, but they lived within their limited income until the stroke occurred. The physician has told her that eventually her husband may be able to resume most of his previous responsibilities, but he now needs to focus on relearning speech and strengthening his right side.

Now there are extra expenses; for instance, she spent "a small fortune" on buses and, occasionally, taxicabs to and from the hospital and still must use buses for essential shopping trips. She is very troubled about having to use money from their savings account this month and is ashamed to admit to anyone that she does not know how to go about obtaining savings from the bank.

An added problem is the reluctance of her two daughters to help her as much as she had anticipated. They cannot assume errand and shopping responsibilities, as both are employed outside the home and are busy meeting the demands of their husbands and teenage children when they are at home. One is married to an alcoholic, who has brief episodes of drinking followed by months of sobriety, but he has been on a binge since Mr. Harley was rushed to the hospital.

The daughters might help her learn again to drive, but their cars seem to be always breaking down. Mr. Harley has kept their automobile, although it is very old, "in top shape," but Mrs. Harley fears she might have an accident in their car while she is learning again to drive. She has heard her husband say many times that there is a $150 deductible fee on their automobile insurance policy. She would hate to have to pay that amount. Driving lessons are out of the question, as they too are expensive.

The social worker begins with the most immediate problems: overcoming Mrs. Harley's resistance to relearning to drive and locating the means to help her to assume responsibility for banking and other finances.

Mrs. Harley has been very dependent on her husband, but she has coped well so far with her husband's disabling stroke. She managed at home while he was hospitalized, and she seems capable in areas other than handling financial matters.

The social worker expresses her understanding of Mrs. Harley's reluctance to resume driving, but reminds her that she did drive for many years. She will not have to drive on the freeways, for there are city routes to the outpatient clinic and to a nearby shopping center. It will be wise for her to use their automobile, for she would eventually use the deductible amount if she continues taking buses and taxis. She reminds Mrs. Harley that her husband is striving toward one small goal at a time and that she can use the same techniques in relearning how to drive. She can tackle each skill separately before moving to another, just as her husband does. She can also start learning how to handle financial matters one step at a time.

Mrs. Harley first objects, commenting that her husband will soon be all right and that she will wait until he can attend to those matters. The social worker recognizes the denial present in the response. She answers that the time needed for rehabilitation is undetermined, for it is a slow process that requires a great deal of patience on the part of patient and family, and the outcome is uncertain, as there are so many factors involved. She would like, at this point, for Mrs. Harley to consider her suggestions.

Mrs. Harley believes that she needs more time to think about the suggestions. She invites the social worker to return, as she needs a "friend" who "knows the business world." The social worker recognizes Mrs. Harley's reluctance to admit that she is asking for assistance on a professional basis. There is a tacit understanding that counseling will be informal.

The following day, the social worker receives a telephone call from each of the daughters. The social worker finds that Mrs. Harley called them after her visit the day before. Mrs. Harley had asked them whether they could arrange time to help her relearn driving and whether one of them will assist her in learning to deal with financial matters. Both daughters are willing to help and to encourage their mother toward becoming more independent, but both are concerned about the time it will take. The daughters complain about their mother's dependency on them, even prior to their father's stroke. They believe that their mother, having never worked outside the home, has little understanding of the tight schedules both women must maintain. They also believe that she expects too much of her teenaged grandchildren in terms of sitting with their grandfather. The teenagers have part-time jobs, as well as attending school, and can stay only briefly with Mr. Harley. One daughter openly expresses resentment toward her mother, as she "quit noticing my children when they were twelve or thirteen" and now "notices" them only because she needs their help. Both daughters express their feelings of being pressured by their mother's "constant demands" and feelings of irritation in regard to her dependency.

The social worker acts as coordinator in planning with Mrs. Harley, her children, and grandchildren in settling on specific times for them to help, and the families appear to respond more willingly. She arranges an informal meeting with the daughters and their mother to discuss their helping Mrs. Harley become more independent in handling financial concerns. Although the daughters appear skeptical of their mother's ability to handle her own affairs, one agrees to help her learn. The other agrees to help her regain her driving skills.

The social worker and the other members of the home health agency team share their impressions and the progress that has been made with the patient. Mr. Harley is benefiting from therapy and making marked improvement in physical therapy. His speech is not improving as rapidly, but he appears to have good comprehension. He is working with intense concentration and great determination. There is general agreement that the wife needs as much social assistance as the patient needs in the form of speech and physical therapy. Fears are expressed that Mrs. Harley's anxieties may be communicated to her husband and impede his progress. All have noted Mrs. Harley's mounting anxieties and are being supportive to her, as well as to the patient, during their professional visits.

On a subsequent visit to the home, the social worker finds that in some ways, Mrs. Harley is faring much better than before. The early crises have been resolved. She is driving in the neighborhood and handling the family finances, both of which have built her confidence and pleased her daughters. The social worker reviews this progress with Mrs. Harley and warmly commends her for overcoming fears and carrying out many activities that were new and stressful.

Mr. Harley is responding to physical and speech therapy and seems to be making progress in both areas. Mrs. Harley mentions that she misses the morning coffee she had formerly enjoyed with a neighboring widow and sharing a soap opera daily with another friend. However, she is enjoying the closer contact with the daughter who is helping her with banking and comments that even this sad event (Mr. Harley's stroke) has had some good things to come out of it. She adds with a note of surprise that her grandchildren seem to be "growing up at last" and have been much more helpful than she had anticipated. She believes Mr. Harley is enjoying their presence for the first time in years.

The social worker listens, but observes that Mrs. Harley frequently sighs and her eyes tear slightly as she talks. When she pauses for a moment, the social worker comments that she appears troubled and asks her how she can help. Mrs. Harley bursts into tears. She readily admits that she feels dejected and despairing, but she feels she should not, for her husband is improving and she feels closer to her two daughters than "since they were babies." She cannot understand why she feels so terrible and suspects it is some lack within herself. The social worker recognizes that Mrs. Harley is experiencing a grief reaction. She assures her that her feelings are "normal." She talks with her about the fact that the main crises are over and that day-to-day living is more difficult for most people than handling a crisis. Mrs. Harley is now trying to adjust to this new situation on a day-to-day basis. Even though she may be thankful for her husband's progress, she knows there have been many losses, and she is undergoing a normal grief reaction for them.

Mrs. Harley begins again to weep and adds that she misses the lively, teasing communication she formerly had with her husband. She especially misses his keen sense of humor and recalls with sorrow many of the funny, clever remarks he has made. Her husband seems so different now that he can express himself only in fragmented speech or print broken sentences. He appears grim, serious, and distant, and is occasionally very irritable. She knows their life together will be different in some ways, and she can tolerate that, if her husband could only joke with her again.

The social worker reminds her that her husband is making many adjustments and has experienced many losses that he is trying very hard to regain. He is probably feeling extremely frustrated, as it is a slow process. When he is less preoccupied with making adjustments and trying to relearn so much at once, their communication is likely to improve. There may be evidence now of Mr. Harley's playful sense of humor that Mrs. Harley has not recognized. The social worker suggests that Mrs. Harley recall and recount to her husband some of the incidents that she and her husband found amusing in the past. The social worker also urges Mrs. Harley to make more effort to have some time away from home, to make arrangements for a sitter other than the grandchildren, as Mr. Harley now needs less care. She assures Mrs. Harley that taking time to be with old friends will help her to be a better caregiver. The social worker and Mrs. Harley agree that a new goal is now to widen her social activities.

A short time later, the social worker receives a telephone call from Mrs. Harley. She sounds as if she is laughing and crying at the same time. She and her grandson have just returned from taking her husband to the drugstore. Mr. Harley had slowly made his way with the walker to the greeting card section. Once there, he selected a card with a humorous message that holds a special meaning for only the two of them. This confirms to Mrs. Harley that the joyful spirit of her husband is still intact, and that he has found a way to communicate that fact to her. It is, Mrs. Harley says, "the light at the end of the tunnel."

In this case, the social worker is aware of many of the family dynamics but does not engage in trying to work out underlying family conflicts. As the contacts with the family will not be long-term, the brevity of the client-worker relationship is an important factor in planning.

The social worker provides a supportive relationship to the client and family throughout her contacts with them. She identifies the major problems and uses a task-oriented approach to resolve them. She helps the client focus on specific problems that she is encountering in daily living. Clear targets are set and task accomplishment is reviewed, then new tasks are undertaken. As the client's skills increase and she gains more confidence, it is hoped that her newly learned abilities will generalize into other areas that she had formerly left completely to her husband.

The social worker recognizes that there is a family support system available, but too many demands have been made too suddenly on all concerned. In the height of a crisis, family members often initially promise more than they can possibly deliver. Some actions, such as the premature purchase of the wheelchair, are taken in haste. The spouse frequently must assume unfamiliar responsibilities that may appear overwhelming. More social work intervention early in the discharge plan may have helped to prevent the development of the situation discussed in this case example.

ONCOLOGY

Oncology is the term used for the study and management of malignant growth. An *oncologist* is the individual who specializes in this subject. The subspecialty of medical oncology was recognized in the early 1970s and is now one of the largest in internal medicine.

The specialty of oncology social work is also relatively new. The First National Conference on Practice, Education & Research in Oncology Social Work, sponsored by the American Cancer Society, was held in March, 1984.

Causes of Cancer

Although the causes of neoplasia (new and abnormal growths) are unknown in many cases, some forms of cancer can be caused by radiation and a variety of industrial chemicals and tars, including cigarettes. It is probable that certain viruses may also bring about cancer in animals and possibly in humans.[37]

Malignant growths cause harm in different ways, including the following:

1. They invade and destroy neighboring tissues, including blood vessels.
2. They spread to more remote organs and tissues. Malignant cells enter the blood vessels and lymphatics and settle in other areas. These secondary deposits (metastases) themselves begin to grow and invade local structures. Thus a carcinoma of the bronchus can cause metastases in the liver and brain.
3. They produce toxic substances which can damage the function of the nervous system, including the brain and peripheral nerves.
4. They can produce hormones such as ACTH...which lead to symptoms due to excess hormonal effect.
5. They lead to metabolic disorders and a general malaise, wasting and exhaustion known as *cachexia*.[38]

Treatment

The successful treatment of most kinds of cancer is dependent on early diagnosis and surgical treatment by operative removal, *radiotherapy*, and *chemotherapy*.

Chemotherapy

Chemotherapy, the administration of drugs, may be considered particularly when surgical treatment has failed to prevent the spread of disease. Such drugs are called *cytotoxic* drugs. Some kinds of cancer, including Hodgkins' disease, carcinoma of the prostate, and acute leukemia in children, often respond well to chemotherapy.[39]

Chemotherapy may consist of one or several anticancer drugs which may be given in combination with surgery or radiation. Chemotherapy may be administered orally, intramuscularly, or intravenously. The medication must enter the bloodstream so that it can reach the cancer cells. The cells that divide most often, such as cancer cells, take up most of the drug. The medication acts by interfering with the duplication and growth of cancer cells that are eventually destroyed. The rate of destruction of cancerous cells is different with each type of cancer. Anticancer drugs can also affect normal, rapidly dividing cells as well; however, normal cells have a tremendous capacity to regenerate themselves. Normal cells that might be affected include those in the bone marrow, gastrointestinal tract, reproductive system, and hair follicles.[40]

Anticancer drugs produce side effects in some but not all individuals. Each drug can produce different reactions in different people, and they can vary in severity from treatment to treatment. Most side effects are temporary and will gradually disappear when treatment is stopped. The gastrointestinal tract, mouth, bone marrow, hair, skin, reproductive system, urinary tract, and emotions may be affected.[41]

Radiation Therapy

Radiation therapy is sometimes referred to as radiotherapy, X-ray therapy, cobalt, or irradiation. *External radiation therapy* involves use of a machine, at some distance from the body; *internal radiation therapy* places small amounts of radioactive material (implants) inside the body or directly on the cancer. Radiation destroys the ability of all cells within its reach, whether cancerous or normal, to grow and reproduce. Cancer cells are more sensitive to radiation than normal cells. If radiation is given just as the cancer cell is about to reproduce, the cell division will be prevented and the cell will die. As cancer cells grow more rapidly, more cancer cells are in the process of dividing and are more susceptible to radiation than normal cells.[42]

Radiation may be used alone to destroy the cancer or, in some kinds of cancer, may be used with chemotherapy. It is sometimes used before surgery to shrink the cancer, after surgery to prevent any cancer cells from growing again, and it is used to reduce pressure, bleeding, pain, or other symptoms of cancer.[43]

The amount of radiation that is given is usually expressed in "rads," meaning "radiation absorbed dose." The treatments are usually given five days a week for several weeks. Side effects vary; some people have few or none, but others may experience serious problems. The severity depends mostly on the part of the body being treated and the amount of radiation. The person's general health also affects how the body reacts to treatment. The most common side effects resulting from radiation treatment are fatigue, skin problems, and lack of appetite. Other side effects result from treatment to a specific part of the body: for example, hair loss associated with treatment of the head.[44]

When internal radiation therapy is given, a small container of radioactive material (radium, cesium, irridium, or other similar material) is implanted into the body, close to, or directly into, the cancerous tissue. Implants are in the form of needles, wires, seeds, capsules, wax molds, and other devices and are usually left in place less than a week. As the radioactive substance may transmit rays into the area around the patient's body, nursing staff and others are not able to spend a long time in the patient's room. Once the implant is removed, there is no longer danger of any radiation. For treatment of some cancer sites, such as the prostate, the implant may be permanent; thus, the patient may need to stay in an isolated room for a few days until the radiation weakens. The implant loses energy each day, so that by the time of discharge, the radiation will be much weaker. The physician will advise implant patients if any special precautions are needed after discharge.[45]

Incidence

The incidence of cancer increases with age and is the only major cause of death for which death rates among the elderly continue to rise. Presently, it is the second leading cause of death among the elderly.[46]

Major Sites of Cancer in the Older Population

Older adult males are likely to have cancer of the lung, colon, rectum, prostate, and bladder. For the older female, the breast, colon, rectum, lung, pancreas, and uterus are the major sites.[47] The age-standardized lung cancer death rate for women is more than that of cholectoral cancer, and has surpassed breast cancer as the number one cause of cancer mortality in women.[48]

Lung Cancer

The statistics for survival of lung cancer are very low. Only 13 percent of lung cancer patients (all stages, black and white) live five or more years after diagnosis. The rate is 33 percent for cases detected in a localized stage, but only 24 percent are discovered that early.[49]

Symptoms include a persistent cough, sputum streaked with blood, chest pain, or recurring attacks of pneumonia or bronchitis. Risk factors for lung cancer are cigarette smoking, history of smoking twenty or more years, and exposure to certain materials, such as asbestos, particularly for those who smoke.[50]

Early detection is very difficult since symptoms often do not appear until the cancer has advanced considerably. Treatment depends on the type and stage of cancer. Surgery, radiation therapy, and chemical therapy are options, with surgery usually chosen for many localized cancers. In small cell cancer of the lung, chemotherapy alone or combined with surgery has largely replaced surgery alone as the main treatment used. A large percentage of patients experience remission, and, in some cases, a long remission.[51]

Cancer of the Prostate

Cancer of the prostate is one of the most common forms among older men, the average age being 70 years. Early symptoms may involve difficulty in starting the urinary stream, unexplained cystitis, urinary bleeding, dribbling, and bladder retention.[52]

Radical prostatectomy is effective treatment for localized lesions when there is no evidence of metastases in a healthy male under 70. There is a 60 percent five-year survival with localized disease when a radical prostatectomy is performed. Cancers that are locally invasive are treated with radiation therapy. Patients who are not candidates for surgery or radiotherapy may be treated with chemotherapy.[53]

In 90 percent of cases, radical prostatectomy has resulted in sexual impotence and in urinary incontinence in 2.5 to 5 percent of patients. However, a new technique has been developed that preserves potency, and it is now being adopted by surgeons worldwide.[54]

Cancer of the Bladder

Cancer of the bladder is most common in the 50- to 70-year-old population with many more men having it than women. Bleeding is the most common clinical symptom but it is usually intermittent. This may delay diagnosis as examination may be postponed if the urine appears clear.[55]

Several factors must be considered before determining treatment. This includes the stage and location of the tumor, general health, associated genitourinary problems, previous surgery or radiation therapy, and the ability of the patient to tolerate and care for any appliance that may be used following surgery.[56]

Surgery and radiation therapy are the treatments used. A systemic chemotherapeutic regimen for treatment of metastatic bladder carcinoma has not been established, but chemotherapy is being studied. The best results reported in the literature occur when the urologist, radiologist, and medical oncologist work together and integrate all modes of treatment.[57]

Colon and Rectum Cancer

The combined incidence of colon and rectum cancer is second only to that of lung cancer, with the exception of skin cancer. When colorectal cancer is detected and treated in an early localized stage, the five-year survival rate is 87 percent for colon cancer and 79 percent for rectal cancer. After the cancer has spread to other parts of the body, the percentages are 40 percent and 31 percent respectively.[58]

Early symptoms include bleeding from the rectum, blood in the stool, and change in bowel habits. Risk factors include personal or family history of colon and rectum cancer or polyps in the colon or rectum, and inflammatory bowel disease. There is also evidence that bowel cancer may be linked to diet. A diet high in fat and deficient in fiber content may be a significant causative factor.[59]

Surgery combined at times with radiation is the most effective treatment method. Chemotherapy is being studied to determine its role in treatment of advanced cases. Permanent colostomies are seldom needed in cases of colon cancer and infrequently required for patients with rectal cancer.[60]

The stool blood slide test is a simple method of testing feces for hidden blood. The patient obtains the specimen at home and returns it to the physician, hospital, or clinic for examination. The American Cancer Society recommends the test every year after age 60.

Ostomy Surgery

An "ostomy" (opening) may be performed on patients who have bladder or colorectal cancer. There are several kinds of ostomies that are performed, depending on the area of dysfunction; for example, a *urostomy* becomes necessary when the diseased or injured bladder or ureters cannot be treated or because nerve damage or impairment prevents the body from functioning properly. If part of the colon must be removed, a *colostomy* is necessary. If it is necessary to remove the colon completely, an *ilieostomy* may be performed. Some types of ostomies, due to disease, trauma, birth defects, and other conditions, are temporary. Other types are permanent.

A colostomy is an opening on the surface of the stomach which provides an exit through which the bowel discharges feces. A colostomy may be made in any part of the colon and is named for the segment of the colon in which it is located.[61]

Colostomy control is established through regular irrigations and by proper diet. An irrigation (essentially the same as an enema) cleans out the colon just as a normal bowel movement would. Irrigation is necessary for some people every day, although a few people are able to have regular timed bowel movements without it. A dressing over the opening is worn, or a colostomy bag may be worn for awhile after surgery, or while traveling, or on occasions when the person feels insecure about irrigation. The discharge from the bowel is collected in this container, which is fitted snugly around the colostomy opening.[62]

An ileostomy is an opening in the abdomen through which wastes from the small intestine are discharged. It substitutes for the functions that were formerly performed by the colon. The major functions of the colon are absorption of water and electrolytes, storage and solidification of intestinal contents, and transportation of wastes to the outside. The small intestine can carry out some of these functions. An individually fitted, properly attached appliance is worn at all times.[63]

A urostomy substitutes for some of the functions of the bladder and urethra. It is an opening in the abdominal wall by surgery to divert urine to the outside of the body. Although there are several kinds of urostomies, the most frequent types are ileal and colon conduits. These conduits are made from a small segment of the intestines (either ileum or colon) that is separated from the mainstream but kept alive and anchored within the abdomen. After one end is sewn closed, ureters are implanted so that urine can flow from the kidneys into this conduit. The other end is brought out through the abdomen and urine flows out of the ostomy as it arrives in the conduit. In the meantime, the intestinal mainstream has been reconnected for normal bowel function. A fitted, properly attached appliance is worn at all times and emptied as needed.[64]

Having a colostomy, ileostomy, or urostomy does not harm the general health of the body and does not have to be a handicap to normal living. There are thousands of individuals who have had this surgery who are gainfully employed and living normal happy lives.

Most hospitals employ *enterostomal therapy nurses* who are trained to help in selecting the proper equipment and teaching the proper care of the ostomy. There is a United Ostomy Association of ostomy chapters throughout the United States and Canada that is dedicated to the complete rehabilitation of all ostomates. Activities of members of this organization include providing help in the formation for new chapters, advice to individuals needing help, and dissemination of information through brochures and their magazine, the *Ostomy Quarterly*.

Breast Cancer

About one out of every ten women will develop breast cancer at some time during their lives. The five-year survival rate for localized breast cancer is 90 percent, as compared to 78 percent in the 1940s. If the cancer is *in situ*—not invasive—the survival rate approaches 100 percent. If it has spread, it is 60 percent.[65]

Warning signs include breast changes such as a lump, thickening, swelling, dimpling, skin irritation, distortion, retraction or scaliness of the nipple, nipple discharge, pain, or tenderness. Risk factors are age (over 50), personal or family history of breast cancer, never having had children, or having the first child after age 30.[66]

A monthly breast self-examination is recommended by women 20 years and older as a good health habit. *Mammography*, a low dose X-ray examination, is effective in screening women without symptoms and a valuable diagnostic technique for women who have findings suggestive of cancer. The American Cancer Society recommends a mammogram every year for asymptomatic women age 50 and over. In addition, a professional breast examination is recommended every year for women over 40. There are also guidelines for younger women in relation to professional breast examination and mammography.[67]

Treatment of cancer of the breast may consist of surgery varying from local removal of the tumor to mastectomy, radiation therapy, chemotherapy, or hormone manipulation. Two or more methods are often used in combination. In recent years, new techniques have made breast reconstruction possible after mastectomy with good cosmetic results. Reconstruction has become an important part of treatment and rehabilitation.[68]

Uterine Cancer

Cervical cancer is most common among lower socioeconomic groups, but all groups are at risk. Diagnosis of endometrial cancer, which affects mostly mature women, is usually made between the ages of 55 and 69. Overall the death rate from uterine cancer has decreased more than 70 percent during the last forty years, which is attributed to the Pap test and regular check-ups. The five-year survival rate for cervical cancer patients is 66 percent. For patients diagnosed early, the rate is 80 to 90 percent, and 100 percent for cancer *in situ*. The figures for endometrial cancer are 84 percent for all stages, 91 percent early, and 100 percent for endometrial precancerous lesions.[69]

Warning signals include intermenstrual or postmenopausal bleeding or unusual discharge. Risk factors for cervical cancer include early age at first intercourse, and multiple sex partners. Risk factors for endometrial cancer include history of infertility, failure of ovulation, prolonged estrogen therapy, and obesity.[70]

Uterine cancers are usually treated by surgery or radiation, or by a combination of the two. Precancerous endometrial changes may be treated with the hormone progesterone. In precancerous stages, changes in the cervix may be treated by *cryotherapy* (the destruction of cells by extreme cold), by *electrocoagulation* (the destruction of tissue through intense heat by electric current), or by local surgery.[71]

Cancer of the Pancreas

Cancer of the pancreas is the fifth most common fatal cancer in the United States. The highest frequency of incidence occurs in people between the ages of 65 and 79. No known causes of cancer of the pancreas have been identified, but some studies, which have not been confirmed, suggest an association with chronic pancreatitis, diabetes, and cirrhosis.[72]

Pancreatic cancer is a rapidly progressive disease. Early symptoms include asthenia (weakness), anorexia, weight loss, gaseousness, and nausea, with loss of weight the most common symptom. A dull or boring pain confined to the epigastrium, the upper middle region of the abdomen, or back occurs in a majority of patients.[73]

More than 90 percent of pancreatic tumors have advanced beyond the pancreas, or metastasized, by the time they are diagnosed.[74] Ninety percent of patients who have untreated carcinomas of the pancreas die within a year of the time the diagnosis is made. There is an intense search for innovative diagnostic and treatment approaches to this disease.[75]

Reactions to Diagnosis of Cancer

The word *cancer* is one that inspires feelings of fear and dread. Hardly any person escapes knowing intimately a friend or relative who endures a long drawn out, losing battle with this disease. Severe emotional distress is likely to result as the patient and family experience the fears associated with a diagnosis of cancer—fears of suffering and death, disfigurement, helplessness, and abandonment.

Some older people may have fears that are related to experiences of family members or friends who had cancer forty or fifty years ago. They may not be aware of some of the advances in surgery and other treatment that may make their particular prognosis more favorable or their treatment more comfortable.

Stonberg points out that cancer is a "family disease" that imposes role changes, the provision of nursing care, and a number of financial, social, and psychological strains. All systems with which the patient interacts require social work intervention. Periods of remission and relapses are particularly devastating to the patient and family and may necessitate repeated social work assistance.[76]

The modes of treatment for cancer are stressful to the patient and family. Misunderstandings and confusion often exist in relation to the course and the effects of radiation and chemotherapy that add to the stress already experienced. In order to comply with the scheduling of radiation therapy, work schedules may be disrupted and financial hardships may occur. If the facility offering treatment is at a distance from the patient's home, the problem of transportation can seem almost insurmountable.

Although chemotherapy has increased the life expectancy of many cancer patients, the side effects are so devastating that some patients refuse to accept treatment. The nausea and vomiting associated with chemotherapy may be a result of the pharmacological properties of the drug or may be conditioned responses. In the latter, sights, smells, or anything associated with the chemotherapy process produce anxiety and vomiting.

Myths Associated with Cancer

In addition to the other problems cancer patients experience, there are also many myths connected with cancer that encourage avoidance of people with cancer. Employees of nursing homes and hospitals, particularly less-educated employees, are not immune from hearing about, believing, and perhaps perpetuating these myths.

As depression is the most prevalent psychiatric symptom encountered in cancer patients, this may account for the myth that every patient who has cancer is clinically depressed. Studies seeking to determine the prevalence of depression vary considerably in regard to the frequency of depression among cancer patients. In a study comparing 80 advanced cancer patients with 80 physically able persons who had recently attempted suicide, profound depression such as that seen in a psychiatric population was not the norm. There also did not seem to be a link between increasing nearness of death and the degree of depression. Significant depressive symptoms occurred in approximately one-third of cancer patients, with one-seventh experiencing some suicidal ideation. Age significantly affected the self-report of depressive symptoms, but not psychiatric interview ratings of depression. On a depression inventory, younger patients reported more negative feelings about themselves and the future than older patients.[77]

Although every cancer patient may experience despair and some depressive feelings initially, or at different stages, the assumption must not be made that there is no treatable cause for the depression. Every patient with cancer who is depressed must be evaluated as carefully as any other person with symptoms of depression.

There may be an organic cause, such as endocrine disturbances and metabolic factors resulting from the cancer. These conditions may produce symptoms that are identified as depression. Metastases of cancer to the brain may cause depressive symptoms. Some of these conditions may respond to medical treatment. Streltzer notes that organic brain syndromes are common complications of cancer that are frequently undiagnosed and are often treatable.[78]

Loss of control may be a significant factor precipitating depression. There has been documentation of studies as to the way that depression predictably follows learned helplessness, "a condition in which there is a shattering of the expected link between actions and responses: 'Nothing you or I do makes any difference, so why bother?' "[79]

Angry reactions and noncompliance may be efforts to establish some control. Goldberg suggests giving patients appropriate opportunities to exercise choices over therapy and their environment. Such actions as continued involvement in financial issues or learning behavior relaxation to decrease side effects of drugs may increase the sense of competence in some patients. The physician may enlist the patient as an ally in monitoring therapy, as a means of providing intellectual mastery to the patient. Fostering altruistic behavior, such as having appropriate patients helping other patients to overcome barriers, may also increase feelings of mastery and control.[80]

Even though there appears to be a medical basis for depression, the psychosocial aspects must be determined and assessed. It is important to know about earlier episodes of depression that the cancer patient has experienced, the individual's life and situation, just as it is with any depressed patient. The stress of illness may cause depression in someone with a history of recurring depression.

Depression may be the result of feeling abandoned by family and friends, if they fail to visit, or by fear of abandonment. Relatives and friends may actually be withdrawing from the patient due to the many fears and myths associated with cancer.

Another myth that may interfere with visits to the cancer patient is the fear of contamination. Visits may not be made due to fear of catching the disease by breathing the air in the room of the patient or by touching the person or the person's clothing. There may also be anxiety about carrying the disease home to children and other relatives.

In addition to fears of contagion, there may be the mistaken belief that the patient has become radioactive as a result of radiation therapy. This myth probably emerged as a result of the possibility of exposure to radiation when radiation implants are used, as described earlier.

It is important to keep in mind that lesser-trained members of staff may be influenced by these myths. They may be fearful of contagion or radiation and avoid doing anything more than is absolutely necessary for the patient. Their feelings of anxiety and discomfort may be communicated to the patient or patient's family. If questioned by family or visitors about the possibility of contagion, they may not speak with confidence and assurance due to their own doubts.

Other Reasons for Withdrawal from the Cancer Patient

Even close friends and relatives may feel uncomfortable about visiting because they do not know what to say. They do not know whether to refer to the illness or to ignore it. They may be concerned about the feelings that may be evoked, not only their own feelings but those of the person visited. There is often anxiety about the possibility as to the ill person's "breaking down" or about themselves losing control when they see the ill relative or friend. Anxiety may be experienced as to whether the person will talk about dying and the kinds of responses that should be made if such thoughts are spoken.

Staff members may share these same fears and also feel uncomfortable about how to converse with cancer patients. They may be reluctant to reveal their feelings, doubts, and fears to their peers, fearing that they would not sound professional.

Feelings of guilt and anger on the part of family members toward the aging relative have been discussed in association with difficulties in other aspects of aging. When they are present in regard to patients with terminal illness, these feelings may cause withdrawal from that individual. The feelings may appear irrational, such as the spouse being angry because the mate is dying and leaving when he or she is most needed.

Feelings of anger may dominate the reaction of both patient and family to cancer. Anger regarding this turn of events may be displaced onto the physician. They may believe that the patient would not be ill now if the physician had made an earlier diagnosis or had planned a different treatment. As the patient also fears being abandoned by the physician if this anger is expressed, it may be displaced again, this time to staff members or to family members.

The terminal cancer patient also often feels abandoned by the physician when everything has been done, in terms of medical treatment, that can be done. Admission to the nursing home, or to assistance from a home health-care agency at home, is a signal that vigorous treatment efforts are at an end. Radiation or chemotherapy may be discontinued, or almost so, and the physician may be seeing the patient infrequently. Having been trained to cure or at least arrest or improve a condition, many physicians find it difficult to accept that there is no further treatment to offer. The physician may actually be avoiding the patient, since there is nothing more to prescribe other than palliative measures.

Practice Applications

It is important for social workers to be aware that family members may have different expectations of the older cancer patient than they might have of a younger person with cancer. Improved functioning may not be considered as a possibility even though enhanced functioning of the older person is possible in many cases. Family members may not be aware that it is just as essential for the older patient to participate in planning and treatment as for a younger patient.

There are many modes of social work intervention to help the individual, families, or staff caring for the person with cancer. Barstow observes that social work is "clearly needed in a radiation therapy clinic, not only to increase comfort and compliance with the treatment itself, but to help patients and families deal more effectively with the overall ramifications of their life with cancer."[81] The same comment holds true for chemotherapy clinics and surgical wards.

Social workers can learn and make use of techniques to reduce or ameliorate the conditioned side effects of chemotherapy. Some modes of treatment that are being used with cancer patients are relaxation techniques, including hypnosis, progressive muscle relaxation training, electromyogram (EMG) biofeedback combined with relaxation training, and systematic desensitization. The literature suggests that these techniques can alleviate some conditioned side effects of many cancer patients undergoing chemotherapy.[82]

Goals must be set with the older person in terms of rehabilitation, although they may be very limited. It is crucial to keep in mind that it is likely that functioning can be enhanced, even though the person is old and may have chronic conditions as well as cancer.

Reinforcing education is an important function. The physician should explain the effects and goals of treatment that are being recommended. The social worker can determine when talking with the patient whether there are further questions or need for more information from a treatment specialist.

Counseling the patient and family in regard to the changes in their lives as a result of cancer, planning with them for the future, and seeking needed resources are important measures. Episodes of rehospitalization result in psychological problems for the entire family, as well as giving rise to financial and life-style problems. Locating resources, such as respite care, is a constant need.

Social workers may also become involved with initiating support groups, if there are none readily available. Peer counseling may be provided through the American Cancer Society, or another resource.

Telephone counseling may be necessary to help family members to overcome anxiety about visiting terminally ill cancer patients in nursing homes or hospitals. Although there are no set answers as to what to do or say when visiting someone who is terminally ill, families and friends can be assured that simply being there is a statement in itself. There are many comments that are comforting but which will not interfere with any denial that is taking place, such as specific offers to do something for the patient.

The dying patient may no longer have hope for a miraculous cure. However, other kinds of things may be hoped for that the social worker may be able to make possible: the hope for a visit by a close relative, for a telephone call from an invalid friend, a pleasant event of some kind, such as a holiday celebration in the hospital room or at home. Hopes that have a reasonable possibility of being realized can be discussed and encouraged; for example, some patients receiving chemotherapy may have periods of well-being so that they are able to plan for and attend a specific function.

Spiritual needs may sometimes be overlooked. Social workers must exercise extreme caution not to impose their own religious views on the patient, but they must be aware that religion can be a strong component and a major concern in an individual's life. There may be a tendency to refer hastily any need remotely identified as religious to a chaplain or minister without attempting to learn what the person may be seeking. In some health-care settings the patients are far from home and their own churches and ministers. The patient may need assistance in locating a pastor with whom he or she can communicate with ease, or in participating in religious activities or church programs that have been important sources of comfort. A major service the social worker extends may well be to assist the patient in continuing participation in these events.

Resources

In addition to resources described in Chapter 12, the American Cancer Society provides some resources for those affected by cancer. Services that may be provided include transportation of cancer patients to and from medical appointments, the provision of home care items, information and guidance services, and rehabilitation programs. A wide variety of reading material in relation to cancer, care of the patient, and treatment is also available from the American Cancer Society.

The service and rehabilitation programs of the American Cancer Society include *CanSurmount, Reach to Recovery,* the *Laryngectomy Rehabilitation Program,* and the *Ostomy Rehabilitation Program. CanSurmount* is a short-term visitor program for patients with many types of cancer and for their families. *Reach to Recovery* is designed to help women who have or have had breast cancer. Literature and services to help husbands and families are also available. The *Laryngectomy Rehabilitation Program* and the *Ostomy Rehabilitation Program* assist patients who have had laryngectomies and ostomies respectively. All of these programs are not available in all communities.

Oncology social workers are helpful consultants to social workers in community agencies who have had less experience in working with cancer patients. They provide information in regard to cancer treatment, the kinds of stresses encountered by the patient, and other relevant material.

NOTES

1. Ruth B. Weg, "Changing Physiology of Aging: Normal and Pathological," in *Aging: Scientific Perspectives and Social Issues*, ed. Diana S. Woodruff and James E. Birren (New York: D. Van Nostrand Co., 1975), 232.

2. *1989 Heart Facts*, American Heart Association, National Center, Dallas, Texas, 1988, p. 1.

3. Edwin L. Bierman, "Atherosclerosis and Other Forms of Arteriosclerosis," in *Harrison's Principles of Internal Medicine*, Vol. 2, 10th ed., ed. Robert G. Petersdorf et al. (New York: McGraw-Hill Book Co., 1983), 1465.

4. J.M. Neutze et al., *Intensive Care of the Heart and Lungs*, 3rd ed., (Boston: Blackwell Scientific Publications, 1982), 217.

5. Ibid., 218.

6. F. I. Caird and J. L. C. Dall, "The Cardiovascular System," in *Textbook of Geriatric Medicine and Gerontology*, ed. J. C. Brocklehurst (New York: Churchill Livingstone, 1978), 136.

7. Christine W. Cannon, "Coronary Artery Disease" in *Combatting Cardiovascular Diseases Skillfully*, eds. Helen Hamilton et al. (Horsham, Pa.: Intermed Communications, Inc., 1978), 80.

8. Amy Morrison Karch, *Cardiac Care: A Guide for Patient Education* (New York: Appleton-Century-Crofts, 1981), 46, 47.

9. *Webster's Third International Dictionary*, 2nd. ed., s.v. "ventricular fibrillation."

10. Susannah Cunningham, "Physiology and Pathology of Heart Disease," in *Cardiac Care*, 20.

11. Alison M. F. Storrs, *Geriatric Nursing* (Baltimore: The Williams and Wilkins Co., 1976), 77.

12. *An Older Person's Guide to Cardiovascular Health*, 5. Copyright, 1983, American Heart Association.

13. Christine W. Cannon, "Coronary Artery Disease," in *Combatting Cardiovascular Diseases*, 76.

14. Meyer Friedman and Diane Ulmer, *Treating Type A Behavior and Your Heart* (New York: Alfred A. Knopf, 1984), 31.

15. Theodore Irwin, *Living with a Heart Ailment*. Public Affairs Pamphlet No. 521 (New York: Public Affairs Committee, Inc.,) 16.

16. Ibid., 14.

17. Amy Morrison Karch, *Cardiac Care*, 76.

18. Susannah Cunningham, "Physiology and Pathophysiology of Cardiac Disease" in *Cardiac Care*, 21.

19. Eugene Braunwald, "Heart Failure," in *Harrison's Principles*, 1355, 1356.

20. Maureen Harvey, "Physical Assessment: A Tailored Approach for Patients in Heart Failure," in *Congestive Heart Failure*, ed. Cydney R. Michaelson (St. Louis: The C. V. Mosby Co., 1983), 372.

21. Amy Morrison Karch, *Cardiac Care*, 84.

22. Ibid., 85, 86.

23. *1989 Stroke Facts*, American Heart Association, National Center, Dallas, Texas, 1988, 1.

24. Charlotte Eliopoulos, *Gerontological Nursing* (New York: Harper & Row, Publishers, 1979), 243.

25. *An Older Person's Guide to Cardiovascular Health*, 10.

26. Rosemary Jarlath Maloney, "Hypertension: Risk Factor in Atherosclerosis," in *Combatting Cardiovascular Diseases*, 67.

27. K. A. Flugel, "Stroke," in *Geriatrics 1*, ed. Dieter Platt (Berlin: Springer-Verlag, 1982), 406.

28. Arthur S. Freese, *Stroke: New Approaches to Prevention and Treatment*. Public Affairs Pamphlet (381 Park Ave. So., N.Y. 10016, November 1979), 9.

29. Charles J. Gibson and Bruce M. Caplan, "Rehabilitation of the Patient with Stroke" in *Rehabilitation in the Aging*, ed. Franklin T. Williams (New York: Raven Press, 1984), 147, 148.

30. Ibid.

31. Arthur S. Freese, *Stroke: New Approaches*, 9.

32. Charles J. Gibson and Bruce M. Caplan, "Rehabilitation of the Patient with Stroke" in *Rehabilitation in the Aging*, 151.

33. Jane Henry Stolten, *The Geriatric Aide* (Boston: Little, Brown and Company, 1973), 264.

34. Ralph R. Leutenegger, *Patient Care and Rehabilitation of Communication-Impaired Adults* (Springfield, Ill.: Charles C. Thomas, 1975), 76.

35. Gibson and Caplan, "Rehabilitation," 149.

36. Ibid., 150.

37. Arnold Bloom, *Toohey's Medicine for Nurses*, 13th ed. (Edinburgh: Churchill Livingstone, 1981), 27.

38. Ibid., 27, 28.

39. Ibid., 28.

40. Ibid., 3.

41. U. S. Department of Health and Human Services, *Chemotherapy and You: A Guide to Self-Help During Treatment*, (NIH Publication No. 86-1136. Revised January, 1985), p. 2.

42. U. S. Department of Health and Human Services, *Radiation Therapy and You: A Guide to Self-Help During Treatment*, (NIH Publication No. 86-2227. Revised January 1985), 3, 4.

43. Ibid.

44. Ibid., 17.

45. Ibid., 13, 15.

46. *Cancer Facts and Figures–1989*, (New York: American Cancer Society, Copyright, 1989), 3.

47. Joan M. Birchenall and Mary Eileen Streight, *Care of the Older Adult*, 2nd. ed. (Philadelphia: J. B. Lippincott Co., 1982), 226.

48. *Cancer Facts and Figures–1989*, 9.

49. Ibid.

50. Ibid.

51. Ibid.

52. U.S. Department of Health and Human Services, *Cancer of the Prostate: Research Report*, Report prepared by Joan Chamberlain, (NIH Publication No. 87-528, Revised November, 1986), 2.

53. Ibid., 8, 9.

54. Ibid., 8.

55. Irwin N. Frank, Henry M. Keys, Craig S. McCune, "Urologic and Male Genital Cancers," in *Clinical Oncology*, 6th ed., ed. Philip Rubin (American Cancer Society: 1983), 205.

56. Ibid., 207.

57. Ibid., 209.

58. *Cancer Facts & Figures–1989*, 9.

59. Ibid.

60. Ibid.

61. Edith Lenneberg and Alan N. Mendelssohn, *Colostomies: A Guide*, Copyright 1971, United Ostomy Association. Revised 1974, p. 10.

62. Ibid., 17.

63. *Ileostomy: An Introduction*. Pub. by the United Ostomy Association, Inc., 1976.

64. Linda Gross, *Urostomy: An Introduction*. Pub. by the United Ostomy Association, Inc., Los Angeles, CA. Revised 12/82.

65. *Cancer Facts & Figures 1989*, 10.

66. Ibid.

67. Ibid.

68. Ibid.

69. Ibid., 10, 11.

70. Ibid., 10.

71. Ibid., 11.

72. Ibid., 14.

73. James T. Adams, Colin A. Poulter, and Kishan J. Pandya, "Cancer of the Major Digestive Glands: Pancreas, Liver, Bile Ducts, Gallbladder," in *Clinical Oncology*, 6th ed., ed. Philip Rubin (American Cancer Society: 1983), 178.

74. Ibid., 179.

75. Ibid., 182.

76. Marion F. Stonberg, "Oncology," *Health and Social Work*, 6, no. 4 (November 1981): 705.

77. Marjorie Plumb and Jimmie Holland, "Comparative Studies of Psychological Function in Patients with Advanced Cancer: Interviewer-Rated Current and Past Psychological Symptoms," *Psychosomatic Medicine*, 43, no. 3 (June 1981): 250, 252.

78. Jon Streltzer, "Psychiatric Aspects of Oncology: A Review of Recent Research," *Hospital and Community Psychiatry* 34, no. 8, (August 1983): 722.

79. Richard J. Goldberg, "Management of Depression in the Patient with Advanced Cancer," *Journal of the American Medical Association* 246, no. 4 (July 24/31, 1981): 375.

80. Ibid.

81. Linda F. Barstow, "Working with Cancer Patients in Radiation Therapy," *Health and Social Work* 7, no. 1 (February 1982): 37.

82. Thomas G. Burish et al., "Behavioral Relaxation Techniques in Reducing the Distress of Cancer Chemotherapy Patients," *Oncology Nursing Forum* 10, no. 3 (Summer 1983): 32–35.

3

CHRONIC DISEASE
recurring challenges

The previous chapter presented material on the three leading causes of death among older people. Chapter 3 is concerned with other common problems that may be of special interest to social workers in terms of presenting opportunities for social work intervention. These diseases and conditions include arthritis, osteoarthritis, osteoporosis, respiratory problems, hypothermia, hyperthermia, presbycusis, and vision impairment. The first condition to be considered in this chapter is one that may occur at any age but is associated especially with middle and old age: arthritis.

ARTHRITIS

The terminology in regard to arthritis is confusing. Many older people complain of rheumatism and may insist they do not have arthritis. Most physicians use three terms interchangeably: rheumatic disease, arthritis, and rheumatoid arthritis. To add to the confusion, the medical specialists in arthritis are called rheumatologists.

The problem with terminology reflects the complexity of arthritis, for arthritis is not a single disease but consists of a great number of related disorders with widely varying characteristics. Although the causes of some types of arthritis are known, many more are unknown.

Arthritis occurs in individuals of every age. The Arthritis Foundation estimates more than 30 million Americans suffer from arthritis. Nearly every individual over 60 has arthritis to the extent that it can be identified on X-rays.[1]

Rheumatoid arthritis (RA) and *osteoarthritis* are major forms that trouble older individuals. Although the cause of RA is unknown, it seems to be related to the body's immune system. The joints that are most frequently involved are those of the hands and feet, wrists, knees, elbows, ankles, shoulders, hips, and temporomandibular (temple and jaw).[2]

Rheumatoid arthritis is two to three times more common in women than in men.[3] Although RA is primarily a disease that affects the joints, it can be systemic and affect the heart, lungs, eyes, and nervous system. Such involvement may indicate a prognosis that is much more serious than the disability of the joints. Many individuals have a mild degree of arthritis which clears up completely or affects only a few joints. There is little or no impairment of function. Usually there is a tendency toward relapse, or inflammation of the joints continues. In a minimum of cases, the disease course is rapid and marked by relentless joint destruction.[4]

RA is an inconsistent disease. Individuals with RA may feel good one day and be in great pain the next; remissions or pain may last for long periods of time. Treatment results vary among individuals. Treatment that appears to be effective for one person may be nearly useless for another. It is sometimes questionable as to whether a specific treatment actually helps an individual, or whether relief is the result of a spontaneous remission.

One of the consequences of the severity of pain and the inconsistent nature of the disease is the readiness of many arthritis sufferers to try almost any remedy. Even though there is no known cure for the disease and no certain way to bring about remission, many individuals have fallen prey to false advertising and have wasted money needed for necessities on false remedies and so-called "cures."

Arthritis is treated by the utilization of rest, drugs, splints, physical therapy, and orthopedic surgery. Drugs used in treatment can be classified as anti-inflammatory, remission-inducing agents, and immunosuppressive agents. Aspirin and indomethacin are among the anti-inflammatory drugs used in the treatment of arthritis. Gold is usually the initial agent used in the hope of inducing remission. Immunosuppressive drugs are reserved for patients whose progressive disease is not responsive to the anti-inflammatory and remission-inducing agents.[5]

Physical therapy plays an important role in the treatment of arthritis. Application of heat to the painful area followed by prescribed exercises may relieve joint pain and muscle spasm. Exercises can preserve the range of motion of joints and strengthen muscles.

The progressive nature of RA usually poses the need for a long-term, patient-physician relationship. Problems may occur in maintaining patient compliance with the medical regimen. Many rheumatologists are aware that the psychological and social needs of the patient warrant attention. Gallagher and others suggest that intervention by a social worker or psychologist with patients experiencing high levels of stress may not only aid in patient compliance with the medical regimes but possibly influence the course of the disease.[6]

Practice Applications

The two aspects of rheumatoid arthritis which are probably most apt to disrupt relations between the patient and family are the inconsistent nature of the disease and the severity of pain. The arthritic patient is sometimes likely to complain at some length. As the disease is inconsistent in its course, the individual may feel unable to do any kind of work at one time but be ready for various chores a short time later, or there may be long remissions between onsets of pain. Those who are unfamiliar with the erratic course of this disease are often disbelieving when the arthritic sufferer complains one day or one month and appears comfortable the next.

Suspicions are aroused by the sudden inability to perform a task that was performed easily a short time earlier. Many patients believe family members are unsympathetic and don't understand; family members sometimes doubt the severity, but not usually the presence, of pain. The consequences may be disruptive or strained marital and family relationships.

Most people react to pain with anxiety and depression, but the ways in which any individual responds to pain may depend largely on that person's past use of coping skills. Some may turn to drugs or alcohol to reduce pain; others may stoically accept their pain, and still others may seek constructive ways to reduce or adjust to pain. Total dependency on spouse and other relatives sometimes occurs, even though the individual can be partially independent.

Social workers can assist family members who become annoyed over their relative's expressions of pain to obtain a better understanding of arthritis and the inconsistency of the course of the disease. Simply the recognition by family members that pain exists can be comforting to the older individual whose complaints have been met with irritation or anger.

Social workers sometimes find that older individuals who complain heavily about pain have little else to occupy their minds. They are frequently socially isolated or living in such emotionally deprived circumstances that preoccupation with their illnesses provides their primary means of relating to others. Working toward involving the person in some constructive way with others in the home or the community may be the only way to interrupt the preoccupation and improve the quality of their lives. Day-care centers may prove helpful in such situations by providing opportunities for socialization and giving the patient and family respite from each other.

Family members who describe the older person with arthritis as constantly complaining may be taught desensitization techniques. Instead of responding irritably to pain complaints, being bored and indifferent to pain statements but warmly attentive to conversation on any subject other than pain may guide the person away from constantly complaining. Setting and working toward attainable goals may divert attention to activities rather than feelings. Helping the individual to become as independent as possible and encouraging every independent act, however small, focuses attention on desirable behavior. Family members may need to be reminded that behavior that is rewarded by acts of attention and love is likely to be repeated.

Occupational or physical therapists in outpatient clinics, home health services, or public health services can identify and set attainable goals that are needed to motivate the patient to work toward independence. Exercises to increase range of motion, learning to use aids to help in dressing, and learning to design or make use of tools that make household chores easier are among the plans that therapists may devise to make life more satisfying for the arthritic patient.

OSTEOARTHRITIS(OA)—DEGENERATIVE JOINT DISEASE

Osteoarthritis is a degenerative joint disease which is characterized by cartilage degeneration and formation of new bone at joint surfaces. Contributing factors include age, trauma, mechanical stress, and genetics. Although the disease advances with time, it rarely becomes as severe as RA. Early symptoms of osteoarthritis include tenderness of the affected joint on pressure, pain on motion, and mild heat. The weight-bearing joints—hips, knees, and lumbar and cervical spine—are usually the affected areas.[7]

Repeated injuries to joints, such as injuries sustained by football players, may eventually lead to osteoarthritis.

OSTEOPOROSIS—BONE DEGENERATION

Osteoporosis is a gradual thinning of the bones. It is a progressive disease that is much more prevalent in women than in men. Although all individuals seem to experience a decrease in bone mass with age, some individuals have a more rapid loss. In women, the reduced levels of estrogen as a result of menopause are associated with rapid loss.[8]

It is generally agreed that osteoporosis occurs as a result of a prolonged negative calcium balance due to a leaching of calcium from the bones. There is disagreement as to whether this occurs as part of physiologic aging and as primarily due to hormonal changes or by a low-calcium, high-phosphorous, high-protein diet. Although there seems to be no doubt that calcium supplementation and a reduction of the intake of phosphorous and protein will not cure this condition after it has begun, calcium supplementation and reduced phosphorous intake are recommended for older people in general in the hope that calcium loss from bone composition can be diminished to some extent.[9]

Although there is no treatment at this time that can reverse bone loss, one of the most effective preventive measures may be diet during the young adult years when bone density is increasing. The diet would include an adequate intake of both calcium and Vitamin D, the latter being an important factor in the absorption of calcium, and a limited intake of carbonated soft drinks containing phosphoric acid, until the effects of excess dietary phosphorous are determined.[10]

When bones become thinner, fractures are more likely to occur. Falls that would not cause fractures in younger people can be very damaging to older people with osteoporosis. For this reason, extra care must be taken to help patients with severe osteoporosis to avoid falls. The following safety precautions would be helpful in evaluating the safety of the homes of all older clients:

- Add nonslip treads or carpet to stairs.
- Paint the top and bottom steps a light color for ease of identification.
- Staircase handrails should be extended beyond the last step, and should be of sufficient distance from the wall as to allow for a solid grasp.
- Staircase handrails should be installed on both sides of the stairs.
- Bathtubs should have nonslip rubber mats, horizontal grab bars, and a stool for resting.
- Polished wood and waxed tiled floors should be minimized; total carpeting with short nap or possibly cork flooring is preferred.
- Scatter rugs should be eliminated or at least nonslip backing should be applied to them.
- Rugs should have their edges tacked down.
- Large pieces of glass (i.e., shower doors and patio doors) should be shatterproof and marked so that the glass is visible to aging eyes.
- Housekeeping should be stressed; spills should be wiped up immediately and objects should not be left in unexpected places to be stored at a later time.
- Use sturdy furniture of the proper height for ease of getting up and down.
- Provide adequate lighting in stairways, storage areas such as basements, and nightlights for bedrooms and bathrooms.
- Place telephone jacks strategically so that the telephone can be moved about the house (i.e., near the bed at night).
- Design shelving low enough so that the use of chairs and stools for climbing is minimized.
- Wear shoes with solid bottoms and with laces and snug fit to support the foot...[11]

SYNCOPE (FAINTING)

Syncope, a temporary loss of consciousness as a result of insufficient blood supply to the brain, is another common cause of falls among older people.[12]

Although some causes of syncope are not difficult to identify, there are other types of syncope that pose great problems in diagnosis. In one study the records of 121 patients hospitalized for syncope of unknown origin were reviewed. A definitive cause was determined through extensive diagnostic studies in only 13 of the patients.[13]

Causes of syncope range from benign to severely life-threatening disorders. *Vasodepressor* or *vasovagal syncope* is generally situational, such as syncope in relation to fear and anxiety or after a medical procedure. There are also some unusual syndromes associated with syncope: cough syncope, micturition syncope, and alcoholic blackouts. More serious causes of syncope include complete heart block, tachyarrhythmias, bradyarrhythmias, pulmonary embolism, and reactions to drugs.[14]

The carotid sinus is very sensitive to stretch. Syncope may be caused by turning the head, by a tight collar, or, more rarely, by shaving over the sinus region.[15]

A commonly observed cause of falling in older people is the *drop attack*. The cause for this type of syncope has not been adequately explained. The legs of the older person suddenly give way, although consciousness is not lost; there seems to be complete flaccidity of the legs and the individual is unable to rise. This may last from a minute to hours. If the soles of the feet can be pressed against a firm object, tone and power immediately return and the person can get up and continue as if nothing had occurred.[16]

As fainting is common among older people, there may be a tendency for the older individual to take it lightly. There may be no mention of fainting episodes to the visiting nurse or family physician. As the causes are so diverse and could be serious, clients who are known to have episodes of fainting should be urged to report this to a health professional. Although some syncopes are difficult to diagnose, causes can be determined for many kinds and prevention or treatment provided.

RESPIRATORY PROBLEMS

There is a decline in pulmonary function with aging. This is partly attributed to changes in the skeletal and muscular systems that can adversely affect the respiratory system. These changes include the following:

1. The rib cage becomes rigid as the costal cartilages calcify.
2. Osteoporosis and kyphosis (humpback) cause a stooped posture which decreases the ability of the chest to expand with each inspiration.
3. The abdominal muscles usually become weaker and lack tone, and then the diaphragm, an important organ of respiration, is affected.
4. The lungs lose some of their elasticity. Bronchioles and alveoli enlarge and decrease in number; their walls become thin and less elastic.
5. Arterioclerosis prevents the forceful circulation of the blood: thus it is harder to circulate blood through the lungs.[17]

Older adults are more prone to have pneumonia and influenza, for resistance to airborne bacteria is also diminished with age. It is important to note that in spite of the changes listed, older people are usually able to breathe normally.

CHRONIC OBSTRUCTIVE PULMONARY DISEASE (COPD)

COPD refers to a group of overlapping diseases: bronchitis, asthma, and emphysema. In COPD there is a persistent obstruction to bronchial airflow which leads to abnormalities in the lung. Shortness of breath on exertion, coughing, wheezing, and expectoration of sputum are frequent complaints of individuals who have COPD. This disease is progressive and chronic and requires patients to continually change their life-styles, conserve resources, and learn to cope with new symptoms, as well as with medications and complications, as they arise.[18]

A comment by Bither helps in understanding the extent of strain imposed by this condition:

> People with COPD must work very hard to breathe owing to increased resistance to airflow and increased muscle work. They become very tired during the day just because they are working so hard at something others take for granted—breathing.[19]

Management includes drugs, adequate hydration and nutrition, maintenance of activities within the physical limitations of the patient, breathing treatments, chest drainage, patient education, and modification of life because of the increased work of breathing.[20]

Cigarette smoking and environmental pollution are thought to be major factors in the development of this syndrome.

Practice Applications

A major role of social workers regarding COPD may be in relation to whether the patient and family have a good understanding of the specific demands of the condition and the means to make whatever adjustments are necessary. When considering the possibility of impaired sight and vision and poor memory, lack of understanding may well interfere with treatment. Experiencing difficulties in breathing is very frightening and anxiety producing, not only to the patient but to the family. Patients and families need to be thoroughly educated to reduce anxiety. In addition, breathing machines are sometimes prescribed which patients may find difficult to operate. The safe operation of these machines and other equipment, such as humidifiers, is essential. It may be necessary to call the physician's attention to the patient's lack of understanding or to suggest referral of the patient to the local public health department for a visit by a nurse or therapist.

HYPOTHERMIA

Hypothermia is a dangerous condition that is not infrequently fatal. It occurs when the body temperature drops below 95 degrees F or 35 degrees C. There are usually two factors associated with hypothermia: low environmental temperature and poor regulation of body heat by the physiological systems.[21]

Symptoms of hypothermia are usually pallor, loss of consciousness or extreme sluggishness, and a fine tremor without actual shivering.[22]

Since heating costs have increased so drastically over the past decade, most families have been forced to lower their thermostats. For younger people, discomfort may be the only consequence, but for the elderly, living in cold rooms poses a real hazard. Besdine observes that older people have become hypothermic in mildly cool environments, usually between 50 to 60 degrees, and possibly even at 65 degrees.[23]

In Great Britain researchers found that between 3 and 5 percent of all patients over age 65 admitted to the hospital in the winter had hypothermia. Extending these figures to the United States results in a conservative estimate of about 50,000 cases per year.[24] Hypothermia poses a health hazard which social workers can help prevent by being observant of the older client's environment.

HEAT ILLNESSES

Environmental temperatures rising above body temperature, which are sustained for one or more days, may cause hyperthermia. Older people have a decreased ability to sweat and are unable to lower body temperature through sweating. It is not necessary for the older person to be out-of-doors to succumb to the heat, for this can occur in a poorly ventilated residence without air conditioning.[25]

In addition to heat exhaustion and heat stroke as a result of the burden of heat stress, heart failure and stroke can also occur.

The risk of developing heat-related medical problems in very hot weather is increased by the presence of physical conditions including a weak or damaged heart, hypertension, emphysema, circulatory problems, diabetes, previous stroke, infection or fever, overweight, diarrhea, skin diseases or sunburn, or any debilitating illness. Medication can also be a factor as some medications can depress or interfere with the body's natural temperature system.[26]

Since heat stress causes physical and mental changes which signal the onset of more serious problems, heat illnesses can be avoided by taking notice of warning signs which include the following: dizziness, rapid heartbeat, nausea, throbbing headache, dry skin (no sweating), diarrhea, chest pains, great weakness, breathing problems, mental changes, vomiting, and cramps. If any of these signs are experienced, medical help should be sought as quickly as possible.[27]

Policy Issues

In the past decade costs for heating and cooling have escalated to the extent that people of all income levels have been affected. Older adults who had lived comfortably on fixed incomes suddenly found their purchasing ability, which was already shrinking as a result of inflation, inadequate to meet their basic needs. The poor and near poor have suffered even more. Many older men and women have had to cut back expenditures on both heating and cooling, and some have experienced disastrous effects. Federal and state efforts have been made to provide assistance. However, the ongoing problems related to rising fuel costs have not been adequately addressed.

The Low Income Energy Assistance Program (LIEAP) is a federally funded program designed to *assist* householders with low incomes to meet their fuel bills. The intention of this program is to supplement heating costs and assist in weather crisis situations. It is often administered at the state level by the Department of Human Services or community action agency. To be eligible, the household's total income cannot exceed 125% of the current Federal Poverty guidelines.

The Weatherization Assistance Program is also a federally funded program with the same income requirement as the LIEAP. This program is directed toward decreasing consumption of energy and reducing the impact of higher fuel costs on low income families, particularly the elderly and the handicapped.

In response to the recognition that rising energy costs were a serious problem for many of the elderly and that a coordinated approach was needed, the National Energy and Aging Consortium (NEAC) was initially organized in 1980 through the efforts of the American Association of Retired Persons. The NEAC consists of approximately 40 diverse national organizations which share information and develop programs and resources for older people.[28]

The NEAC has also fostered the development of state consortia involving government, business, consumer, and social service organizations that are concerned about energy issues and the ways the elderly are affected. The consortia include utility companies and other energy suppliers, state and local area agencies on aging, social service and energy assistance providers, legislative and regulatory bodies, consumer organizations, energy trade associations, and older membership groups. A manual is available to individuals that are interested in developing energy and aging consortia in their states.[29]

On a state and local level, many utility companies provide information about energy conservation and refer needy customers to federal, state, and local programs. Partial payment plans are sometimes available.

A number of utility companies have also developed direct assistance programs, sometimes referred to as "fuel funds," to help low income consumers. The utility may supply seed money to start the fund and pay for initial administrative costs, match donations up to a maximum amount, and perhaps solicit additional funds from local businesses and charities or the government.[30]

New programs related to meeting problems resulting from increased energy costs are being developed or proposed in various areas of the country. Social work input may be a valuable aid in developing such programs.

PRESBYCUSIS—IMPAIRED HEARING

Presbycusis is the term used for the decline of auditory acuity that occurs with increased age. Although only about 8 percent of older people have severe hearing problems, about 50 percent have some hearing impairment.[31]

Presbycusis begins as a high tone loss but gradually becomes a generalized loss of hearing. Rapid speech and loud background sounds increase hearing difficulty. Since hearing loss occurs gradually, older men and women often compensate, without realizing it, in such ways as facing the person who is speaking and through lip reading.

It is important to note that the person who complains of vertigo (dizziness), tinnitus (ringing in the ear), and ear pain should seek medical attention, for these conditions are not normal.[32]

Hearing deficits are irritating and frustrating to others, because they drastically impede communication. Having to repeat words or sentences interferes with the train of thought. Being misunderstood adds to the frustration, sometimes leading to shouting responses which do not help either party. The usual result is breaking off an attempt at serious conversation and settling for a few simple questions and answers. There is even the assumption, many times, that the individual who cannot hear is retarded or mentally ill.

Some older individuals with impaired hearing are sensitive to the irritation of others and withdraw from making efforts to converse. Others work at learning to lip read or try to remedy their loss with the use of hearing aids. In some cases, hearing aids can be helpful, but they do not help with profound hearing loss.

Numerous investigations of the delivery system and pricing of hearing aids have revealed serious abuses. These include the sale of hearing aids to people who do not need them, inadequately trained hearing aid dealers, false advertising, and misleading promotional schemes.[33]

Unfortunately, many older people believe hearing aids can resolve any type of hearing problem. Social workers may need to urge their older clients to seek a hearing evaluation from a medically qualified hearing specialist before purchasing a hearing aid.

Practice Applications

It is so difficult to communicate with the hearing impaired that it may be tempting to skimp on time spent with these individuals. Since communication is probably the most vital component of social work services and must take place, regardless of the frustration that may ensue, social workers may find the following suggestions helpful.

The interview should be planned carefully, allowing ample time. Communicating with a client who has difficulty in hearing requires much more time than with someone with normal hearing. Irritation can be avoided by perceiving this as a challenge instead of an obstacle. The schedule must be arranged so that the social worker can be unhurried, relaxed, and receptive.

A private place for the interview should be located *before* the interview takes place. Confidentiality must be protected. Speaking loudly in the presence of others about a subject that requires confidentiality produces discomfort on the part of both client and social worker. If there is no privacy, clients may avoid discussions that are vital to their welfare.

Background noise should be kept to a minimum. This is an aspect to be considered when locating the place for the interview. Background noise seriously interferes with the quality of hearing experienced by the client with impaired hearing.

It is important for the interviewer to keep his or her face turned toward the client. Even if the client is not trained in lip reading, seeing the speaker's face and expression aids in understanding what is said. Speaking slowly and distinctly, enunciating each word, is important. Shouting or raising the voice excessively is a hindrance. Most hearing-impaired people understand words spoken clearly in a slightly loud voice. If it is necessary to increase loudness, do so gradually until voice range reaches what is needed for this particular client. The bearded social worker may have difficulty in communicating with a client who is very dependent on lip reading.

Most important of all, keep in mind that the person who experiences difficulty in hearing has a constant struggle in communicating with others. This interview is very likely one of the few opportunities that this individual has to express concerns. If frustrations are kept to a minimum, it can be a highly rewarding and enriching experience for both the social worker and the client.

VISION IMPAIRMENT

Most older people wear glasses for farsightedness; except for that condition, about 80 percent have reasonably good eyesight until the ninth decade or later.[34] Macular degeneration, cataracts, glaucoma, and diabetes retinopathy are the most common causes of impaired vision in people over 65.[35]

In *macular degeneration,* a part of the retina is affected which leads to central vision loss, but peripheral vision is not disturbed. In *glaucoma,* increased tension inside the eyeball and hardening of the eyeball occur. *Diabetic retinopathy* is deterioration of the retina caused by diabetes. A *cataract* is an opacity of the eye lens.[36]

When older people experience an increase in visual impairment and this loss is not corrected, they may stumble, grope for support, and have difficulty in moving about in strange surroundings. They may even be labeled demented simply because such actions have made them appear bewildered and confused.

Older adults also may be experiencing unnecessary discomfort because they assume their impaired vision is a natural state and therefore do not inquire about it. However, helpful devices are available. Older people should seek evaluation by a professional clinician who will analyze the effect of the eye problem on the person's vision and consider the tasks the person wishes to perform. All low vision devices are prescribed individually and require thorough instruction to ensure that the patient will benefit through correct use. Examples of low vision devices include magnifying glasses that may be set in eyeglass frames, a telescopic system which ranges from hand-held to complex units mounted in spectacle frames, and absorptive lenses that absorb ultraviolet light or increase/decrease light intensity.[37]

Practice Applications

Blind or nearly blind individuals, if hearing is unaffected, are not greatly hampered in their understanding of speech. However, if they cannot see faces clearly, there may be uncertainty as to the interpretation of the emotions of the other person. The ability to interpret speech depends to some extent on nonverbal communication, even though there is often not a conscious awareness of this element. Sitting so that the client with visual impairment can see the face of the speaker as well as possible may aid in communicating. In order to do so, there must be an understanding of the nature of the client's visual loss—for example, the extent of loss and whether peripheral vision is affected.

Most older people are fearful of falling and incurring fractures. Those who have poor vision are usually even more fearful that they will stumble and fall. Offering one's arm to the person with visual impairment provides much better support than gripping the individual's arm in an attempt to furnish guidance.

Keeping furniture in the same place is important. When they are in their own homes, most visually impaired people can manage to get around with little difficulty. Away from home, they often encounter problems unless someone takes the responsibility to look after them when they move about. Visiting relatives and friends occasionally may move furniture around for more comfortable seating. If they forget to put it back into place, they are presenting hazards to the person with visual loss.

In addition to the other problems caused by impaired vision, this condition also interferes with socializing with others. Many older people who would remain active and involved in social events become withdrawn when severe vision problems occur. Admission to a nursing home may result, even though that individual is able-bodied except for visual impairment.

Wineburg points out some major inadequacies in services to the blind, including the following: limited reimbursement by Medicare and Medicaid, which does not provide for eye examinations, services for those with poor vision, or rehabilitation; insufficient resources for service agencies for the blind; federal budget cuts in recent years which have affected systemwide efforts that were just beginning to expand services for the elderly blind; and the lack of emphasis on blindness and other visual impairments of the aged so that professionals and paraprofessionals are often not attuned to working with the blind.[38]

Much of the vision loss that occurs could be avoided through prevention and treatment.[39] Glaucoma screening tests are recommended for everyone over 40. Active efforts must be made by social workers, as well as other community workers, to learn about resources in the community for detection and treatment of glaucoma and other visual problems and to provide their clients with this information. As resources are generally scarce, social workers may attempt consciousness-raising tactics and enlist the help of other concerned health-care professionals in the community in order to provide screening and treatment programs for the elderly.

Visual impairment, like so many other chronic conditions of older people, is an area that requires an emphasis on prevention. This is another area that could provide fertile ground for social work advocacy.

Resources

For those who have severely impaired sight, the public library offers some resources, such as recorded books (talking books) that can be heard instead of read.

Vocational Rehabilitation assists in paying for some restorative services to the elderly, such as eye surgery, provided the individuals are able to maintain themselves. Services of a rehabilitation teacher are available to older people in institutions or living with relatives. The teacher helps them to cope with and adapt to their disabilities in handling everyday tasks. Leisure activities, such as macrame, are also taught. Eligibility for services depends on income and amount of sight loss. Legal blindness or a condition that will lead to blindness, tunnel vision, and double vision are some of the conditions that meet eligibility requirements.

The following brief examples present some of the ways social workers may intervene to aid individuals who are experiencing difficulty with some of the chronic conditions described in this chapter.

CASE EXAMPLE: CORRECTING MISINFORMATION—ARTHRITIS

Agnes Barton comes to the attention of a social worker at a senior citizens center when she comes into his office seeking help in regard to transportation to the center. While there, she complains at some length about the painful arthritis in the joints of her hands and wrists. She supplements Social Security by doing domestic work. When she has jobs that require rubbing and polishing furniture, silver, and brass, the joints in her hands become swollen and red. She was advised by a physician at the city hospital to avoid using her hands in the same activity for long periods of time. A large dosage of aspirin was prescribed, but nothing else. She was disappointed because they did not give her any "real" medication. She does not bother to take the aspirin. She is taking "some pills" she ordered from an advertisement. They are expensive, and they aren't helping now, but she thinks they eventually will.

The social worker suggests that Mrs. Barton comply with the physician's recommendations in regard to aspirin. If it does not help her condition, she can return to the clinic physician and seek further help. He warns her that the medication she ordered from the advertisement may be harmful. He reminds her that a public health nurse attends the senior citizens center once a week and suggests she make an effort to come that day and talk with the nurse.

The social worker makes a mental note to suggest at the next staff meeting an informational program at the center on arthritis. Mrs. Barton has been the third person in the past few days to mention buying a "wonder drug" for arthritis from an advertisement of some kind.

CASE EXAMPLE: PREVENTING HYPOTHERMIA

Joan Grant, a 78-year-old widow, is referred to a church-supported community center for social work services by a volunteer who delivers lunches for Meals on Wheels. Mrs. Grant lives with her son and his wife, both of whom are employed, in a small house in a suburban development. Mrs. Grant has osteoporosis to the extent that her spine has begun to crumble. She experiences a great deal of pain and has difficulty walking. She is recuperating from the effects of a fall which fractured both arms. Unable to return home following hospitalization, she was discharged to her son's small home. The volunteer brings a noon meal five days each week and is concerned, for Mrs. Grant seems to be "so pitiful" and "becoming sicker." She has also observed that the house is usually cold and uncomfortable.

The social worker telephones the son and arranges to make a home visit the following day. The son is polite on the telephone but cool, saying that his mother is fine. However, if there has been a complaint, he would like for the social worker to visit and check it out.

When the social worker arrives, she is immediately aware of the coldness of the house. Mrs. Grant is wearing a dress and sweater with the lower part of the sleeves cut off, because both arms are in splints. She can use her hands enough to open the door, but with difficulty. She appears very frail and weak as she slowly makes her way to a chair near the television and pulls a blanket over her knees.

The social worker comments on the coldness of the day and asks whether Mrs. Grant is comfortable. She replies that she is. She quickly adds that everything is fine, she feels good, and she is sorry the volunteer called anybody. Her son takes her to the clinic when she is supposed to be there and looks after her "the best he can."

The social worker talks with Mrs. Grant about her move into her son's home and how hard it must have been to leave her own home. Mrs. Grant freely describes her feelings of loss and loneliness, her reluctance to be a "burden," and her wish to live independently again. She admits she is cold "all the time" but wearily adds that this is not her house. She must not turn up the heat. Her son and daughter-in-law have too many bills already, and their utility bills are very high, even with the house so cold. She is afraid they will "put her away" in a nursing home if she adds to their expenses.

The social worker learns enough about the family to tentatively determine that Mrs. Grant is not being neglected or physically abused by her son and daughter-in-law. She believes their failure to keep the house warm is a result of ignorance.

The social worker inquires into Mrs. Grant's finances before she came to her son's home and learns that Mrs. Grant receives a pension from her husband's employment that she is now turning over to her son as soon as it arrives each month. Mrs. Grant was able to live on it, but now she is afraid to live alone. She has been advised by the city hospital physician that she will become even less able to function independently due to her osteoporosis. Her greatest fear is being placed in a nursing home.

The social worker persuades Mrs. Grant to increase the heat before she leaves. She tells her that it is unhealthy to be in such a cold house and that her physician would want her to have the house warmer. She assures her that she will call and talk to Mrs. Grant's son so that he will understand.

The social worker finds, as she thought, that Mrs. Grant's son has no knowledge of hypothermia. Before his mother came, he and his wife had set the thermostat back to 50 degrees when they left to go to work and turned it up "some" when they came home. They have set the thermostat up "a little" since his mother's arrival. He is alarmed to hear that it is possible that his mother's life could become endangered by living in a poorly heated home.

The social worker does not close the case. She believes that Mrs. Grant has made the choice to stay with her son without assessing the alternatives. She visits Mrs. Grant again and discusses with her the alternatives of a boarding situation, congregate-care facility, or spending some of her daytime hours in a day-care center provided by a community health agency until such time that Mrs. Grant needs more care. Mrs. Grant is interested but wants the social worker to talk to her son before making a decision.

The social worker meets with the family and finds that none of them has firsthand knowledge of living facilities for older people. She suggests some places for them to visit. After much discussion and visits to several facilities, Mrs. Grant moves into a small boarding home which provides custodial care and opportunities for socializing with others.

In each of these cases, the social work contacts are brief, but may have extensive impact on the client's health and life. Both cases involve the prevention of further health problems. Medical knowledge does not need to be extensive to enable the social worker to identify and resolve some problem areas.

NOTES

1. Arthur S. Freese, *Arthritis: Everybody's Disease*. Public Affairs Pamphlet No. 562. (New York: Public Affairs Committee, Inc., 1978), 2.
2. Ruth Beckmann Murray, M. Marilyn Wilson Huelskoetter, and Dorothy Lueckerath O'Driscoll, *The Nursing Process in Later Maturity* (Englewood Cliffs, N.J.: Prentice-Hall, Inc., 1980), 398.
3. *Primer on the Arthritic Diseases*, 7th ed., Gerald P. Rodnan, ed., *The Journal of the American Medical Association*, 224, no. 5 (supplement) (April 30, 1973): 688.
4. Ibid., 687.
5. Bruce C. Gilliland and Mart Mannick, "Rheumatoid Arthritis," in *Harrison's Principles of Internal Medicine*, Vol. 2, 10th ed., ed. Robert G. Petersdorf et al., (New York: McGraw-Hill Book Co., 1983).
6. Dolores Gallagher et al., "Psychological Correlates of Immunologic Disease in Older Adults," *Clinical Gerontologist* 1, no. 2 (Winter 1982): 57.
7. Murray, Huelskoetter, and O'Driscoll, *The Nursing Process*, 397.
8. Elizabeth A. McGuire, "Nutrition for Life," in *Educational Horizons*, 60, no. 4 (Summer 1982): 176.
9. "Recent Advances: Osteoporosis and Periodontal Disease" in *Nutrition and Health* 1, no. 6 (1979): 3.
10. Elizabeth A. McGuire, "Nutrition for Life," 176.
11. James H. Price, "Unintentional Injury Among the Aged," *Journal of Gerontological Nursing* 4, no. 3 (May-June 1978): 40.
12. L. Wollner and J.M.K. Spalding, "The Autonomic Nervous System," in *Textbook of Geriatric Medicine and Gerontology*, 2nd ed., ed. J.C. Brocklehurst (New York: Churchill Livingstone, 1978), 258.
13. Wishwa N. Kapoor et al., "Syncope of Unknown Origin," *Journal of the American Medical Association* 247, no. 19: 2687–2691.
14. Ibid.
15. Robert G. Petersdorf, "Faintness, Syncope, and Seizures," in *Harrison's Principles*, 76.
16. John Agate, "Common Symptoms and Complaints," in *Clinical Geriatrics*, 2nd ed., ed. Isadore Rossman (Philadelphia: J.B. Lippincott Co., 1979), 160.
17. Joan Carson Breitung, *Care of the Older Adult* (New York: The Tiresias Press, 1981), 149.
18. Suzanne Bither, "Respiratory Problems," in *Nursing Management for the Elderly*, ed. Doris L. Carnevali and Maxine Patrick (Philadelphia: J.B. Lippincott Company, 1979), 429.
19. Ibid., 431.
20. Ibid., 427.
21. G.L. Chalmers, *Caring for the Elderly Sick* (Bath, England: The Pitman Press, 1980), 104.
22. Ibid., 107.
23. Richard W. Besdine, "The Content of Geriatric Medicine," in *The Geriatric Imperative: An Introduction to Gerontology and Clinical Geriatrics*, ed. Anne R. Somers and Dorothy R. Fabian (New York: Appleton-Century-Crofts, 1981), 44.
24. Ibid., 46.
25. I. Rossman, "Hyperthermia" in *Clinical Geriatrics*, 471.
26. W. Moulton Avery, "Hypothermia and Heat Illness," *Aging*, no. 344, (April-May 1984): 45.
27. Ibid.
28. Jane Marden-Stephens and Ann Shalit, *How to Establish an Energy and Aging Consortium in your state*, Manual, National Energy and Aging Consortium, printed by the American Association of Retired Persons, 1986, 3,4.
29. Ibid., 5,6.
30. David C. Sweet and Kathryn Wertheim Hexter, *Public Utilities and the Poor* (New York: Praeger, 1987), 83.
31. C. Carl Pegels, *Health Care and the Elderly* (Rockville, Md.: Aspen Systems Corp., 1980), 139.

32. Mathy Doval Mezey, Louis Harnett Rauckhorst, and Shirlee Ann Stokes, *Health Assessment of the Older Individual* (New York: Springer Co., 1980), 55.

33. House Subcommittee on Aging, *Medical Appliances and the Elderly: Unmet Needs and Excessive Costs for Eyeglasses, Hearing Aids, Dentures, and Other Devices*, 94th Cong., 2d sess., Sept. 1976, 21–23.

34. Robert N. Butler and Myrna I. Lewis, *Aging and Mental Health, Positive Psychosocial and Biomedical Approaches*, 3rd ed. (St. Louis: C.V. Mosby Co., 1982), 140.

35. Ibid., 139.

36. Ibid.

37. Eleanor E. Faye and Clare M. Hood, "Perspectives in Low Vision: Low Vision Devices and Their Prescription," *Aging and Vision News*, 1, no. 1 (July 1988): 2.

38. Robert J. Wineburg, "Geriatric Blindness: A Neglected Public Health Problem," *Health and Social Work* 9, no. 1 (Winter 1984): 37.

39. Butler and Lewis, *Aging and Mental Health*, 140.

4

MENTAL DISORDERS OF LATER LIFE
terminology and differentiation

Chapters 4, 5, and 6 are involved with mental disorders. The entity of mental disorders includes many types of conditions and diseases that have similarities in symptoms but are extremely different in regard to causes, treatment, and outcome. Chapter 4 is concerned with types of mental disorders with a physiological cause, such as overmedication, that can be corrected or cured. Chapter 5 is devoted to a discussion of senile disease, Alzheimer's type (SDAT), a mental condition that is progressive and incurable. Chapter 6 focuses on depression. However, there is much overlapping in these various kinds of mental disorders, which gives rise to difficulties in making diagnoses and prescribing treatment. This will become obvious as the reader progresses through these three chapters. The initial discussion in this chapter is concerned primarily with the confusing terminology and with the difficulties in differentiating between a progressive, deteriorating brain disease such as Alzheimer's disease, and a disorder such as one resulting from a head injury which can be diagnosed, treated, and reversed. As both conditions may present similar symptoms, such as confusion, there may be problems in making a correct diagnosis.

ATTITUDES TOWARD MENTAL DECLINE

Individuals of every age dread and fear the mental losses that are assumed to be the accompaniments of old age. To become old has been the equivalent of becoming "senile," "demented," dependent on others, and useless to society.

Incidences of forgetfulness that would be ignored by a younger person take on an ominous significance when displayed by an older individual. Any evidence pointing to memory loss, however slight, is often construed as a sign of impaired intellect. This in turn becomes a cause for anxiety, fear, and depression, which may become the cause of further incidences of memory loss.

Psychiatry has neglected mental disorders associated with cerebral disease. However, more interest is currently being displayed, as a result of several factors: a new classification of mental disorders in the recent editions of the *Diagnostic and Statistical Manual of Mental Disorders* (DSM-111 and DSM-111-R)[1] and explicit diagnostic criteria for organic mental disorders; the growing awareness that organic mental disorders are a major health problem; advances in the neurosciences which have produced better techniques and methodology for research; and the present focus on chronic disease which has highlighted the psychiatric aspects of cerebral disorders.[2]

An encouraging aspect of the new interest in studying mental disorders is the emphasis on the social environment of the older adult. Throughout much of the current medical literature on dementia, the social aspect of mental disorders receives attention. There appears to be more awareness of the importance of the family role in maintaining the patient outside the institution. There is wide recognition of the emotional losses that are incurred with advancing age and the ways in which these losses may affect mental functioning. Concern is expressed for the older man or woman who is judged incompetent and institutionalized, sometimes as a result of misdiagnosis or inadequate family supports instead of as a result of debilitating mental functioning.

The need for careful planning in regard to maintenance of older adults in the community is recognized and the lack of resources is acknowledged. Although some of the literature stops short of naming social workers as the professionals essential to helping older adults with mental disorders, some clinicians specify the great need for social work skills.

Results of longitudinal studies in regard to memory and cognition in later life are helping to change the negative, pessimistic attitudes toward aging in relation to mental loss. The concept of a natural progression of impaired mental functioning as one grows older is no longer accepted.

Henig summarizes the conclusions from a number of studies on mental functioning and aging as follows:

- most old people remain throughout life as intelligent as they ever were;
- the decline in intelligence test scores that does occur with age usually is on those tests in which speed of performance is an important factor;
- on self-paced tests, even those involving the incorporation of new types of abstract information, old people perform better than they do on timed tests, and usually perform almost as well as young people do;

- on certain tests of accumulated knowledge, such as vocabulary tests, persons actually perform better as they get older;
- persons with a higher educational level and higher initial IQ scores decline less over time than do their less educated or less intelligent peers, either because the education itself provides some protective effect or because it is associated with a lifestyle in which the mind is always used;
- many people seem to become forgetful with age, but this may be due primarily to a slowdown in the retrieval of information, rather than to a total obliteration of the memory trace;
- if old persons can be taught to store new information more efficiently, their ability to retrieve it later improves significantly.[3]

Henig also points out that of the 23 million Americans now past 65, serious intellectual impairment is shown by only about 5 percent and mild to moderate memory loss by only about 10 percent.[4] The proportion is small, which is encouraging from the standpoint of statistical risk, but in terms of numbers it amounts to a great many people.

Clinicians have found that many of the causes of "incurable" mental disorders can be reversed, halted, or even prevented. Even those older adults who have mental conditions deemed irreversible at this time can have improved functioning if they receive treatment.

IMPACT ON THE FIELD OF SOCIAL WORK

Social workers, more so than probably any other community workers with older adults, have more avenues for intervention with the small proportion who experience severe problems with mental functioning: in hospitals and mental health clinics, family services, home health and protective services, rehabilitation units, nutrition programs, senior citizen centers, public housing, and in their communities as private citizens. Many of the older men and women who come to the attention of social workers have outlived relatives and friends who would normally provide support systems for them. Social workers are sometimes their only advocates.

One of the stumbling blocks that social workers may experience is a lack of familiarity with mental disorders as results of an organic cause. Some understanding of the reasons for intellectual decline, problems in diagnosing mental disorders, and suggested treatment is vital in attending to the needs of older individuals.

Although progress has been made in understanding many mental disorders, in terms of both cause and treatment, the terminology has tended to become more confusing, or, as one physician phrases it, "notoriously muddled."[5] A wide variety of terms are used, and the meanings of some of the terms vary from one clinician to another. Some terms that were used five or ten years ago are still being used, but the meanings have changed. Old medical or case history records often present problems of interpretation. The existing confusion is noted throughout the scientific literature.

The confusion in terminology reflects the complexity of the entity of mental disorders and the incomplete, constantly changing knowledge that exists. Fortunately, there appears to be a current trend toward making the terminology more explicit and uniform.

The following section on terminology includes descriptions of terms in past or current usage which social workers may encounter in old or current medical records or in present-day discussions of the mental health of older adults.

TERMINOLOGY OF ILLNESSES AND CONDITIONS
THAT INTERFERE WITH INTELLECTUAL FUNCTIONING

Senile dementia has been referred to as a "wastebasket term," as it has been used very loosely to mean any one of a great variety of mental conditions. Dementia is derived from the Latin word *demens,* meaning "out of one's mind." "Senile" was added to indicate older people who were demented. The word senility lost its original meaning of merely "old" and became synonymous with craziness in old age. Consequently, the terms *senile* and *senility* have become repugnant to most older adults and to those who have close working or living relationships with older men and women.[6]

Wang notes that the meaning of *dementia* has undergone three identifiable changes in the past century. In the first stage, during the latter part of the nineteenth century, dementia was equated with insanity, and all diseases of the mind were labeled dementia.

In the second stage, from around 1900 until the 1940s, *senile dementia* was used to mean a specific form of disease, but was used interchangeably with *senile psychosis* or was considered as one of several diseases categorized under the heading of senile psychosis. During the forties, *dementia* began to be used to define a syndrome of behavior, but was also used as a diagnostic term.

The third stage began about 1950. *Dementia,* as a diagnosis, was nearly tossed out of the medical vocabulary, but as time passed it began to reappear in medical writings and has continued to do so. Although *dementia* is commonly used as a descriptive term for a syndrome of behavior, it is still used in a diagnostic sense.

Wang observes that the three stages were not distinctly separated. All of the usages were employed by different writers during the same period, leading to confusion in the literature and in the field of neuropsychiatry.[7]

For many years, one of the most common alternatives for the term *senile dementia* appears to have been and continues to be *organic brain syndrome.* *Syndrome* may be defined as a "constellation of signs and symptoms which recur in a consistent manner."[8] This term was further classified into chronic brain syndrome and acute brain syndrome. *Chronic* and *acute* are two words used in a medical sense; *chronic* refers to conditions that are long-standing, whereas *acute* conditions are of recent onset or within the immediate present.

The terms *irreversible* and *reversible* are used to describe whether the progress of the condition can be stopped. In irreversible conditions of the brain, the actual brain cells are damaged or dead, resulting in mental deterioration that is permanent. Reversible mental conditions include other conditions that cause mental deterioration, but, once the cause is found, can be reversed. Although these terms continue to be used with those meanings, they do not seem to appear in the medical literature as often. However, they may be prevalent in common usage among some medical professionals.

Primary and *secondary dementia* were and are used to denote irreversible and reversible conditions: *primary dementia* for those brain diseases and conditions that cannot be reversed and *secondary dementia* for those that can be reversed. Still another pair of terms that have been and are still being used in the same sense are *organic* and *functional*. *Organic* refers to a physical disorder; *functional* to an emotional disorder. The mental function of individuals with organic brain disease cannot be restored, as this is an irreversible condition in which brain cells are permanently damaged. The person with functional disorder can have improved mental status or a return to normal functioning, as the condition is reversible.

Although the preceding paragraph sounds relatively simple, the overlapping makes it complex. An example of overlap is depression. Some drugs can cause depression, but it may also be the result of loss of a cherished object. The individual who presents with symptoms of clinical depression may be bereaved after 30 years of marriage and may also be taking a medication known to cause depression. Depression may be a symptom of the effects of a certain medication. On the other hand, depression may be the major disorder that should be treated. The person may be clinically depressed as a result of the reactivation of unresolved conflicts and the medication is contributing to the cause.

In addition to the problem of overlap, an objection to labeling conditions *reversible* or *irreversible* lies in the possibility that the diagnosis of a disorder as irreversible may lead to feelings of futility in regard to treatment. A recurring theme in the medical literature is an emphasis on the treatability of all kinds of mental disorders. Although every disorder may not be cured, functioning of many individuals even with incurable brain disorders can be helped.

TERMINOLOGY AND DEFINITIONS OF THE DSM–111–R

In response to the changing thought in regard to dementia, the four editions of the *DSM* have changed their diagnostic categories of mental disorders with each edition (1952, 1968, 1980, and 1987). *DSMS-I* and *II* did not give the full range of the various manifestations of cerebral dysfunction. The *DSM-II* did not include mental disorders resulting from metabolic problems, drug and poison intoxication, or brain lesions. The DSM-111 referred to the organic *brain syndrome*, but the DSM-111-R replaced this term with organic *mental syndrome*, which refers to a "constellation of psychological signs and symptoms without reference to etiology," such as organic anxiety syndrome. Organic *mental disorder* refers to a particular organic mental syndrome in which the etiology is known or presumed.[9] Primary degenerative dementia of the Alzheimer type is included in this category.

It is noted in the DSM-111-R that in the past, the term, *dementia* often implied a progressive or irreversible course. In this manual, the definition is based on clinical symptoms alone and does not indicate prognosis. Dementia may be progressive, stationary, or in remission, depending on the cause.[10]

DELIRIUM AND DEMENTIA IN THE DSM-III-R

The terms *delirium* and *dementia* are classifications used by psychiatrists to denote two types of behavior. Although they overlap, they are not identical.

In *delirium*, the total duration is usually brief, about one week, and rarely more than a month. Awareness fluctuates. There is a reduced ability to appropriately shift attention to new stimuli. Speech is rambling and irrelevant in some cases and pressured and incoherent in others. Engaging the person in conversation is difficult due to the inability to sustain attention. Thinking appears fragmented and disjointed. In severe delirium, thinking is totally disorganized.[11]

As perceptual disturbances are common, misinterpretations, illusions, and hallucinations may occur. The person may "see" people when no one is there or have the illusion that the bedclothes are animate objects. The sleep-wake cycle is also almost invariably disturbed. The person may fluctuate between hypersomnolence and insomnia and be subject to vivid dreams and nightmares that may merge with hallucinations. Psychomotor activity may be affected. There may be sudden shifts from one extreme to another, from hyperactivity to sluggishness. This fluctuation in symptoms is one of the characteristics of delirium.[12]

Emotional disturbances are common and variable. Fear, depression, crying, cursing, and moaning are common manifestations of the disturbed emotional state of people with delirium.[13]

The criteria for diagnosing *dementia* include the loss of intellectual functioning which is sufficiently severe to interfere significantly with work or usual social relationships with others. An underlying causative organic factor is always assumed; however, in some clinical states, a specific factor may be difficult to identify. Dementia may begin quite suddenly or there may be a gradual onset, depending on the cause.[14]

The prominent symptom of dementia is impaired memory. In mild dementia, memory loss is more marked for recent events, such as forgetting names, directions, conversations, and events. In advanced stages, the person's occupation, education, birthday, names of close relatives and even his or her own name are forgotten.[15]

Before discussing diagnosis and treatment of dementing illnesses and conditions, it may be helpful at this point to review the terminology discussed in the past few pages.

Terms that are or have been in use for the entity of mental disorders include *organic brain disorders, dementia, senile dementia, senile psychosis, organic brain syndrome, organic mental syndrome, organic mental disorders, senile brain disease, progressive idiopathic dementia, intellectual deficits, mental fallaway,* and *mental disorders.*

Combinations of terms used with very similar meanings to indicate a condition that is irreversible/reversible include organic/acute brain syndrome; primary dementia/secondary dementia; organic mental disorder/functional mental disorder; dementia/delirium.

It is important to remember that some mental disorders may be reversed or stopped, and others cannot be reversed. In addition, there is a great overlapping of these conditions. Some reversible disorders may become irreversible if left untreated. Both may be present in one individual.

MENTAL DISORDERS THAT CAN BE REVERSED OR PREVENTED

Potentially reversible conditions include the following:

> Diabetic acidosis, liver failure, dehydration, uremia, emphysema, hypothyroidism (myxedema), brain tumors, general surgery, blindfolding during eye surgery, drastic environmental changes, and bereavements...hypercalcemia, caused by metastatic carcinoma of the lung or breast...multiple myeloma, or Paget's disease.[16]

Some of the reversible causes of impairment which may cause delirium and dementia are described in the following section: cardiac conditions, malnutrition and anemia, infections, inappropriately prescribed or administered medication, drug intoxication, head trauma, pernicious anemia, hypothyroidism, dementia in carcinoma, major surgery, hepatic disease, viral infections, normal pressure hydrocephalus, dialysis dementia, internal changes and external environmental changes, and depression.

Cardiac Conditions

Decreased cerebral flow may lead to a confusional state. As described in Chapter 2, congestive heart failure occurs when the heart cannot pump enough blood to supply nutrients and oxygen to the brain. Butler estimates that about 13 percent of acute myocardial infarctions receive medical attention mainly as confusional states.[17]

Malnutrition and Anemia

Poor nutrition can lead to behavior that may be misdiagnosed as dementia. New advances in nutrition are leading to an increased awareness of the broad role nutrition plays in the maintenance of mental health. For example, vitamin B_{12} deficiency may be accompanied by mental changes.[18] Future research in nutrition may greatly influence treatment programs for those with mental disorders.

Infections

As older adults do not have the same amount of autoimmunity as the young, there is more likelihood that infections can occur. If left unattended, fever can cause dehydration and fatigue, resulting in confusion that can lead to a misdiagnosis.[19]

Medication

Over- or under-medication and drug interaction can produce symptoms that may be misdiagnosed as an irreversible brain disorder. Heart medications may deplete the body's supply of potassium, resulting in mental confusion and hallucinations. Antihypertensive medication may lead to cerebral vascular insufficiency, resulting in depression and confusion. Corticosteroids prescribed for relief from arthritis may alter electrolyte imbalance and produce personality disturbances. Other medications with possible mental effects include diuretics, antihistamines, and anticonvulsants. The troublesome drug effects are also found in the nursing home population. The Senate Subcommittee on Long-Term Care estimated that 30,000 nursing home deaths occurred each year as a result of improper combinations of drugs.[20]

Drug and Alcohol Intoxication

Due to the high incidence of drug usage in the past few decades, there is likely to be more incidence of mental disorders associated with substances such as alcohol, barbiturates, amphetamines, tranquilizers, cocaine, phencyclidine (PCP), cannabis, and others. These states are usually confusional states that are reversed when drug use is discontinued.

When mental disorders are caused by drugs, the history of the disturbance is usually quite short. There may be visual hallucinations and delusions, with symptoms becoming exacerbated in the evening.[21]

Memory impairment is the most pronounced intellectual defect associated with alcoholism. When nutrition is improved and the use of alcohol discontinued, there is often, but not always, a quick reversal of effects.

Head Trauma

Head injuries may result in subdural hematomas, causing confusion. Head trauma can begin as a reversible condition but sometimes becomes chronic and irreversible.[22]

Pernicious Anemia

Pernicious anemia usually presents with a fluctuating delirious state. Treatment often but not always reverses cognitive impairment and personality changes. When treatment does not help, it may be that anemia has caused irreversible neuronal loss or has potentiated preexisting damage from other causes.[23]

Myxedema—Deficient Functioning of the Thyroid

Myxedema may be associated with dementia. Although intellectual impairment may be reversed by treating with thyroid, this does not always occur. It has been recently discovered that hypothyroidism in its masked atypical form may give rise to symptoms of depression. The patient may appear apathetic and have experienced significant weight loss. These symptoms are sometimes mistaken for early dementia or depression.[24]

Dementia in Carcinoma

Some individuals who have cancer may have progressive dementia. Metastatic carcinoma of the breast or lung can produce *hypercalcemia*, an elevated level of serum calcium. This condition usually produces lethargy and confusion and may account for some of the mental changes that occur in cancer patients.

Close to one-half of all brain tumors seen in a general hospital are metastatic cancer which originated primarily from the lung or breast.[25] There are other as yet unexplained causes of dementia associated with cancer.

Cerebral Tumors

In addition to tumors associated with cancer, the brain can also have nonmalignant tumors. Dementia may occur as a result of brain tumors in the frontal or temporal lobes.[26]

Environmental Changes

Transfer from a familiar setting to a strange one, such as from home to hospital, may trigger the "sundowner's syndrome." Familiar stimuli are lacking, particularly if the change is made at night, and confusion results.[27] Exposure to environmental contaminants, such as insecticides, solvents, and heavy metals, may also affect the brain. Many of these chemicals are used in vocations or hobbies, and harm can be avoided through use of safety precautions.

Postoperative Depression

Occasionally an individual may develop symptoms of dementia following major surgery, especially when a general anesthesia is used. Some patients may experience a reversal after several weeks or months.[28]

Depression

The characteristics that are noted in depression of younger people are usually not present in the depression of older adults. As discussed in Chapter 1, older people of today grew up at a time when feelings were not expressed as freely as they have been in the last 20 years. Difficulties in concentrating, poor memory, and weight loss are symptoms in the elderly that sometimes are misdiagnosed as dementia. Depression is discussed in more detail in Chapter 6.

Practice Applications

A major function of social workers in health-care facilities, in relation to mental disorders, is to provide a psychosocial history that will aid the physician in diagnosing the presenting condition. If the social worker is in contact with the older delirious or demented person in the community, it is equally important to obtain a detailed history and to make certain that the individual receives a complete medical evaluation and care. In cases in which family members report that the older individual has been diagnosed as having senile dementia or Alzheimer's disease, there should be careful questioning as to how, when, and by whom the diagnosis was made. A detailed and complete evaluation of the person may not have been made.

Practice applications in relation to mental disease and disorders will be given fully at the end of each of the next two chapters when they will be more meaningful. However, it may be useful at this point to present the following case example in order to demonstrate the way that delirium could be differentiated from dementia when delirium is a result of disorientation from a dramatic change in surroundings.

CASE EXAMPLE: DELIRIUM

Mrs. Burns is an 85-year-old widow who is admitted to the hospital emergency room with vomiting, delirium, and a high fever. She is placed in isolation while tests are made, for meningitis is suspected. As Mrs. Burns's physician for the past 35 years is on vacation, his associate, whom she has never met, is assuming care for Mrs. Burns.

Throughout the first night, Mrs. Burns is delirious and terrified of the masked and gowned strangers who come into the isolation room. When her fever begins to subside, she continues to scream when anyone comes near her. Although the physician tries to reassure her, she is even more frightened of him than anyone else, for she does not recognize him. She does know that he is *not* her physician of 35 years. The nurses try to tell her that she is in a hospital, but she believes they are lying. She does not know where she is, but she begins to believe that she has been abducted and that these strange, masked figures are trying to kill her.

The next two days are just as frightening. As her temperature lowers and tests reveal that she does not have a contagious disease, she is removed from isolation to a private room. Mrs. Burns tries to get out of bed and twice manages to make her way down the hall. Consequently, the nurses place restraints on her wrists and pull the guard rails around her bed. She is improving, but the physicians are still puzzled as to the diagnosis of her physical symptoms. She is still having digestive problems and vomiting. She shouts to everyone that she is being poisoned and refuses to take anything to eat or drink unless someone first tastes it. Throughout these two days, she asks for her sister. It is at this point that the physician refers Mrs. Burns to the social worker. He specifically wants to know Mrs. Burns's state of mind prior to admission to the emergency room.

The social worker visits Mrs. Burns but is immediately rejected. Mrs. Burns screams at her to leave. The social worker then calls Mrs. Burns's sister, Mrs. Ames. Mrs. Ames is very distressed. She has been beside herself over her sister's hospitalization. She has called the hospital but has been given no information other than that her sister's condition is "guarded." She was told that no visitors were allowed. She is afraid to visit, anyway. Neither she nor her sister has ever been hospitalized. They have not been to the hospital to visit in years. Too, she fears she may catch something and also become ill. There would be no one to look after either of them. She called the physician, but he is out of town, and she has not known anyone else to call.

The social worker assures her that her sister is in no immediate danger. She learns that neither of the two sisters has spent a night away from home in over 20 years. Both are widowed and live together in a small house in the old part of the city. Attending church is the only activity that takes them out of the neighborhood. They are the last survivors of a large family, their remaining relatives being nieces and nephews whom they seldom see. They enjoy working in a small garden and looking after their cat. Both have been in reasonably good health. Mrs. Burns was "jolly and happy" the day she became ill and she has never had any "mental problems."

Mrs. Ames assures the social worker that she wants her sister home as soon as she is able to leave the hospital. She is confident that she will be able to look after her sister if she does not have to be lifted or turned in bed. She asks the social worker to tell Mrs. Burns that the cat had kittens and that the chrysanthemums finally bloomed this morning.

The social worker acquaints the physician with the home situation. He regrets having known so little about the patient when she came into the hospital. The information will be helpful in planning the discharge.

The social worker returns to Mrs. Burns's room. An aide is standing outside the door, laughing heartily. She tells the social worker that she has just been in "that senile Mrs. Burns's room" to clean up the floor. A male nurse had come into the room while Mrs. Burns was on the bedpan. Mrs. Burns was "so senile" and "demented" that she had started screaming and had thrown a pitcher of ice water at him.

The social worker does not laugh with her, but remarks that Mrs. Burns has never been hospitalized before and probably does not know that there are nurses who are male. She was very likely frightened to find a man in her bedroom, particularly when she was using the bedpan.

The social worker goes in and speaks to Mrs. Burns soothingly, but the patient turns her face away from her. She then relays the messages from Mrs. Ames, and Mrs. Burns turns her head so that she can see the social worker's face. She stares at her for several seconds, then asks how many kittens were born. The social worker believes she has captured her attention, at least for a few minutes. She promises to obtain more information about the kittens. She is reassuring and explains to Mrs. Burns why she is hospitalized. Although Mrs. Burns does not respond verbally, she appears to be listening at first, then begins to moan softly, turning her head away.

The social worker talks with the charge nurse, explaining Mrs. Burns's lack of familiarity with hospitals. She expresses her concern about some of the aides' lack of understanding and their casual assumption of senility. She wonders whether the charge nurse can assign only female nurses to Mrs. Burns, at least for a couple of days.

The nurse agrees that some of the staff have probably contributed to the problems Mrs. Burns is experiencing. She is willing to reassign the male nurses. When they have their daily charting meeting, she will talk with them about distinguishing between delirium and dementia.

Later in the day, the social worker stops again in Mrs. Burns's room. Again, Mrs. Burns stares at her for several moments, then asks where her sister is. The social worker responds that Mrs. Ames is at home, waiting for her sister to get well and come home. She asks whether there is a message she can give Mrs. Ames. There is no answer. When she turns to leave the room, Mrs. Burns calls to her to have her sister come after her. The social worker starts to explain why the sister cannot take her home, but a noise in the hall distracts the patient and the strand of communication is broken.

On the fourth day of hospitalization, Mrs. Burns no longer manifests physical symptoms of any kind, and she appears less paranoid. However, she is still disoriented. She is less distracted and is willing to allow the nurses to care for her, although she is still suspicious and watchful. She seems to trust only two of the nurses and the social worker, whom she believes to be the "manager" of the hospital. As she no longer appears extremely agitated, the restraints are removed. The decision is made to discharge Mrs. Burns to her home with follow-up by a public health nurse to evaluate Mrs. Burns's mental state. The social worker is responsible for coordinating the discharge plan.

The social worker contacts Mrs. Ames and explains that Mrs. Burns is expected to recover fully once she is in familiar surroundings. She describes Mrs. Burns's present behavior and tells Mrs. Ames that she must not be alarmed, if her sister continues to be disoriented at times in the next few days. Mrs. Ames sounds concerned but not fearful. She remembers her mother being confused when she had pneumonia. She is glad that she may call the social worker is assistance is needed between the public health nurse's visits.

The social worker obtains information from Mrs. Ames as to finances. The two women seem to be managing reasonably well, having combined their resources many years earlier. Members of the church are also helpful in supplying clothing and groceries from time to time. The social worker promises that she will call in a few days to see how they are managing.

The follow-up call by the social worker results in a favorable report. Mrs. Burns is glad to be home and does not require any special care. She is almost "like her old self." Mrs. Ames appreciates the social worker's concern and is relieved to know there is someone she can call, should her sister suddenly become worse, if the nurse or doctor cannot be located.

The follow-up note by the public health nurse is sent to the hospital ten days later. Mrs. Burns is doing well. She still has brief, temporary spells of disorientation, but only upon awakening from a night's sleep or from a nap, and it is of short duration. Mrs. Ames is able to reorient her quickly to her surroundings. The public health nurse will not visit again unless directed by the physician.

The social worker receives the report with relief, but she believes there should be continuing contact with the two women. She arranges, through the veterans' hospital in the community, to have Telecare services for the two sisters. She also contacts the minister of the church that has helped the sisters in the past. The social worker finds that the church has a volunteer visiting program and that they will call on the two women on a regular basis. If anything happens that requires attention, there will be someone to take action.

In this case the social worker is able to establish a tenuous relationship with the delirious patient, providing a line of communication from the patient to the closest relative. She shares information about the patient that is appropriate to share with the nursing staff, in an effort to improve patient care. When the patient is discharged, she does not end her own contact immediately with the family, but continues in a supportive role. Lastly, she arranges follow-up as ongoing protection for these frail, but determinedly independent, older women.

NOTES

1. *DSM-111-R: Diagnostic and Statistical Manual of Mental Disorders*, 4th ed., Task Force on Nomenclature and Statistics (Washington, D.C.: American Psychiatric Association, 1987).

2. Z.J. Lipowski, "A New Look at Organic Brain Syndromes," *American Journal of Psychiatry* 137, no. 6 (June 1980): 674.

3. Excerpts from *The Myth of Senility* by Robin Marantz Henig, (Glenview, IL: Scott, Foresman and Co., 1985), 15. Copyright 1981, 1985 by Robin Marantz Henig. Reprinted by permission of Scott, Foresman and Company/AARP, and the author.

4. Ibid., 18.

5. Lipowski, "Organic Brain Syndromes," 674.

6. H. S. Wang, "Dementia of Old Age." Adapted by permission of the publisher from pages 8–10, Chapter 1 in *Aging and Dementia*, eds. W. Lynn Smith and Marcel Kinsbourne, (Jamaica, New York: Spectrum Publications, Inc., 1977).

7. Ibid.

8. S. L. Kushnir, "Reflections on Alzheimer's Disease," *Canadian Journal of Psychiatry* 27, (February 1982): 18.

9. *DSM-111-R: Diagnostic and Statistical Manual of Mental Disorders:* 97.

10. Ibid., 104.

11. Ibid., 100.

12. Ibid., 101.

13. Ibid.

14. Ibid., 103.

15. Ibid.

16. Robert N. Butler and Myrna I. Lewis, *Aging and Mental Health, Positive Psychosocial and Biomedical Approaches,* 3rd ed. (St. Louis: The C.V. Mosby Co., 1982), 107.

17. Ibid.

18. Leslie S. Libow, "Senile Dementia and 'Pseudosenility': Clinical Diagnosis," in *Cognitive and Emotional Disturbances in the Elderly,* ed. Carl Eisdorfer and Robert O. Friedel (Chicago: Year Book Medical Publishers, Inc., 1977), 85.

19. Ibid.

20. T. L. Brink, *Geriatric Psychotherapy* (New York: Human Sciences Press, 1979), 101.

21. Martin Roth, "The Diagnosis of Dementia in Late and Middle Life," in *The Epidemiology of Dementia,* ed. James A. Mortimer and Leonard M. Schuman (New York: Oxford University Press, 1981), 37.

22. Libow, "Senile Dementia," 85.

23. Roth, "The Diagnosis of Dementia," 34, 35.

24. Ibid., 35.

25. Libow, "Senile Dementia," 85.

26. Ibid.

27. Charles B. Schaffer, Patrick T. Donlon, "Medical Causes of Psychiatric Symptoms in the Elderly," *Clinical Gerontology* 1, no. 4 (Summer 1983): 12.

28. Libow, "Senile Dementia," 86.

5

SENILE DISEASE, ALZHEIMER'S TYPE
helping families to cope

The previous chapter was concerned primarily with the kinds of mental disorders that usually can be prevented or reversed. This chapter singles out the most prominent irreversible organic brain disease, *senile disease, Alzheimer's type,* for discussion. The terms discussed in Chapter 4 that are sometimes used in reference to Alzheimer's disease include *primary dementia, organic brain disease, chronic brain syndrome, senility, senile dementia, senile brain disease,* and *organic mental disorder.*

Alzheimer's disease has received widespread publicity, not only in medical journals, but in nearly every type of publication. The intense interest displayed by the press in this disease is probably due to the more recent developments in the understanding of Alzheimer's type of senile disease, the reported prevalence, and the progressive, irreversible nature of this disease.

Although Alzheimer's disease has received the most attention in the last few years and is the most prevalent of the dementing diseases, there are others that occur, although far more rarely, including Pick's disease, Huntington's chorea (which may or may not affect the brain), and Cruetzfeldt-Jakobs disease.

Since no prevention and no cure have been discovered for Alzheimer's disease, there is increased interest in trying to improve the functioning of the individual with Alzheimer's disease. Emphasis is placed on keeping the patient at home as long as possible, when this is feasible, instead of considering early nursing home placement. Social workers, particularly in health-care settings, are called upon for services in relation to providing support and planning with families in regard to the way the patient will be maintained during the progressively downward course of the disease.

Some understanding of the disease process is essential in working with other professionals and with the patient and family members.

ALZHEIMER'S DISEASE

Alzheimer's disease was named for Alois Alzheimer, who published a paper in 1907 describing the neuropathological aspects of the autopsy of the brain of a 55-year-old demented woman.[1]

For many years Alzheimer's disease was thought to have no relation to aging. As aging populations increased, more older people began to exhibit symptoms of Alzheimer's disease. Alzheimer's disease began to be classified as "presenile Alzheimer's disease" (usually occurring in the person's forties or fifties) and "senile Alzheimer's disease" (after age 65). In the mid-1970s medical professionals began to question the separate classification of "presenile" and "senile" Alzheimer's disease, as there appeared to be evidence that they had the same origins.

The question has also been raised as to whether Alzheimer's disease exists as a distinguishable, separate disease. There is conjecture that there may be a group of several diseases of unknown etiology that are very similar to each other instead of a single disease. While research continues in this area, some clinicians refer to "senile dementia, Alzheimer's type" (SDAT) instead of to "Alzheimer's disease."

Etiology

Several explanations have been advanced to explain the origins of Alzheimer's disease. They include hypotheses that Alzheimer's disease is the result of (1) a viral infection or a slow virus; (2) the presence of a toxic agent in the brain; (3) a chromosomal cause; (4) hereditary factors; and (5) a defect in the individual's immune system.[2]

The viral concept is considered a possibility, for it is known that certain viral infections affect the brain, sometimes many years after the infection occurs, as in cases of subacute sclerosing panencephalitis, an infection associated with measles. The slow virus concept is associated with studies of slow virus diseases which cause dementia, such as Creutzfeld-Jakob disease. The incubation period of the virus is measured not in days or weeks, but in years.[3]

The finding of 10 to 30 times the normal level of aluminum in the brain has given rise to the theory that a toxic agent may cause the disease. Research suggests that aluminum may interact with DNA and cause lesions of the brain.[4]

The chromosomal concept has arisen as a result of the finding that all Down's syndrome patients who survive to adulthood eventually develop lesions in the brain which resemble those of Alzheimer's disease. Down's syndrome is thought to be caused by an extra chromosome. This twenty-first chromosome may be related to the cause of Alzheimer's disease.[5]

Most investigators believe there is the possibility of multiple genetic factors which result in the variety of ways that Alzheimer's disease presents itself.[6]

Prevalence

Alzheimer's disease is considered by many clinicians as the fourth or fifth leading cause of death.[7] Diseases of the brain, such as Alzheimer's disease, are rarely named on death certificates as cause of death. Nonspecific causes, such as bronchopneumonia, are commonly listed.[8]

It has been estimated that the senile form of Alzheimer's disease accounts for 50 percent of the dementia that occurs during old age. Henig estimates the numbers of Alzheimer's disease as about 600,000 to 1 million Americans over age 65 with 60,000 of those in their fifties and sixties.[9]

Some research has indicated that Alzheimer's disease occurs with more frequency among women than men, and others have shown an equal prevalence among both sexes. Still others have shown that findings of Alzheimer's pathological changes are not predominant in women.[10]

Diagnosis

The diagnosis of Alzheimer's disease is made by exclusion (ruling out all other causes of intellectual impairment). Sometimes the diagnosis can be made only after treatment is begun for other suspected cause or causes. Alzheimer's disease at this time can only be diagnosed with certainty by brain autopsy.

Pathologic findings of the brain include neurofibrillary tangles (threadlike nerve fibers which are tangled), neuritic plaques (clusters of neurofibrillary tangles and other abnormal tissues), and atrophy of the brain. The plaques and tangles occur in the hippocampus and the cerebral cortex, areas of the brain responsible for memory and intellectual functioning. Widespread destruction of individual nerve cells occurs. The plaques interfere with the passage of electrochemical signals between cells, which causes impairment of intellect and memory according to the location and size of the plaques.

Criteria for the diagnosis of Alzheimer's disease is described by Roth as follows:

> Three of the following features must be present: (1) a gradual and continually progressive failure in work performance and some of the common activities of daily life, not due to impairments in general health or physical handicap; (2) impairment in memory with difficulty in reordering and retrieving recent personal experiences and current happenings; (3) deterioration in general intellectual ability with impairment of grasp, capacity for reasoning, inference, and conceptual and abstract thought; and (4) disorganization of personality and its characteristic features with

deterioration in self-care, blunting of emotional sensibility, and impairment of social adjustments through fall-out of personality assets.

The following criterion of exclusion also has to be satisfied. The dementia should not be attributable to associated causes such as cerebrovascular disease; cerebral lesions due to other specific causes; or systemic diseases, deficiencies, and intoxications liable to give rise to interference with cerebral function.[11]

As noted in discussions of conditions often confused with Alzheimer's disease in the previous chapter, one of the great problems has been the misdiagnosis of older people. A recurring theme in the literature is the need for accurate diagnosis of symptomatology. The recommendations for accurate diagnosis include a complete history taking; physical and neurological examination, administration of several laboratory tests, including a test for neurosyphilis; a mental status test of orientation, concentration, language, and praxis function; thorough assessment by a neuropsychologist; a detailed profile of cognitive functions and test-taking behaviors.[12]

Treatment

There is no drug at this time that can cure or prevent Alzheimer's disease, but there are drugs that are being prescribed to which some patients seem to respond. Two classes of drugs are being used: cerebral vasodilators, such as papaverine, and cerebral metabolic enhancers, including dihydroergotoxine which is probably the most widely used agent in treating dementia.[13]

Prognosis

After onset of symptoms, the average length of survival ranges from five to ten years, with considerable variation. The disease is gradual, progressive, and ends in death.

The kind and quality of care in relation to the patient's nutrition and general health may affect the longevity of the patient.

Progress of the Disease

Although many articles about Alzheimer's disease refer to stages, it is generally agreed that it is difficult to separate every aspect of the symptomatology into stages, for individual responses to the disease vary. However, there are symptoms that are more apt to occur early, midway, or late during its course. It is in this sense that stages are referred to in the following material.

Alzheimer's disease is a progressively deteriorating disease, with the first stage characterized by loss of recent memory and changes in behavior and personality. The first stage may last from two to four years.[14] The first clear-cut symptom recalled by some family members is an episode in which the patient became hopelessly lost while traveling to a location that should have been reached without undue difficulty.[15]

There is apt to be an impoverishment of ideas and impairment of the ability to think abstractly. For example, it would be difficult for the patient to explain the similarities between an apple and an orange. Each type of fruit may be described accurately, but there is a lack of ability to make the connection that both are fruit, both are round, and so on.

Friends and family members may not notice very early mental changes. After many changes have taken place, they begin to recall earlier incidents indicating mental impairment that may have disturbed them vaguely. This gradual onset makes it difficult for family members to determine a beginning point of the disease. It may also account partially for the difficulties in determining the duration of Alzheimer's disease.

When the disease is diagnosed at an early stage, the patient requires counseling. According to Fisk, most of the individuals with mild to moderate Alzheimer's disease are aware of their problem of intellectual decline. Anxiety and depression are likely to be exacerbated by withholding information. Family and patient need open communication, understanding, and trust.[16]

If the diagnosis is made in the early stage, the patient and family may place their focus on making the necessary plans for the future. Wills may need to be made, executors named, possibly a guardian appointed or power of attorney executed.

By the end of the first stage, employed people with Alzheimer's disease are experiencing difficulty at work. They may be unable to perform basic arithmetic or carry out simple tasks.[17] If the family has been overlooking or denying the individual's mental deterioration, it is necessary now for them to come to terms with it.

The second or middle stage, which may last several years, is even more difficult. The diagnosis of Alzheimer's disease is likely to be made during this period. It is characterized by further memory loss. There may be difficulty in speaking and continued loss of earlier skills, although there may be less awareness of the disabilities that are occurring. The person may be combative and may "shadow" (follow close upon) the caregiver. Paranoid symptoms may become more pronounced.[18]

The individual may appear less able to handle frustration, be more impulsive, and may experience drastic changes in mood. There may be outbursts of temper and physical or verbal aggressiveness. Personality traits may become exaggerated; for instance, a person who has been slightly passive or slightly assertive may become more passive or more assertive.

It is in this stage that the patient may begin to require extensive care. The care has some similarities to infant and child care, except the individual is a mature being, requiring around-the-clock care, who must be bathed, dressed, and fed, have personal needs attended to, and be protected from the environment and from accidental self-harm.

The third (terminal) stage of Alzheimer's disease is usually brief, not lasting more than one year. Many who are in the terminal stage stop eating and do not communicate or try to communicate with others. Some become incontinent or have convulsions.[19]

The individual may require nursing home placement, a difficult decision for most family members to make. Relatives sometimes care for the demented person until they too become ill. This may also be a time of financial hardship in addition to the mourning of the present and anticipated losses.

Even though many who have Alzheimer's disease stop communicating and may appear to have little comprehension, many caregivers believe that they are still sensitive to the feelings of those around them. The person with Alzheimer's disease may be aware of unexpressed irritation or annoyance, as well as feelings of love, affection, tenderness, and other caring attitudes.

The family and the patient require sustained services and support throughout the duration of the disease. The stress of caregiving may disrupt marital and family relationships. Social workers may provide counseling or refer family members for therapy. Continuity of care is needed during the illness and the bereavement.

There is another progressive condition which should be noted, as it resembles Alzheimer's disease; however, it can be treated to prevent further progression: multi-infarct dementia.

MULTI-INFARCT DEMENTIA

Multi-infarct dementia (MID) is a chronic disorder with symptoms so similar to those of Alzheimer's disease that they are sometimes difficult to differentiate. *Infarct* means tissue death.

Multi-infarct dementia is associated with damage to the blood vessels through arteriosclerosis. In MID there is an insufficient supply of oxygen and nutrients to the brain. It is a progressive disease which usually does not present symptoms until later life.[20]

The onset may be gradual or sudden. The cases in which memory loss is gradual are similar to Alzheimer's disease. However, the impairment of memory is different from Alzheimer's, as the person may forget one minute and retain complete memory the next. The course of the disease is not steadily downhill, but is up and down, with periods of lucidity. There may be hallucinations and delirium, indicating the insufficiency of cerebral circulation. Speech disturbance and an abnormal gait may also be noted.[21]

There may be remissions in some cases. Hypertension and vascular disease may be treated in an early stage to prevent further progression. Stroke, arteriosclerotic heart disease, or pneumonia are the usual causes of death.[22]

Practice Applications

As noted in the previous chapter, the diagnosis of Alzheimer's disease can be made mistakenly, for so many conditions may present with symptoms similar to those of Alzheimer's. The individual who has symptoms of dementia should be referred for a complete medical evaluation, including testing.

History Taking

A social worker in a community agency is sometimes the first professional person to interview an older person who is displaying symptoms of dementia. A very careful history should be taken to aid physicians in ruling out possible causes for observed or reported confusion, difficulties in concentration, memory loss, depression, loss of appetite, personality change, and other changes indicating mental disorders.

Questions may include inquiries about recent surgery, accidents or injuries, physical conditions and medication taken for them, difficulties with vision and hearing, nutrition, recent change of environment, recent events (retirement, bereavement, divorce, etc.), and exposure to environmental contaminants. The kind and extent of memory loss should be determined. When was memory loss first noticed? Is the person spasmodically forgetful? Are recent memories forgotten but older memories retained? Has the loss been gradual and progressive or abrupt? Does the person forget only temporarily? Questions to determine the individual's present mental status may be asked: day of the week, month, year, president's name, name of hospital or place in which the person is interviewed, home address, telephone number, name of siblings, and so on. The patient, family, and caregivers should be interviewed and the full information given to the examining physician as an aid to diagnosis.

Helping Patients and Families in the Early Stages

Some patients with Alzheimer's or related diseases experience a period of time in which they are aware of their mental deterioration. Denial of the symptoms and of the diagnosis by patient and family members is usually the first reaction; it may interfere drastically with planning, at least for a time. A great deal of resentment and anger may be directed toward the medical staff or physician. There may be a feverish search for a cure that delays planning realistically for the future.

The reactions of patients and family members are often similar to those of relatives of stroke patients. They may ask, "Why did this happen to me?" Anger, frustration, and guilt usually accompany the question. Some may believe they are being punished by God. There is a grief reaction, as the patient grieves over the losses of function and family members mourn the loss of the former relationship. Grappling with these emotions and worrying about the future often leaves little strength for constructive action.

Social workers help families to acknowledge and express their feelings. The assurance that their emotions are normal is often helpful. Putting families in touch with others who have gone through this experience is usually beneficial. Information about self-help groups for families of patients with Alzheimer's disease can be obtained from the local chapter of the Alzheimer's Disease and Related Disorders Association (ADRDA). The local mental health association, inpatient and outpatient services in hospitals, or other clinics may provide group meetings.

Providing information on whatever federal and state medical insurance is available, locating community resources, and steering the family through the various steps of application are concrete services that can be offered. Legal services should be considered. A durable power of attorney or guardianship may be needed. Chapter 12 describes legal measures that may be used. Planning constructively may help the patient and family members to feel less helpless and the patient to feel more in control of his or her life.

Family members also need to be advised about the kinds of changes the patient will undergo. The care of demented people is fraught with problems that inexperienced caregivers have never considered, much less encountered. Preparation of the family before undertaking care is essential. Discussing the provision of resources for supportive assistance during the ensuing months and/or years is equally important.

Assisting with Behavior Problems

As intellectual impairment inevitably increases, behavioral problems are likely to occur. Social isolation may become a problem for the family more than for the patient, as friends may stop visiting when they do not know how to deal with the situation. The family may stop trying to take the patient outside the home, due to embarrassment, shame, or simply the difficulties of caring for the patient in strange and possibly upsetting surroundings.

The family that has been warned of possible paranoid symptoms such as suspicion, complaints of having items stolen, and so on may be better able to handle these symptoms when they occur. Remaining calm and reassuring, explaining any conversation or incident that may have confused the patient, may restore harmony. If the confused person also has impaired hearing, the inability to distinguish clearly what is said may contribute to paranoid reactions.

With loss of mental function, there may be misunderstandings of conversations because the patient may be able to understand some words but not others. If someone is complaining about noisiness of a child in the home, the patient may believe the complaint is directed at himself. Startling noises, such as a shout, may be frightening and an explanation may not be understood. Speaking clearly and slowly and remaining calm may provide reassurance, whether the patient understands the explanation or not. Arguments should be avoided, as this will only intensify the distress that is being experienced.

Rabins notes that catastrophic reactions ("a massive, emotional over-response to minor stress") may occur. The reaction may consist of explosive rage or tearful outbursts over a minor change. Reacting to an outburst non-combatively and in a supporting manner may lessen difficulties that occur in the future.[23] It is easier for families to react supportively when they understand that the behavior, which may have been perceived as simply being willful or obnoxious, is a result of the disease.

The family may need reminders that the demented person needs to feel loved. Being demonstrative with affection, expressing love, and giving praise is comforting to the patient and may help when other responses fail.

Establishing a Routine

Encouraging the patient's family to establish an environment that allows freedom but provides structure may be helpful in management. A daily schedule in which each activity occurs at a certain time and familiar objects are placed in sight may help the patient remain familiar with his environment. Frequent efforts at orientation, using calendars and clocks, and reporting of current events to the patient may also help.[24]

Providing Recreation

The family may not realize that the patient can still experience enjoyment. There are variations among patients as to which activities will be experienced as pleasurable. Some leisure activities such as television may be enjoyable or frustrating. The family can test different kinds of activities with the patient instead of assuming that they will not be enjoyed.

Recalling the kinds of hobbies and pleasures that the person had prior to illness will help in identifying activities that may give pleasure. Individuals who enjoyed reading may still find looking through magazines a pleasurable activity. Listening to music on the radio or taking a ride in a car may be gratifying.[25]

Maintaining Physical Health

Exercising regularly has been observed as helping patients with dementing illness to be calmer and less agitated. It is also a way to keep an impaired person involved in activities. Other benefits from regular exercise include better sleeping during the night and more regular bowel habits.[26] Being active also helps to avoid pressure sores. Consulting with the physician as to the amount and kind of exercise is advisable.

Good nutrition is also important. Keeping a mealtime schedule may be difficult, for demented patients often cannot remember when they have eaten. If they want to continue eating, it may be necessary to lock the food out of reach.

If coordination is impaired, bowls and spoons may be used. If the patient has abandoned the use of tableware, food that can be eaten with the fingers may be prepared.

Keeping the patient clean is necessary to avoid skin rashes and infections. Continuance of the usual routine, such as bathing and teeth brushing, should be encouraged. The patient should be allowed to do as much as possible for himself or herself, but supervision may be needed in personal care. The patient should be supervised in the bathroom or shower for safety reasons, as well as elsewhere.

The Need For Respite From Care

Throughout the illness, family members may need to be urged to seek respite from care. Reassurances to families of patients with Alzheimer's disease that no amount of care will prevent further damage may relieve those who feel they should always be doing more, even though they may be exhausted. Reminders may be needed that there is no known cause of Alzheimer's disease and no known cure, that the disease is not contagious, and that severe mental deterioration is not a part of the aging process, but is due to the disease.

Resources for the Family

The preceding suggestions are merely indicators of the innumerable problem areas that arise when caring for a demented person. Family members should be urged to attend group meetings for caregivers so that they may learn how others have coped with various problems. A book that is frequently recommended to help family members deal with patients with dementing disease is *The 36-Hour Day* by Nancy L. Mace and Peter V. Rabins, (Baltimore: The John Hopkins University Press, 1981.)

The following case example demonstrates some of the kinds of problems that may occur.

CASE EXAMPLE: COPING WITH ALZHEIMER'S DISEASE

Mr. Heath is 73 years old. He was diagnosed as having Alzheimer's disease a year before the social worker came into contact with him. Mr. Heath was widowed when he was 60 and married a woman 12 years his junior a short time later. He has two daughters by his first marriage who strongly disapprove of his remarriage. They are both in their late forties and live in the same city as their father. Mr. Heath has repaired and restored antique furniture since his youth. Only in the past year has he become too disabled by Alzheimer's disease to continue working.

Mr. and Mrs. Heath come to the attention of the social worker when they move into a city housing project that provides small independent housing units to older people. The social worker knows from the record that Mr. Heath has been diagnosed as having late-onset diabetes and Alzheimer's disease. She is familiar with the fact that the disease is progressive, with no known cause or cure, but that is about all.

The social worker does not know what to expect when she visits the home. Mr. Heath comes to the door with his wife. Mrs. Heath is an attractive, youthful-appearing 61-year-old woman who looks very tired. Mr. Heath is neatly dressed, and repeats the social worker's name twice when she introduces herself. He does not speak again at any time during the visit. However, every time his wife moves, he stays at her side.

The apartment is furnished with beautiful antique furniture. The social worker comments on the furniture, but Mr. Heath does not respond or appear to understand. He sits on the couch, very close to his wife, and folds a newspaper very carefully into precise folds over and over again throughout the interview.

Mrs. Heath volunteers the information that she is very lonely since they moved from the old neighborhood on the far side of the city in which she lived for most of her adult years. They moved to this housing at the stepdaughters' insistence. Mrs. Heath has no children by her previous marriage but has a sister who lived nearby, whom she misses. They have been very close all their lives, and especially so during the ten years she was widowed before marrying her present husband. Now she rarely sees her sister, as she lives so far away.

She also speaks fondly of the trips she and her husband made to flea markets and auctions until his forgetfulness became severe. She tells the social worker, with a note of pride in her voice, that she learned quite a bit about antiques during their marriage. Her husband often entrusted her to attend auctions without him. She also frequently made money by reselling items she located on her own.

Mrs. Heath relates the incident that made her realize her husband's memory had become a cause for concern. About a year earlier Mr. Heath lost his way from an antique shop to their home, a route he had taken thousands of times, and drove until he ran out of gas. A policeman brought him home and recommended she take him to a doctor. Mrs. Heath had taken him to a physician and had been told the diagnosis was "probably" Alzheimer's disease. She had then taken him "to doctor after doctor" to please the stepdaughters, until the Heaths' savings were nearly exhausted. She then remarks that her husband will surely get better soon, for she looks after his every need.

The social worker hesitates, then comments that it is her understanding that Alzheimer's disease is a progressive and incurable disease. This remark is met with silence. Mrs. Heath then remarks softly that he can get better even if he isn't cured and abruptly changes the subject. Shortly thereafter she declares she must run an errand she had forgotten earlier and terminates the interview.

The social worker telephones the medical social worker at the hospital clinic that Mr. Heath attends. She learns more about Alzheimer's disease and the problems that caregivers encounter. The medical social worker remembers the Heaths, as he has very recently called Mrs. Heath and her stepdaughters about a group that is being formed for families of patients with Alzheimer's disease. He found that all three were denying the extent of Mr. Heath's present problems and were insistent that he will improve, even though they recognize that he "mightn't become well." He tells the social worker that there is a group for relatives of patients with Alzheimer's disease which will start meeting in about a month in the outpatient clinic. He adds that a series of community education programs on Alzheimer's disease are periodically presented by the mental health association. He offers to send the social worker some material on Alzheimer's disease that includes suggestions she may wish to relay to Mrs. Heath.

When the social worker informs the client about the meetings, Mrs. Heath is reluctant to attend, saying that she does not want to leave her husband. She agrees to think about it.

About six weeks later the social worker receives a call from the medical social worker suggesting that she visit Mrs. Heath. He saw her in the clinic corridor, and she appears close to exhaustion. She had refused to talk with him but had agreed she would talk to "that social worker that made the visit to my home."

The social worker telephones Mrs. Heath and asks her to come to her office, as she thinks it will be difficult to talk with her in the presence of her husband. Mrs. Heath responds that she dare not leave her husband. The social worker then says she will come to their apartment. Mrs. Heath hurriedly agrees to arrange for her sister to stay with her husband.

The social worker is shocked at Mrs. Heath's appearance. She has lost weight since the home visit was made and seems exhausted. She admits she is extremely tired and depressed, as her husband shows no signs of improvement. His behavior is becoming more bizarre. In addition to staying at her side every moment, he is changing clothes every few hours. He insists that every item be washed before wearing it again. Fortunately, Mrs. Heath found that he does not remember whether they are washed. Although she feels uncomfortable about doing it, she lies about washing the clothes.

The social worker first responds with some suggestions which may help Mrs. Heath cope with her husband's "shadowing." She suggests that Mrs. Heath try to imagine how Mr. Heath is feeling. His memory has failed and he is confused. It is likely that Mrs. Heath represents security to her husband, much as a mother does to a young child. As his sense of time is also confused, he cannot remember how long she is gone if, for instance, she tries to take a nap. The social worker suggests that she try to think of simple chores for her husband to do. If he is occupied some of the time, this will give her some freedom. Other suggestions are made in regard to structuring his day, asking the physician about an exercise program, and trying to find an activity her husband may enjoy.

She then firmly tells Mrs. Heath that she must have some respite from caring for her husband. The social worker does not respond to the repeated comments about Mr. Heath's "getting better, as long as I keep trying." She focuses only on the need of Mrs. Heath for rest. Without rest, she too may become ill and unable to care at all for her husband. It is on this basis that Mrs. Heath begins to consider seeking some relief from the constant care. The social worker suggests she call her stepdaughters; at first, the client refuses. They have not visited for weeks. She does not want to ask them for help, but she realizes she cannot continue to provide full care.

While Mrs. Heath is in her office, the social worker contacts the leader of the Alzheimer's group for information on resources for respite care. She learns there is a group of volunteers who will stay on an emergency basis for short periods until regular help is located. She also obtains the name of a few sitters who are willing to come in for a few hours in the evening for a small sum. She gives the names to Mrs. Heath and suggests she use her phone to call a sitter for the next day, then leaves the office for a short time. On her return, she finds that Mrs. Heath has made emergency arrangements for care for her husband the following day. She agrees to make plans to spend some time with her sister and other friends in the old neighborhood. Then she will call her stepdaughters.

The following months are difficult for Mrs. Heath, but her first step in obtaining respite care enables her to take further steps. Mrs. Heath attends the last two meetings of the family group and further meetings, as the group votes to continue meeting once a month on their own, without a leader. She attends the informational meetings provided for the community by the mental health association. She finds a great many suggestions given by speakers and by other family members that help her to cope with her husband's behavior.

Mrs. Heath's stepdaughters are surprisingly cooperative, taking turns to give her some relief. They express concern over her fatigue. Mrs. Heath cannot help wondering whether they are helping primarily because they are worried about her becoming ill and unable to care at all for her husband. She then feels guilty for the thought and seeks assurance from the social worker that she is not being malicious and ungrateful. She also expresses concern about the angry feelings toward her husband, his daughters, and toward the world that she sometimes experiences. The social worker assures her that such feelings are normal, and helps her to understand why they occur.

Mrs. Heath slowly begins to accept the finality of her husband's growing mental impairment. The acceptance is accompanied by a period of mourning for the life she shared with her husband and all that the relationship meant to her. The emotional support and discussions provided by the group members and by the social worker help her to deal with her loss as well as with her husband's increasingly withdrawn and apathetic behavior. In addition, she gains more insight in relation to her own feelings of guilt and anger, as well as to some of the behavior of her stepdaughters.

The social worker continues to counsel with her about problems as they occur, helping her to focus on events other than those involved in her husband's care. She begins to encourage Mrs. Heath to attend an auction occasionally and suggests that she resume collecting and selling articles. Mrs. Heath follows the suggestions with some reluctance, but admits that getting out makes her feel better.

Mr. Heath's condition worsens, then seems to remain on a plateau. He is barely able to communicate in any way with his wife. He refuses to eat and fails to recognize his daughters when they come to stay with them. He is incontinent and has lost bowel control. There finally appears to be no way to continue to look after him at home.

As difficult as the step is to take, Mrs. Heath is able to make plans with the social worker for nursing-home care. The social worker suggests that they try to locate a bed in a nursing home near the neighborhood in which the Heaths formerly lived. It is no longer necessary for her to remain so far from her sister and old friends. She and the stepdaughters will be able to visit together occasionally if they wish. Mrs. Heath comments that, as strange as it seems, she will miss her stepdaughters. Now that she has a better understanding of them, they no longer seem as threatening as they once did. She believes she can handle any reaction they may have in regard to the decision to seek nursing-home care.

The social worker considers the case closed, but Mrs. Heath comes to see her just before she moves. Her husband has been in the nursing home for two weeks. She visits her husband daily, but she is "ashamed" because she feels happier than she believes she should feel. The social worker helps her client to accept her natural feelings of release and freedom. When Mrs. Heath leaves, the social worker reminds her that she will be available if Mrs. Heath feels she needs her help.

At the beginning of this case, the social worker knows little about Alzheimer's disease, but she seeks information immediately after contact with the client. She continues to work with the client by responding to each problem as it arises and by locating resources when they appear to be needed. She helps the client to overcome her initial denial in relation to her husband's illness. The social worker provides supportive therapy along with some insight therapy which helps the client become more independent and able to increase her coping skills, reducing anxiety. If Mrs. Heath had been disabled or feeble, the social worker probably would have taken a more active role in terms of providing concrete services.

This experience acquainted the social worker with some of the needs of the client who is caring for a relative with Alzheimer's disease. With the next such client, the social worker may be able to anticipate some of the problems that may arise and work toward preventing them.

NOTES

1. Michael K. Schneck, Barry Reisberg, and Steven H. Ferris, "An Overview of Current Concepts of Alzheimer's Disease," *The American Journal of Psychiatry*, 139, no. 2 (February 1982): 166–173. Copyright 1982, the American Psychiatric Association. Adapted by permission.

2. Ibid., 170–171.

3. Ibid., 170.

4. Ibid.

5. Ibid., 171.

6. Ibid.

7. Joseph C. Parker, "Alzheimer s Disease—A Major Health Problem," *Journal of the Tennessee Medical Association* 78, no. 1 (January 1985): 9.

8. James A. Mortimer, Leonard M. Schuman, and L. Ronald French, "Epidemiology of Dementing Illness" in *The Epidemiology of Dementia*, ed. James A. Mortimer and Leonard M. Schuman (New York: Oxford University Press, 1981), 18.

9. Robin Marantz Henig, *The Myth of Senility* (New York: Anchor Press/Doubleday, 1981), 19.

10. Schneck et al., "An Overview of Current Concepts," 168.

11. Martin Roth, "The Diagnosis of Dementia in Late and Middle Life," in *The Epidemiology of Dementia*, 26, 27.

12. Wilma G. Rosen, "Update on Dementia," *Journal of the American Medical Women's Association* 37, no. 8 (August 1982): 214.

13. Harold L. Klawans and Nina Genovese, "Pharmacology of Dementia" in *Neurologic Clinics*, ed. J. Thomas Hutton (Philadelphia: W. B. Saunders Company,) 4, no 2 (May 1986): 86.

14. Lisa P. Gwyther and Mary Ann Matteson, "Care for the Caregivers," *Journal of Gerontological Nursing* 9, no. 2 (February 1983): 93.

15. Barry Reisberg, "An Overview of Current Concepts of Alzheimer's Disease, Senile Dementia, and Age-Associated Decline," in *Alzheimer's Disease*, ed. Barry Reisberg (New York: The Free Press, 1983), 7.

16. Albert A. Fisk, "Management of Alzheimer's Disease," *Postgraduate Medicine* 73, no. 4 (April 1983): 238.

17. Gwyther and Matteson, "Care for Caregivers," 93.

18. Ibid.

19. Ibid.

20. Robert N. Butler and Myrna I. Lewis, *Aging and Mental Health, Positive Psychosocial and Biomedical Approaches*, 3rd. ed. (St. Louis: The C.V. Mosby Company, 1982), 103.

21. Ibid., 104.

22. Ibid., 105.

23. Peter V. Rabins, "Management of Irreversible Dementia," *Psychosomatics* 22, no. 7 (July 1981): 592.

24. Ibid.

25. Nancy L. Mace and Peter V. Rabins, *The 36-Hour Day*, (Baltimore: The John Hopkins University Press, 1981), 61.

26. Ibid., 60.

6

DEPRESSION, SUICIDE, ALCOHOLISM, PARANOIA
social work intervention

Chapter 6 is primarily involved with the identification and treatment of depression which may or may not be associated with Alzheimer's disease or reversible mental disorders. A serious complication of depression—suicide—also receives attention. As alcoholism is sometimes a factor in suicide and depression, and as paranoid ideation is also frequently encountered in old age, these topics are also reviewed in this chapter.

According to epidemiological data reviewed by Busse and Pfeiffer, the aged appear to either receive little or no psychiatric attention or have lengthy hospitalization. They seek or receive little psychiatric treatment on an ambulatory basis. Several factors are suggested to account for the lack of care, including those that follow. Mental illness may be tolerated to a certain degree by the aged or their families, for such behavior may be perceived as normal aging. There may be a reluctance to seek care for financial reasons and because psychiatry may not be as well accepted by older as by younger people. There is also the possibility that therapists may be reluctant to take older people as patients. This may be due to the lack of training in working with the aged, the belief that the older patient will not respond to therapy, or gerontophobic attitudes on the part of the therapist.[1]

It is hoped that research findings in the past few years are contributing to a change of attitude by mental health workers, as many myths held about aging are being discarded. Older people are perceived as being able to benefit from psychotherapy. As noted in earlier chapters, there is recognition that physical health is a strong determinant of psychological functioning in old age and that aging, in itself, does not cause the personality to deteriorate.

It is generally accepted that the 60-, 70-, or 80-plus-year-old has the same general personality characteristics that existed in youth. The neurotic patterns that emerged in younger years are essentially no different in old age, and many of the same treatment methods are used with older patients as with younger ones. Older men and women who were able to deal effectively with the problems of youth and middle life are more likely to be able to manage the problems that occur with aging.

PREVALENCE OF FUNCTIONAL MENTAL DISORDERS

Functional psychiatric disorders, with the exception of severe depression, rarely occur for the first time in the latter decades. However, the conflicts that seemed to have been resolved in earlier years may be reactivated in old age. The most common psychiatric problem that may make its appearance for the first time in old age is depression, which is discussed in the following section.

DEPRESSION

Reactive depressions are mild depressions that arise as a result of a loss or accumulation of losses, such as loss of a spouse, financial loss, loss of hearing or sight, loss of mobility, and so on. Clinical depression differs from normal bereavement when it is out of proportion to the cause, with symptoms that persist beyond the usual mourning time and interfere with normal functioning. If left unrecognized and untreated, these symptoms may become more severe.

It is important to note that most older men and women survive the changes and losses of old age without becoming severely depressed. Only a minority of older people have a "clinically significant" depression.[2]

Some patients have recurrent *endogenous depressions* ("a state of deep melancholy unrelated to an obvious cause")[3] throughout their lives which may be more severe and more frequent as they grow older. Others may have *involutional depressions* (associated with life-span problems and biological deterioration)[4] during the middle years, which may be reactivated in old age.

Symptoms of Depression

Depression may range from mild to severe. The moderately depressed older person carries out daily tasks with difficulty, forcing himself to do so. Withdrawal from others is typical. The symptoms of mild depression may not be recognized as readily as those of the severely depressed person. The lack of energy displayed by the mildly depressed person may be diagnosed as a physical problem.

In severe depression, the individual feels depressed, not only about the actual loss, but in regard to all aspects of life. There is an intense feeling of despair. This feeling may be accompanied by feelings of worthlessness and guilt and by delusions. Behavior is affected; retardation of speech, thought, and action may occur. The opposite behavior may be agitation. The individual is restless, unable to sit still. The patient may be histrionic in attempting to convey the feelings of depression. The agitated depressive individual has the greatest risk of suicide.[5] Agitation may be expressed by pacing the floor, wringing of hands, tearing of hair, gnashing of teeth, and so on.

There are disturbances of appetite and bowel function and a change in sleeping patterns. The depressed person is likely to awaken very early in the morning and to feel more depressed, with a lightening of the depression toward evening.[6]

Hypochondriacal complaints are a major characteristic of depression in old age. There may not be a focus on one pain but on a multitude of seemingly unrelated complaints. These include abdominal pain, headaches, breathlessness, palpitations, and backache. In this way, the older patient may displace the emotional distress that is experienced. As mentioned in Chapter 1, the majority of men and women over 65 today were not encouraged in their youth to express their emotions freely. However, they do feel free to speak about their physical complaints.

The depressed individual may become quite angry and defensive if any mention or suggestion of a psychiatric cause is made. There are reports of patients who were treated and who recovered from a depressed state without ever admitting or recognizing their depression.

As the older person usually has some chronic condition which could be painful, it is often very difficult to determine whether the pain is a symptom of depression or has taken on special significance due to the depressed state of the individual. Often when the depression diminishes, the pain becomes less.

Care must be taken not to mistake an appropriate concern for health as pathological. Stenback points out that taking an active interest in preventive health care and "tenacious care of a chronic disease" are necessary. When one is ill and there is a foreboding of disability and death, the depressive preoccupation with the body must be considered normal instead of neurotic.[7]

Depressed older men and women complain about difficulty in falling asleep and of early awakening, with difficulty in returning to sleep, just as younger depressed people do. However, as changes in sleep patterns occur with age, it is sometimes difficult to determine whether the change in sleeping is associated with depression or is part of a normal change. Sleep complaints must be considered in conjunction with other symptoms.

Confusion of Symptoms of Depression with Those of Dementia

Social workers in health-care settings may hear physicians mention *pseudodementia* in reference to depressed patients. *Pseudodementia* is not a diagnosis but a term which "refers to a presentation of depression in an elderly person where symptoms and signs of dementia are significant enough to suggest the diagnosis of dementia."[8]

The symptoms that may be misinterpreted include mental and motor retardation, agitated behavior, and apathy. Because of their similarity to symptoms of dementia, physicians sometimes prescribe antidepressants as a means of checking both the depression and their diagnosis.

Mental and motor retardation may be so severe that the person may be mute or immobile. If it is less severe, speech responses may be slow. Answers to questions may appear so muddled that they seem to have little relevance to the questions. The patient may be assessed as being confused, due to giving an answer to the first question after a later question is asked.[9] Very slow responses and slow speech are sometimes presenting symptoms which may lead to a misdiagnosis of dementia.

It is important to remember that even if the condition is correctly diagnosed as dementia, depression may also be present and require treatment.

There are also some differences in the symptoms of depression and dementia, as follows:

- In depression, the onset of symptoms is usually more acute and the progression of symptoms more rapid than in dementia.
- The depressed patient usually emphasizes his disability, whereas the demented patient tries to conceal his disability.
- Agitation and confusion are more likely to occur at night in dementia, whereas agitation when present is worse in the mornings in the older depressed individual.
- There is more likely to be a history of previous depressive episodes in the depressed patient.

Causes of Depression

In addition to depression associated with brain disease, depression in older individuals may also be a result of other specific diseases or it may be induced by drugs or due to a nutritional lack. Depression often accompanies the motor disturbances that occur in Parkinson's disease.[10] Hyperthyroidism and hypothyroidism may produce mental impairment in which depression is a presenting symptom.[11] Drugs used to treat hypertension often induce depression.[12] Mental changes, including depression, can be the result of a deficiency of nicotinic acid.[13] There are many other examples of such causes.

Depression is also thought to arise as a result of the various losses that occur in later years; the diagnosis of a fatal illness or the erroneous belief that a fatal illness exists; poor physical health which results in dependency on others; feelings of hopelessness; and frustrated aggression.

Losses in later years. Loss of an external love object is considered a major cause of depression.[14] It has been found that a serious loss that occurs during childhood, such as that of parent or sibling, may indicate the degree of depression that follows other losses in later life.

Loss of a spouse through separation, divorce, or death often means the loss of one's major source of emotional support. It is often the forerunner to a drastic change in life-style, incurring even more losses, including loss of home, community contacts, and old friends.

Fear of one's own death does not seem to play a part in the older individual's depression. There seems to be more anxiety about *not* dying before becoming a burden to the family or society. The depressive concerns that are centered on death are related to how life will be managed in the event of death of the spouse, a beloved child, or another close relative. There may be fear as to the effects of one's own death on the spouse or on others who may suffer.

Loss of employment, often through forced retirement, also may involve a loss of identity along with the loss of working relationships and friends. Retirement may be accompanied by a loss of status, changes in social roles, and decreased income. If the career provided the major goals sought throughout life, these may be sorely missed.

So many losses, sometimes occurring very close together or even simultaneously, undermine feelings of security. There are feelings of loss of control over life's events and over one's immediate world. Feelings of helplessness and powerlessness may become so overwhelming that depression results. Self-esteem may be severely damaged, not only from the changes in the immediate environment, but from the ageism encountered throughout society. Feelings of worthlessness and inferiority may ensue, reflecting the societal viewpoint.

Poor physical health. Poor physical health has long been associated with depression. Coping with the demands of illness drains energy needed to cope effectively with crises that occur. Chronic disease may become more disabling, and new health crises are more apt to occur in later years. Individuals who have been independent all their lives may be confronted with the necessity of depending on others to assist them in even the most basic daily functions.

Fatal illness. Individuals who have a diagnosis of a fatal illness become depressed, sometimes to the extent of opting for suicide rather than living out the remainder of their lives in pain or as an invalid. There are also those who develop a phobia that they have an undiagnosed terminal disease and cannot be convinced otherwise. They may become depressed enough to commit suicide.

Frustrated aggression. Pitt notes that frustrated aggression seems to occur in late life most often between couples who are "stuck with each other." They feel angry and resentful but are unable to quarrel and bring their angry feelings out into the open. Since their aggressive feelings cannot be expressed outwardly, aggression is turned inward.[15] This then becomes manifest through psychosomatic symptoms or suicide.

Assessment of Depression

Arie and Jolley strongly recommend that all patients referred to a psychogeriatric service be assessed initially at home by a psychiatrist, with other members of the team, instead of being taken to a hospital for diagnostic purposes. The reasons given include the following: Psychiatric problems in older people nearly always are in reference to functioning in the older person's usual environment, not functioning in the hospital; visits in the home aid in understanding the characteristics of the setting, such as warmth, food in the larder, presence of bottles, and so on; neighbors, local shopkeepers, and others in the community can provide a collateral mental history which is especially helpful if the patient is confused; the older person's confusion may be exacerbated by the process of moving; hospitalization may preempt more appropriate solutions, for it is sometimes very difficult to resettle an older person once removal from the community has taken place; home visits made initially may establish the resources which may be used in eventual resettlement.[16]

Although most physicians and a great many social workers in this country do not make home visits, they obtain information from the patient, spouse, and other relatives of the depressed patient in regard to sleeping, health, activities of the individual, attitude, mood, living situation, and economic circumstances. Determining the events that led up to the onset of depression is a vital part of the assessment. Information as to problems the person has encountered in the past and the coping mechanisms employed to resolve them is considered essential.

A necessary component of the assessment process is determining the physical health of the depressed individual. Causes of depression, such as illness, medication, nutrition, or other physical cause, must be explored.

Comfort notes that asking specifically whether individuals believe they have cancer or other terminal illness may quickly lead to the basis of the depression.[17]

Assessment of the older individual's income is vital. Poverty may be a contributing factor. Some older men and women do not ask for financial help because they believe it is shameful to do so or because they are not aware that help is available.

Treatment of Depression

The treatment approach depends upon the assessment of the older person: the severity of the depression, the physical condition, psychodynamic factors, socioeconomic situation, and environmental variables. An aggressive approach to treatment of depression is recommended.

Treatment of severe depression includes hospitalization if there is a risk of suicide, or for evaluation and treatment of a severe depression; psychotherapy; and drug therapy. If these are ineffective, electroconvulsive shock therapy may be considered.[18] As mentioned in earlier chapters, antidepressants are sometimes poorly tolerated by older adults or conflict with other medications and cannot always be prescribed.

The goals of treatment are apt to differ from the goals set for younger individuals. A young person can expect many years ahead in which to seek a new career, find another mate, pursue new educational goals, and so on; the older person may be restricted by poor health and other circumstances that can be changed very little or not at all. However, the way the individual perceives the loss and the situation may be changed. The person may learn new ways to interact with the environment which are more constructive. Goals for older adults are usually more specific and more highly focused. They must be realistic to prevent further discouragement and hopelessness, but as each small goal is reached, greater goals may be set.

The defenses that the older individual has established are usually left alone unless there can be a fairly extensive modification of the person's life. Care is taken not to increase feelings of having little control over life. Depressed individuals need to make every decision within their capabilities and circumstances.

The aged who are institutionalized may appear to have no choices, but even in those cases there are opportunities for decision making. For example, the resident may be encouraged to make any decision that is available: selecting items from the menu, choosing from reading material, deciding when to take a walk or sit outside, dining with others or alone.

The technique of "life review" is used by some therapists in treatment of depression. The rationale for the use of life review is that the key to aging successfully lies in the individual's review of his or her past life.

Butler postulated that reminiscing about the past occurs naturally to some degree with every individual and is brought about by the realization of approaching death. It is a means of making sense out of the whole of one's life—a spontaneous, unselective process in which past events and unresolved conflicts become conscious. If the unresolved conflicts can be successfully reintegrated, the life review process can bring new meaning to the individual's life and will become a preparation for death by decreasing fear and anxiety.[19]

By reconstructing the past, the older individual, with the therapist's help, can identify the struggles that have ended in triumph, thereby producing feelings of achievement and self-worth. Writing autobiographies, attending reunions, visiting friends from earlier years, and studying genealogies can help this process occur.

There are objections to the use of life review based on the fact that the person may become too preoccupied with the past to deal effectively with the concerns of the present. Or the individual may remember the most painful parts, the defeats and disappointments, and fail to recall victories. There may in actuality be little to recall that is praiseworthy, and reminiscing may add to despair. Butler notes that life review can occur as a mild nostalgia and regret. However, in extreme cases, there may be intense regret, panic, and even suicide if the person is unable to resolve or accept the problems.[20]

Before using life review as a treatment device, an assessment of the individual must be made as to whether this will be helpful or a hindrance. Studying the techniques is necessary, for life review therapy is not simply reminiscing about the past. It is much more structured and purposive. Discussions of life review therapy are found in the writings of R.N. Butler.[21]

Practice Applications

It is important to keep in mind that older people do not display the same symptoms of depression as those of younger individuals. When taking the history of the person who appears depressed or presents symptoms of depression, it is important to obtain information about the older person's physical health, medication, and treatment, since these may be primary or contributing factors to the depression.

Prevention of severe depression is a major concern. Although many of the losses of old age cannot be prevented, reaching older men and women as early as possible to ameliorate the effects of losses is vital. Since retirement and death of significant others are two losses that may require extensive changes in life-style, early counseling in these areas may prevent the development of severe depression. Bereavement and retirement counseling, as preventive measures, are discussed in Chapter 11.

Treatment for depression requires vigorous action devoted to all aspects of the person's self and environment. The social worker may be involved in treatment as the major therapist or as a member of a specialized team in a health-care setting. The help offered by the social worker is most likely to be crisis intervention, with the major aim of therapy being to restore the person to his or her activity level prior to the crisis that triggered the depression.

Although the setting in which the social worker is employed may not require appointments, firmly setting an appointment time gives the client a specific time and place to anticipate personal, undivided attention. Making sure the client knows that the social worker is available between appointments is also important.

Assessing the coping skills that the older person used in past crises is helpful, provided the present environment is conducive to providing assistance in effective coping. If not, manipulation of the environment may be the first step.

If depression is the result of loss of a spouse or a child, the social worker provides a relationship which may help the client to realize that new and meaningful relationships can be developed. Quite often the older person relates to the social worker as a parent to a mature child. The social worker may respond by being the mature child who provides a hopeful, positive attitude while helping the parent mobilize coping skills.

At some time during the interview, questions must be asked about suicide. The question must be specific as to whether suicide has been considered. If so, the patient's suicidal plan must be determined as well as whether he or she has the means at hand.

If the patient has a definite suicide plan, or if there is any doubt about the risk of suicide, urgent admission to the hospital must be made. Evasive answers should be considered grounds for suspicion, and close observation of the individual by a relative should be advised, pending further psychiatric evaluation of the patient.

Social workers in nursing homes may find that a resident is depressed partly because of dependence on others. If the person is extremely incapacitated, the focus may be on helping the individual accept the dependency role. The resident can be reassured that dependence is age-related and unavoidable. The depression may be due to concerns about losing those on whom the patient has been dependent. Helping the individual to identify each family member and each person on the nursing home staff who is supportive and understanding may ameliorate the patient's fears.

Use of resources. When social workers think of resources for the patient, "family" is the first thought. However, the older patient may initially be unable to identify friends, family members, or neighbors to help or with whom they can confide. Relatives may be in other institutions and inaccessible, or deceased. The therapist may be required to become this friend and confidante until other support systems are located or created. Depressed individuals must not be allowed to feel abandoned or that they must deal with their problems alone.

For clients who need socialization opportunities, group work may be more helpful than one-to-one counseling or may be used in conjunction with counseling. Many older people are not members of any social groups. There are a wide variety of interest groups in most communities, in addition to therapeutic kinds of groups that may be offered by Family Services, the Y, or other social agencies.

Day-care centers are a source of help in terms of providing socialization and care for the socially isolated individual. The center must be carefully selected, as the quality and kinds of services vary widely. Many centers associated with community mental health centers, Catholic Social Services, and some senior citizen centers provide day care supervised by social workers or psychologists who can provide counseling and ongoing assessment of the patient. Other day-care centers may offer mainly custodial care and limited socialization activities.

Glickman and Friedman warn against referral to senior citizens' centers as part of an initial therapeutic plan. Depressed individuals are too preoccupied with themselves to benefit initially from exposure to the opportunities of such centers. Self-esteem may only be further diminished if they are not successful in forming new relationships. Senior citizen centers are helpful after symptoms have subsided.[22]

SUICIDE

Suicide is a more frequent cause of death among the 65 and older population than any other age group. This is mainly due to the relatively high suicide rate among older white men. In 1984 the suicide rate for white men 65 and older was nearly four times the national rate, three times the rate for older black men, six times the rate for older white women, and twenty-four times the rate for older black women.[23]

There is general agreement about suicide in relation to older people, as follows: (1) there are fewer suicide *attempts* in the older population; (2) there are more completed or "successful" suicides in the older population than in the younger; and (3) older men complete suicide more often than older women.

Causes of Suicide

The question as to why some depressed individuals commit suicide and other depressed persons do not has been answered in a variety of ways. Suicide has been related to population density, socioeconomic class, and other environmental factors.

Research studies indicate that the majority of older individuals who commit suicide have been depressed. A smaller number have used alcohol to excess; an even smaller number are individuals with organic brain syndromes; and a very small percentage have an untreatable terminal illness.[24]

The element of hopelessness has been identified as the link between depression and suicidal behavior. Suicidal patients see the future as being highly constricted. In one study, three different diagnostic groups described their current life situations in negative terms, but only the suicidal group rated the future in negative terms.[25]

Although suicide may not be the result of any one factor, bereavement is believed to be a major factor in the development of severe depression and suicide among older individuals. The first year following the death of a spouse or other loved one is considered to be the most crucial time period. Suicide of the survivor occurs most often during this period of time.

Stenback, in a discussion of depression and suicidal behavior in old age, condenses five main factors contributing to suicidal behavior:

> ...first, general and age-specific losses and failures which cause depression with hopelessness and despair; second, an 'egoistic' or excessively individualistic per-

sonality, emotionally shallow or cold; third, a society unable to create social integration by means of family bonds, community interest groups, or supporting social services; fourth, a personality trait of resolving problems by action and not by passive adaptation; fifth, a suicide-promoting environment, either personal (such as suicides in the family) or cultural (such as acceptance and idealization of suicide).[26]

In a study of 301 cases of white males in Arizona aged 60 or older who committed suicide during a five-year span, 1970–1975, eight major patterns of geriatric suicidal behavior were identified. They are as follows:

(1) The reaction to severe physical illness; (2) the reaction to mental illness; (3) the reaction to the threat of extreme dependency and/or institutionalization; (4) the reaction to the death of a spouse; (5) the reaction to retirement; (6) the reaction to pathological personal relationships; (7) the reaction to alcoholism and drug abuse; and (8) the reaction to multiple factors.[27]

Miller points out that the various reactions overlap, adding that there is seldom one reason for suicide. The titles of the first seven reactions represent an attempt to focus on the *salient motivation* for any given case of suicide in an older person.

These studies and others emphasize the need for social workers and other mental health professionals to be as aware of the total environment of the suicidal individual as of the psychodynamic factors that are present. Particular attention must be placed not only on the client's actual health but the person's *perception* of health. Individuals who are convinced that cancer or some other life-threatening illness is present in their bodies are as frightened and desperate as the person with a diagnosed cancer.

"Passive" Suicide

Although suicide may be violent, such as by shooting or hanging, other less obvious means are used. These include refusal to eat, forgetting to take or refusing prescribed medication, delaying life-saving treatment, failing to observe dietary restrictions, and abusing drugs or alcohol. These cases, sometimes referred to as "passive suicides," may be detected by comments made by relatives or spouse in relation to the person's actions or lack of actions, such as failing to take antihypertensive medication.

Prevention

To reiterate an earlier point, the crucial life-saving factor in treating a depressed person is very likely to be the existence of a significant supportive relationship. Whoever provides treatment must see to it that the depressed individual has this relationship. If there is no one in the person's environment to provide the relationship, the therapist must provide it until the patient is able to develop such relationships with others.

Practice Applications

Social workers in community agencies, particularly senior citizen centers, government housing developments, and home health agencies, frequently come into contact with recently retired and bereaved individuals with reactive depressions. These older persons very likely will not identify their need as being for bereavement counseling or retirement counseling. The sensitivity of the social workers to the depressed, hopeless, and despairing person's sadness and discomfort will enable them to identify and respond to the unexpressed needs of these individuals so that appropriate steps can be taken.

ALCOHOLISM

Some older people have been alcoholics since their youth; some have become alcoholic when old. Older alcoholics are often classified in the literature as having an early onset, representing about two-thirds of older alcoholics, or late onset, representing the remaining one-third. Early onset older alcoholics have personality characteristics that seem to be similar to those of younger alcoholics, and they have long-standing histories of alcoholism. Alcoholism of late onset may develop as a result of the stresses of old age.[28]

Prevalence

The literature varies in estimating how much alcoholism exists among older people and how many become newly addicted to alcohol. However, there appears to be substantial documentation for the view that alcoholism is a problem in the older population that warrants attention.

Schuckit, using several studies, estimates alcoholism in the general population over 60 at between 2 percent and 10 percent; alcoholism in nursing-home patients at approximately 20 percent; and alcoholism among psychiatric patients at one-third or more. The high percentage of alcoholic nursing-home and psychiatric patients is due to the association of heavy alcohol intake with both medical and psychiatric pathology.[29]

There are a number of difficulties inherent in attempting to estimate the number of elderly alcoholics. Younger alcoholics are more readily identified because they come to the attention of law enforcement and community agencies. They frequently encounter difficulties in holding their jobs, are arrested for traffic violations, become involved in fights and brawls, and often experience marital difficulties. As the majority of older people are unemployed, many are widowed, and proportionately fewer drive automobiles, there is less chance of attracting attention from the public. Alcoholism may be a more hidden problem among the aged.

Although many alcoholics are admitted to hospitals, some of them have physical problems of such severity that they dominate the medical picture. Their addiction to alcohol may not be diagnosed. Relatives of the older person may not provide information in regard to drinking in order to protect the reputation of the family. Malnutrition, confusion, and injuries resulting from falls may be erroneously attributed to senility. In addition, physicians may be reluctant to apply the additional label of "alcoholic" to an older person beset with a wide array of health and social problems.

Older adults may underreport their drinking habits, just as younger ones do. They may not admit to the amount they imbibe when surveyed or interviewed by a study group.

Vulnerability of the Aged to Alcohol

The elderly person does not need to drink large amounts to have significant problems as a result of drinking. The body becomes less resilient with aging. There are metabolic changes in the body which result in higher blood alcohol levels for older individuals than younger ones who have ingested an equivalent amount of alcohol. In addition, there is an apparent increase in brain sensitivity to drugs that depress the central nervous system so that lowered levels of cognition may occur from modest amounts of alcohol.[30]

Many older people have serious medical problems that can be exacerbated by the addition of alcohol; for example, even one drink can cause decreased cardiac output and decreased cardiac efficiency in a patient with impaired cardiac functioning. For those who are taking medication, alcohol can be a dangerous accompaniment to many prescribed or over-the-counter drugs.[31]

It appears that early-onset alcoholics cut down on their drinking as they grow older. This may be due to the older person's decreased tolerance to alcohol. Some clinicians attribute this cutback to concerns about poorer health and the awareness by the older person that full possession of all faculties is needed for survival. However, as noted earlier in this section, drinking smaller quantities does not prevent problems from developing.

It is likely that chronic alcoholism among the older population may become more pronounced in the future due to better nutrition and health care, increasing the survival of early onset alcoholics.

Causes of Alcoholism Among the Aged

There are many diverse opinions as to the causes of alcoholism. Genetic predetermination, a learned adaptation to psychological stress, a result of societal conditions such as poverty, or cultural acceptance of alcohol are some of the current beliefs as to reasons for alcoholism.[32]

External factors associated with increasing age are often given as the major cause of alcoholism for those over 55. Bereavement, loneliness, and the pressures of retirement, such as the loss of status associated with employment and decreased income, are frequently noted causes.[33]

Treatment of Alcoholism

Many alcohol treatment programs are concerned primarily with detoxification and intensive medical care. According to Zimberg, admission to these kinds of programs is inappropriate for the elderly. The need for treatment of alcohol withdrawal manifestations rarely arises. Treatment approaches that focus on the stresses associated with aging are the most effective. Modes of treatment used successfully include group socialization, social casework and family casework, medical care when needed for physical problems, and, with clinically depressed patients, antidepressant medication.[34]

Practice Applications

One of the problems social workers encounter when trying to help chronic alcoholics known in a community is resistance by agencies that provide support services. In a study of clients with alcohol-related problems that was conducted at a Mental Health Outreach Program for the Elderly, it was found that agencies in the community were reluctant to become reinvolved with chronic long-term alcoholics. During previous contacts there had been instances of clients' falsification of records, refusal to participate in therapy, and paranoid accusations toward agency staff. Once the mental health workers from the Outreach Program emphasized their commitment to these clients and their responsibility for them, the community agencies were willing to become reinvolved.[35]

A second problem that often interferes with treatment is the failure to recognize alcoholism in some older individuals by a number of health-care and community workers, as well as by many family members. It is a sort of "Why not?" attitude based on hopelessness and, possibly, pity. The reasoning appears to be that some of the older individuals living in the community have such overwhelming problems, and those in institutions are so bored by life, that the resort to alcoholism is justified. Instead of addressing the lack of support systems in the community and the practices in institutions that result in boredom, this attitude accepts drinking as a regrettable but reasonable solution to these problems.

Social workers in health care and other community settings can work toward educating their fellow workers, family members of older adults, and members of the community about the effects of even limited drinking on older men and women. They must be made aware of the need for the recognition and treatment of alcoholism.

As noted in the previous section, excessive drinking has been identified as a factor in suicide among older adults. Making this fact known to other health-care workers and to family members may alert them to the need to reevaluate their attitudes toward the drinking habits of older people.

In most cases, social networks are lacking and must be structured to meet the individual's needs. Family members may need to be involved in planning when they are accessible and willing to participate. Building new relationships and new support systems is frequently necessary, as losses of significant others may be contributing to the person's drinking problem.

Helping the client to find new activities is usually necessary. Referral to Alcoholics Anonymous may be made, as this is a means of socializing with others. In some communities AA has a number of activities that provide a means of involvement with others.

Zimberg suggests that alcohol treatment programs be provided through agencies that serve older adults in other ways, such as via senior citizen programs, outpatient medical and psychiatric geriatric programs, nursing homes, and home health-care services.[36] This could be an area for advocacy for a social worker seeking new avenues of helping older alcoholics.

Another component of depression is frequently that of paranoid ideation. A brief discussion of paranoid ideation follows.

PARANOID IDEATION

In the literature on paranoid ideation, there appears to be controversy over the types or categories of paranoia. For this reason, paranoid ideation is discussed in this section in relationship to severity instead of typology.

Before considering paranoid ideation, it may be helpful to consider the characteristics of paranoid personalities.

Paranoid Personalities

A person with paranoid personality has a "chip on the shoulder" attitude and is quick to imagine slights and insults, when none is intended. Actions may consist of two extremes: either extreme sensitivity, with feelings of inferiority, or belligerence, with a readiness to take offense. There is a willingness to go to court over injustices that may be imagined. Grudges may be held tenaciously. Friends and relatives are often alienated long before they reach old age.[37]

Conditions Predisposing to Paranoia

Individuals with paranoid personalities usually become more paranoid with increasing age. It is very likely that the paranoia seen in old age has always been a part of the personality but becomes visible for the first time in old age. It may have been of such a mild nature that normal life stresses occurring in youth and middle age did not activate it.

There are other conditions predisposing to paranoia. These include the use of alcohol and drugs, sensory deprivation, impaired memory, and a change in the environment. Each of these is discussed in the following paragraphs.

Paranoia can be caused by drugs used in the treatment of physical illness, such as steroids, and some drugs used in the treatment of tuberculosis and Parkinson's disease. Amphetamines taken in excessive quantities can cause an acute paranoid state. Similarly, withdrawal of barbiturates from drug-dependent individuals may result in paranoid thinking and behavior.[38]

Sensory deprivation contributes to paranoia, for perception depends on the information provided by sight and sound and by the interpretation of what is heard and seen. When incoming sensory data decreases, there is a tendency toward greater subjective interpretation. Individuals with suspicious traits of personality may tend to believe that those around them, whom they can only partially hear, are conspiring against them.[39] Too, the irritation from trying to communicate with the hearing impaired person may be sensed by the person, and this may contribute to paranoid thinking.

Impaired memory increases the problem. Forgetting where items are placed and where valuables are stored, failure to remember whether checks have been cashed, bills have been paid, or letters written are common occurrences that are likely to accentuate paranoid thinking and lead to unwarranted accusation of others in order to explain them.

Some possible results of a sudden change in environment were demonstrated in the case example presented in Chapter 4, in which an older woman experienced her first hospital admission and suffered from delirium and paranoid ideation. Transfer to a nursing home or even to a relative's home, particularly without adequate preparation, may contribute to paranoid states. Such moves may bring about feelings of loss of mastery over the environment. Some older men and women may resort to blaming the world around them or blaming specific individuals in an effort to make some kind of sense out of what is happening to them.

Range of Paranoia

Paranoid ideation in older men and women ranges in intensity from a mild suspiciousness (often more troubling to family members than disabling to the person) to florid paranoid schizophrenia with marked thought disorder, delusional ideation, unwarranted hostility, and complete loss of insight.

Paranoia can also be transient and situational. This may be a result of isolation and a change in living circumstances; for example, an individual of advanced age may be moved from a familiar environment to an unfamiliar one, such as a working relative's home. The relative, when at home, unthinkingly rearranges furniture when cleaning. The older person, alone all day in a strange environment, may believe that the relative is purposely moving furniture around to cause confusion; hiding food, when in actuality the individual cannot remember where the cupboards are located; and so on.

Treatment

It is probable that most older adults with very mild paranoid ideation do not come to the notice of physicians and mental health workers unless they constantly complain to the police or in some way call attention to themselves. Post mentions that the psychotic conditions of older women frequently are undetected until the spouse dies. It is then discovered that the deceased husband had been covering up for his sick wife or may have shared her delusional beliefs.[40]

Obtaining eyeglasses and hearing aids for those who have untreated visual or auditory impairment may also assist in resolving the problem. It is necessary for the helping person to explain each step that is taken so that the suspicious person fully understands.

The major stumbling block to successful psychotherapy in the older paranoid individual is the person's inability to accept that the slights, insults, and injuries that are experienced are manifestations of his paranoid state. Individuals with severe paranoid ideation frequently need to be hospitalized for their own safety and the safety of others. Psychotropic drugs are often used with varying degrees of success.

Family members are usually aware of the long-standing suspiciousness of their older relatives. Explaining the role of sensory deficits and changed environments in increasing paranoid ideation may help family members understand the importance of communicating as clearly as possible with the older person. Maintaining a patient attitude and interpreting events as they occur allow less opportunity for misinterpretations to arise.

Practice Applications

When confronted with a paranoid client, the possibility of some truth underlying the paranoid ideation must be considered. Complaints must be assessed as to their relation in terms of the reality of the situation. Older adults sometimes do have letters stolen. When hospitalized or out of their homes for some other reason, possessions are sometimes taken from them by neighbors. Some residents of institutions are victimized by employees, and older family members are sometimes abused by their relatives. It may be very difficult to determine whether these events have actually happened, or to what extent they have happened, or whether they are imagined.

Social workers also need to be aware that the diagnostic label of "paranoia" can be used to abuse the older client's civil rights. Pitt mentions three examples of rights that might be infringed upon for the sake of expediency: the matron of a home for older adults who does not get along with a resident; an older lady refusing to move from her home when the area is designated for slum clearance; and a private landlord wishing to be rid of an unprofitable tenant. In each of these instances, pressure may be placed on community or government agencies to take action against a fearful, angry older person who is labeled paranoid.[41]

POLICIES AFFECTING PRACTICE

There are a number of policy issues in regard to mental health that need addressing. They include the discharge policies of mental institutions and mental wards and the restrictive eligibility policies and lack of outreach of many community agencies. The following section is devoted to a discussion of these issues. A description of case management as a means to address the need for coordination and supervision of services follows. The chapter concludes with a case example which demonstrates some of the ideas presented on mental disorders.

Discharge Policies

For the past two or three decades, mental health institutions have had policies of reducing admissions, shortening the stay of those patients admitted, and discharging long-term patients in order to prevent institutionalization. Unfortunately, many institutions have discharged marginally adjusted mental patients into the community to be rehabilitated. Comprehensive community health centers, funded by the Community Mental Health Act in 1963, were expected to provide rehabilitation services to care for those who needed continuing outpatient care, but this has not taken place. Many surveys have revealed that community mental health centers have not served the older population. Older men and women do not seek services from these centers, and there are few outreach efforts directed to older adults.

Such policies affect social work practice with older adults who have psychiatric problems. Social workers in hospitals are under pressure to discharge the patient to living arrangements in the community; social workers in community agencies are under pressure to maintain the individual in the community and avoid institutional placement. Family members are frequently hesitant about providing care for a relative who has a mental disorder. Consequently, a significant number of patients who are discharged from mental wards or who are abandoned by their families to community agencies have been and continue to be moved into residential hotels and boarding homes, with few community supports to contribute to their care. Some patients become street people and fade into oblivion.

Restrictive Policies

It has been frequently noted that older adults do not make as much use of social services as do other populations. This holds true for services provided by crisis intervention and drug- and alcohol-abuse programs. Although one reason may be an unwillingness of today's self-reliant older population to ask for help, another may well be the structure and restrictive policies of the agencies. For example, in a study of a representative sample of alcoholic programs in the Cleveland area, most programs were found to have a policy that restricted admission to those who are ambulatory and not experiencing disabling medical problems. None of the programs had outreach components that might increase the number of old people requesting services.[42]

Crisis centers usually have a walk-in or telephone policy. Some older people are isolated or located far from the agency and do not have transportation; some do not have telephones. Many may not even know of the services. More outreach is needed to acquaint older men and women with agencies that supply emergency services. Moreover, the means for the older client to make use of these services, whether it is transportation, a telephone, or something else, must be provided.

CASE MANAGEMENT

Case management is an old term that has taken on new meaning, when applied to long term care and working with older people. The concepts embodied by the term, as it is now used in social work, are a mixture of old and new. Since the early days of social work, many generalist social work practitioners, particularly those in hospitals, have thought of themselves as case managers in the sense of coordinating discharge planning, locating resources for clients, referring clients to other agencies, and providing or arranging referrals for follow-up services.

The newer concept of case management is an outgrowth of the growing concern over the past several years about the escalating cost of health care coupled with the realization that many older people, if given assistance, could remain in the community instead of being placed in nursing homes. During the last decade or so, government-sponsored programs have been testing the feasibility of providing care and supports to older people to avoid institutionalization and to reduce cost of care. As a result of these pioneering programs, the services provided by the case manager have broadened and are more inclusive than in the earlier concept.

Differences between Case Management and Discharge Planning

Although the concept of case management includes some of the activities that are inherent in hospital discharge planning, there are several characteristics that distinguish between these two services, such as the duration of service, the intensity of the relationship, and breadth of involvement. The discharge planner is mainly concerned with the acute episode that preceded the hospitalization and with arranging the transition in a timely, safe way from the hospital to the living arrangement needed by the patient. In contrast, the case manager is sanctioned to remain involved with the care of the discharged individual as long as needed. This could range from a one-time consultation to several years of monitoring. The short term relationship between the discharge planner and patient usually does not become an indepth relationship. The case manager, however, involved in a long term relationship, may become a surrogate family for clients who lack other informal supports. The case manager's span of involvement may include acquiring much more knowledge of the client's past life, planning more extensively for his or her future, and more involvement with formal and informal segments of the community life that is related to the client's life.[43]

Case Management in a Broader Context

The case management concept is not limited to the field of hospital social work, and the position of case manager does not "belong" to social workers. Child welfare and community mental health are other areas of social work which make use of case managers. There are also social workers in private practice who are primarily involved in providing case management services to older people and handicapped individuals. Although the case manager may be a social worker in a hospital or a community agency, he or she may be a nurse, psychologist, physician, or other designated person with few or no professional credentials. Employment opportunities for case managers include hospitals, home maintenance organizations, home health agencies, and various programs funded by public sources.

Lack of a Clearly Defined Model

There does not seem to be one distinctly defined model which can be identified as "the case management model." The responsibilities and the amount of authority held by the case manager have been described as ranging from authoritarian models in which the case manager determines whether the client is entitled to remain at home or be placed in a nursing home to the least authoritarian model in which the case manager has little more than persuasive power to urge the client to follow a suggested plan.[44]

Major Components of Case Management

Although the case management concept has not been completely formalized, there are four components of case management in long term care that seem to be generally agreed upon, as follow: *casefinding, assessment, care planning,* and *monitoring.* Casefinding involves screening, as it is aimed at identifying clients that need the service. In long term care, this means identifying those individuals who are at greatest risk for nursing home placement and ruling out those who are clearly ineligible. Assessment is concerned with determining functional abilities, cognition, emotional and social well-being, and the strength of social-support systems. Care planning consists of formulating strategies to meet specific needs and requires a thorough knowledge of available and appropriate community resources. Once the plan is made, the services are located, ordered, and implemented.

Monitoring may be focused on the individual's care and on the service providers, if needed. The case manager assesses the client's care at established intervals. Services may be added or removed, according to the client's needs. A case management system may also assess the adequacy of services and identify those the client needs but that are not provided, as well as the cost. In order for the monitoring to be effective, a management information system is a necessity to a case management program.[45]

Major Problems in the Use of Case Management

The *quality* of a case management plan depends on the knowledge, skills, and training of the case manager. The *effectiveness* of the plan depends on the quality and availability of financial assistance and community resources. Social work educators may need to place more emphasis on the development of geriatric social work specialization with an emphasis on case management and to recruit more students into these programs. Changes in Medicare and Medicaid policies are needed to supply funding for the community services and supports needed by older people to avoid institutionalization. Until these two problems are resolved, the potential is very limited for case management to become a viable social work method to help the disabled and frail elderly remain in the community.

The following case example illustrates the use of case management by a social worker in the community whose client is a mildly paranoid, depressed older woman.

CASE EXAMPLE: DEPRESSION

Mrs. Carney is a 76-year-old widow who is taken by her daughter-in-law, Joanne, to the social worker's office in the senior citizens' center. Joanne had called earlier and talked briefly with the social worker, identifying her mother-in-law as "the problem" that needed help. She had explained that she had only recently married Ben Carney, shortly after Ben's mother came to live with him. She and Ben are concerned about Mrs. Carney being alone at home all day, as they both work. They hope she will be interested in coming to the senior citizens' center. She will return for Mrs. Carney later in the day.

The social worker immediately notes Mrs. Carney's apathy and fatigued motions as she settles herself into a chair. She finds that Mrs. Carney has several physical complaints but has not had a complete physical examination in several years.

The social worker learns that Mrs. Carney and her husband were born in the small town in which she lived until she moved in with her only surviving child, Ben, four months earlier. Mrs. Carney's husband was supervisor at a factory in which Mrs. Carney also worked as a seamstress. She has been widowed for 15 years. The couple had two other children, a daughter who died when she was 15 with polio and another son who was killed in World War II, only weeks after his sister's death. The losses were so devastating that both Mr.

and Mrs. Carney worked double shifts in the factory for several months to escape their grief.

Mr. Carney's death is attributed by his wife to having worked too hard all of his life and having too little to do after retiring. Her description of his drinking habits indicate that he was an alcoholic whose drinking habits were exacerbated by retirement.

From Mrs. Carney's account of her excessive grief reaction following her husband's death, the social worker believes that it was associated with a delayed reaction of grief over her children's death. Mrs. Carney was thought to be so close to "breaking down" that her son's wife, Elsie, came to stay with her for several weeks.

Mrs. Carney was 62 at the time and wanted to stop working and stay at home, but Elsie insisted that she continue working at the factory. She also helped her to become active in church work and to make new friends in the community.

When Mrs. Carney retired from the factory, Elsie again "came to the rescue." She helped her to set up a small alterations business so that she could work at home in order to supplement her Social Security check. Mrs. Carney also enjoyed talking with her customers. Altogether, it was "real enjoyable," having Elsie to visit once in a while, going to church in the neighborhood, and making a little extra with sewing. Then her eyesight began to fail and she had to give up most of her alteration work. Her hearing was also slightly impaired.

Her customers and friends from the church continued visiting for a time. Mrs. Carney began to experience difficulty in recognizing and understanding the visitors. She began to be afraid to open the door, because there was so much "meanness" going on. The visits seemed to "stop all at once." Mrs. Carney mentions that she always wondered whether some neighbor "started a story on her" that made them stop coming. She also believed her mail was stolen from time to time, because she rarely received a letter.

At this time, to make matters worse, Mrs. Carney received word that her son and his wife had gotten a divorce. Her son had immediately remarried. To Mrs. Carney this was almost as if Elsie had died, for Elsie returned to her home, which was a great distance away.

Only a few weeks after their divorce and Ben's remarriage, Mrs. Carney tripped on the front steps to her house and sprained her left ankle and left wrist. It was after dark and she was on the steps four hours before a neighbor found her and called her son.

The next events happened so quickly that Mrs. Carney has difficulty sorting them out. Ben was very distressed and thought she should not live alone. He immediately placed her house and furniture up for sale, packed her things, and took her to his home. Almost overnight she had moved 200 miles away from her home of 76 years, into a new environment.

Mrs. Carney describes a number of current difficulties: problems with sleeping, constant fatigue, digestive disturbances, and lack of appetite. She finds it almost impossible to conceal her feelings toward her son's second wife. Mrs. Carney is positive that Joanne took her son away from Elsie. She is certain the only reason Joanne married her son was "to get his paycheck." She rarely sees either one of them, as Joanne goes to work when Ben leaves and comes in about the same time. After they have a meal together (which Joanne prepares), Mrs. Carney feels in the way and goes to bed, even though she knows she won't sleep.

She would like to "help out with the housekeeping." However, she would be expected to use a vacuum cleaner and other appliances that she has never used.

Cooking has always been one of her greatest pleasures, but now poses problems, for her poor eyesight prevents her from reading the labels easily and she has trouble "figuring out" the stove and other unfamiliar appliances. She is fearful of using them because she might break them.

As Mrs. Carney describes her situation, the social worker listens empathetically and reinforces her by responding with brief comments and questions. When Mrs. Carney talks of her feelings of loss at the time of her husband's death, the social worker asks her whether she had thoughts of hurting herself in some way when she was overcome by grief. Mrs. Carney doesn't remember exactly. She might have, for she was "crazy with grief." However, she does not have any such thoughts now. In fact, she thinks she ought to miss Elsie more than she does. It seems like she doesn't have "feelings" like she should.

While the social worker uses her listening skills, she is also evaluating what is being said. Although Mrs. Carney does not use the word *depressed* or at any time use words such as *sad, lonely, unhappy,* or express feelings of worthlessness, her depressed state is apparent. In addition to her despondent attitude and nonverbal actions, the account of the loss of her relationship with Elsie, the many changes in her living situation, difficulty in falling asleep and early awakenings, and somatic concerns indicate depression.

When her children died so closely together, the social worker believes that Mrs. Carney probably had not worked through the grief process, as indicated by the account of the severity of her grief reaction when her husband died. Submerging herself in extra shifts of factory work allowed her to use denial and suppression, so that she delayed coping with the losses of both children at the time but had to deal with them later, along with the death of her husband.

It seems to the social worker that after the death of Mrs. Carney's husband, the relationship with Elsie largely replaced Mrs. Carney's relationship with her husband and may have been more satisfactory, in some ways. Elsie was her mainstay for 11 years. In addition, self-employment provided her with feelings of worth and a means of socializing with others, as well as enabling her to live more comfortably on her income. Involvement with the church provided some spiritual and social satisfactions. As time passed, the situation began to change. Impaired sight and hearing interfered with working at home and were probably largely responsible for the cessation of visiting by old friends and customers. Over time, she developed mild paranoid ideation in order to explain her increasing isolation.

Mrs. Carney must now cope with the loss of the relationship with Elsie, her feelings about her new daughter-in-law, and a drastic change of environment. Although she no longer has the resiliency and the physical strength of youth, her willingness to come to the center indicates that she has not given up.

The social worker notes aloud that Mrs. Carney's health has not been medically evaluated recently. A medical assessment of her health is the first priority. The social worker stresses the importance of taking all her medication to the physician when she has her health checked.

Mrs. Carney reluctantly agrees to have a physical examination after discussing it with her son later that day. The social worker arranges with the nurse at the senior citizens' center for an appointment with a physician for the physical. A summary from the physician is to be sent to the nurse and the social worker. An appointment is made with Mrs. Carney to see the social worker in a few days. Very soon after this initial interview occurs, the results of the physical examination are sent to the social worker. The summary is heartening. The only major illness is congestive heart disease, which is in a very early stage. If Mrs. Carney maintains her prescribed diet and takes only the prescribed medication, there is no immediate danger. Mrs. Carney's vision can be considerably improved, but not fully corrected, by newly prescribed eyeglasses, but her hearing problem is not considered the type responsive to a hearing aid.

The social worker has an interview with Mrs. Carney's son and wife and finds that the situation at home is more intolerable than the social worker had imagined from Mrs. Carney's account. She finds that Mrs. Carney has made clear her dislike and distrust of Joanne.

Ben wishes that his mother could understand that he and Elsie had a poor marriage in which neither had been happy. They stayed together for years for the sake of the children. They might never have divorced had he not met Joanne and realized he did not have to be a "walking zombie." He is happy and feels he owes no apologies to his mother or to his ex-wife.

Ben adds that he has not been around his mother for such long intervals since his boyhood. He and Joanne had been happy until his mother came. He realizes she has many problems in adjusting, but he also feels she is "the problem" in his household at this time. He finds her deafness very irritating and frequently shouts at her, then feels guilty and ashamed.

The social worker is favorably impressed by the way Joanne responds to Mrs. Carney's behavior. Joanne admits that she is sometimes annoyed and angry, but she is not retaliatory. She shows compassion in relation to Mrs. Carney's grief over the loss of Elsie and her home. Joanne has no children of her own, only a few distant relatives, and wants to be on friendly terms with her mother-in-law. She mentions that she was raised by her grandmother, now deceased, and she would "treasure" having a close relationship with Mrs. Carney. She believes she can "win her over," but, at the moment, her mother-in-law is a "real problem."

The social worker learns from Ben that Mrs. Carney's only income is from Social Security. The sale of the house brought very little, as it was in great need of repair and located in an area of little value. Ben has set aside the small amount from the sale of the house to pay any medical costs his mother may have. He and Joanne have obligations that leave little to go toward extra expenses. From a financial standpoint, it would be very difficult for Mrs. Carney to live independently, but she can live comfortably in her son's home.

They discuss the necessity of the three of them learning to live together with some measure of harmony and satisfaction. Ben and Joanne agree that they must do more than passively accept Mrs. Carney's presence. They will cooperate in any way possible. Ben comments wearily that most of all he wants "a little peace" at home.

The social worker enters into a counseling relationship with Mrs. Carney and maintains contact with Ben and Joanne, sometimes seeing them together or with Mrs. Carney. She believes the entire family unit can gain some insight that will help them in their new situation.

Although Mrs. Carney had only an eighth-grade education, she impresses the social worker as intelligent, with a practical approach to problems. The social worker recalls her client's earlier experience with the death of her children. At that time, Mrs. Carney had not dealt with her feelings but had plunged herself into work. The social worker does not want her to repeat the experience. She encourages Mrs. Carney to explore her feelings about Elsie, her son and his "new" wife, and the other changes in her life. Although the social worker does not employ stringent life review techniques, she encourages reminiscing that brings memories of her clients' triumphs over hardship.

The social worker knows most of the members of the senior citizens' center well and frequently brings members together to resolve a problem. At this point she talks with a member, Mrs. Woods, who had a deaf child and is skilled at communicating with the deaf. Mrs. Woods is a widow in her late sixties and in vigorous health. She is a warm, outgoing person who seems to inspire good will and optimism in others.

The social worker explains the difficulties that Mrs. Carney is having with housekeeping and cooking and her desire to be more helpful to her son and his wife. She does not divulge anything other than the facts of Mrs. Carney's living arrangements.

Mrs. Woods quickly sees this as a challenge, and is eager to begin. The social worker recommends that she contact a worker in the state aid-to-the-blind services for suggestions. Although Mrs. Carney is not legally blind and not eligible for state assistance, one of the field workers will probably be willing to provide some helpful ideas. The social worker adds that Mrs. Woods is to be in contact with her as she wants to keep a close check on Mrs. Carney's progress or any problems that may arise.

With Mrs. Woods's help, Mrs. Carney finds that she can contribute significantly to the running of the household. Her greatest pleasure lies in finding that she is able to use her cooking skills and prepare food, which wins Ben and Joanne's honest appreciation. This reinforces her efforts, although it is difficult for Mrs. Carney to respond openly to Joanne's praise.

About this time, Mrs. Carney mentions to the social worker that she is sleeping a little better. Although she is still wakeful at times, she finds she can return to sleep. The social worker explains that wakefulness is often a part of the change that occurs in sleep patterns as one ages.

As church work had helped Mrs. Carney adjust to losses in the past, a second environmental approach made by the social worker is in reference to the church. Ben wants no part of attending church, but, fortunately, this is an area in which Joanne feels very comfortable. She is agreeable to accompanying Mrs. Carney to a church in the neighborhood.

At first Mrs. Carney is reluctant to attend, as she believes her hearing is too impaired. The social worker reminds her that her sight is much improved and she may be able to understand some of the service by lip reading. Mrs. Woods tells her that she is doing more lip reading than she realizes. Mrs. Carney finds that she is able to comprehend the main message of the sermon and enjoys the company of others at the coffee after the service.

Later, Mrs. Carney admits to the social worker that her opinion of Joanne began to change from the time Joanne accompanied her to church. She firmly believes Joanne is going to church for repentance. The social worker does not draw the same conclusion from the remarks made by Joanne, but she doesn't express her doubt to Mrs. Carney.

When exploring resources in Mrs. Carney's neighborhood, the social worker learns that there is a children's day-care center a block away from the Carney family which welcomes older adults as volunteers. The volunteers read or tell stories to the children, teach them to tie their shoes and other skills, but primarily provide them with a caring grandparent relationship. It is a meaningful activity that the social worker makes a note to discuss with Mrs. Carney when she may be ready to spend time in a volunteer activity.

The social worker has kept in contact with Ben and Joanne, for they have been taking Mrs. Carney to the senior citizens' center to talk with her during this planning-and-doing period. Although life is not perfect, they assure her that it is much better. Joanne believes she is winning her mother-in-law's confidence, as she has stopped making hurtful remarks. Ben is more patient with his mother's deafness. He has observed Mrs. Woods's relaxed, easy communication with his mother and is practicing her techniques.

During this time, Mrs. Carney has begun to venture out into the senior citizens' center after the counseling session. She has explored the various rooms used for club meetings, painting, crafts, quilting, and so on. She has inadvertently become acquainted with a few other members and seems to be slowly building new relationships in the center. Mrs. Woods has also helped to make her feel more at ease in the center. Mrs. Carney mentions to the social worker that she has heard from Elsie and that she has a "serious" relationship. She believes Elsie is "right happy" now.

Ben confides to the social worker that since his mother is more pleasant to his wife, this has helped him to have more patience with her deafness when conversing with her. Life is finally "more peaceful."

The social worker believes Mrs. Carney has worked through her feelings about both of her daughters-in-law when Mrs. Carney mentions to the social worker that Joanne reminds her quite a lot of Elsie. Ben, Joanne, and Mrs. Carney appear to be making a reasonably good adjustment to each other and to be working out relationships that are more satisfying to each of them.

Although both the son and daughter-in-law identify the mother-in-law as "the problem," the social worker recognizes that the issue is a family problem. Attempting to treat Mrs. Carney's depression in an isolated counseling relationship would probably be fruitless. It is necessary to involve the family, as well as others in the environment. She strives to help the family work out ways of interacting so that they respect and like each other and are able to live together harmoniously.

The social worker uses problem-solving and life-review techniques with Mrs. Carney and provides supportive therapy to the family, helping each of them to adapt to a change in living arrangements that requires the development of new ways of relating to each other. The social worker makes use of her knowledge of the coping mechanisms that were given in the psychosocial history to help the client deal with the presenting crisis. Through the counseling relationship, she offers the same kind of warmth and interested help that was given by the client's daughter-in-law, but she also works toward replacing herself as Mrs. Carney's major emotional support.

The social worker uses case management skills. In addition to identifying and making use of family resources, she refers the client to the physician, enlists the aid of a volunteer, the state services for the blind, the church, and, for future reference, the day-care center in the community. The social worker remains in contact with the helping persons, constantly checking to be certain that services are being provided effectively and appropriately.

NOTES

1. Ewald W. Busse and Eric Pfeiffer, "Functional Psychiatric Disorders in Old Age," in *Behavior and Adaptation in Late Life*, 2nd. ed. (Boston: Little, Brown and Co., 1977), 170, 171.
2. T.L. Brink, *Clinical Psychotherapy*, (New York: Human Sciences Press), 45.
3. Brice Pitt, *Psychogeriatrics: An Introduction to the Psychiatry of Old Age*, 2nd. ed. (Edinburgh: Churchill Livingstone, 1982), 64.
4. Asser Stenback, "Depression and Suicidal Behavior in Old Age," in *Handbook of Mental Health and Aging*, ed. James A. Birren and R. Bruce Sloane (Englewood Cliffs, N.J.: Prentice-Hall, Inc., 1980), 626.
5. Pitt, *Psychogeriatrics*, 68, 69.
6. Ibid., 68.
7. Stenbeck, "Depression and Suicidal Behavior," 626.
8. Robert H. Gerner, "Depression in the Elderly," in *Psychopathology of Aging*, ed. Oscar J. Kaplan (New York: Academic Press, 1979), 101.
9. J.A. Whitehead, *Psychiatric Disorders in Old Age: A Handbook for the Clinical Team*, (New York: Springer Publishing Company, Inc., 1974), 27.
10. Stenback, "Depression and Suicidal Behavior," 632.
11. Beni Habot and Leslie S. Libow, "The Interrelationship of Mental and Physical Status and Its Assessment in the Older Adult: Mind-Body Interaction," in *Handbook of Mental Health*, 710.
12. Ibid., 707.
13. Ibid., 709.
14. Stenback, "Depression and Suicidal Behavior," 618.
15. Brice Pitt, *Psychogeriatrics: An Introduction to the Psychiatry of Old Age*, 2nd. ed. (Edinburgh: Churchill Livingstone, 1982), 65.
16. Tom Arie and David Jolley, "Making Services Work: Organization and Style of Psychogeriatric Services," in *The Psychiatry of Late Life*, ed. Raymond Levy and Felix Post (Oxford: Blackwell Scientific Publications, 1982), 23.
17. Alex Comfort, *Practice of Geriatric Psychiatry*, (New York: Elsevier, 1980), 27.

18. Busse and Pfeiffer, "Functional Psychiatric Disorders," 176.

19. Robert N. Butler and Myrna I. Lewis, *Aging and Mental Health*, 3rd. ed. (St. Louis: The C.V. Mosby Co. 1982), 58.

20. Ibid., 59.

21. Robert Butler, "The Life Review: An Interpretation of Reminiscence in the Aged," *Psychiatry* 26, no. 1 (February 1963): 65–76.

22. Lewis Glickman and Sandor A. Friedman, "Changes in Behavior, Mood, or Thinking in the Elderly: Diagnosis and Management," *Medical Clinics of North America* 60, no. 6 (November 1976): 1307.

23. *Aging America: Trends and Projections*, 1987–88 Edition. Prepared by the U.S. Senate Special Committee on Aging in conjunction with the American Association of Retired Persons, the Federal Council on the Aging, and the U.S. Administration on Aging, 101.

24. Busse and Pfeiffer, "Functional Psychiatric Disorders," 177.

25. Aaron T. Beck, Maria Kovacs, and Arlene Weissman, "Hopelessness and Suicidal Behavior, An Overview," *Journal of the American Medical Association* 234, no. 11 (December 1975): 1149.

26. Stenback, "Depression and Suicidal Behavior", 645.

27. Marv Miller, *Suicide After Sixty: The Final Alternative* (New York: Springer Publishing Co., 1979), 23, 24.

28. Sheldon Zimberg, "Diagnosis and Treatment of the Elderly Alcoholic," *Alcoholism: Clinical and Experimental Research* 2, no. 1 (January 1978): 27.

29. Marc A. Shuckit, "A Clinical Review of Alcohol, Alcoholism, and the Elderly Patient," *Journal of Clinical Psychiatry* 43, no. 10 (October 1982): 397.

30. Ibid., 396.

31. Ibid.

32. Robert N. Butler and Myrna I. Lewis, *Aging and Mental Health*, 2nd. ed. (Saint Louis: C.V. Mosby Co., 1982), 134.

33. Lawrence Blum and Fred Rosner, "Alcoholism in the Elderly: An Analysis of Fifty Patients," *Journal of the National Medical Association* 75, no. 5 (May 1983): 489.

34. Sheldon Zimberg, "Alcoholism in the Elderly," *Postgraduate Medicine* 74, no. 1 (July 1983): 172.

35. Richard W. Hubbard, John F. Santos, and Mary Alice Santos, "Alcohol and Older Adults: Overt and Covert Influences," *Social Casework* 60, no. 3 (March 1979): 167.

36. Zimberg, "The Elderly Alcoholic," 29.

37. Pitt, *Psychogeriatrics*, 101.

38. Ibid., 102.

39. A.T. Welford, "Sensory, Perceptual, and Motor Processes in Older Adults," in *Handbook of Mental Health and Aging*, 200.

40. Felix Post, "Paranoid, Schizophrenia-like, and Schizophrenic States in the Aged," in *Handbook of Mental Health*, 596.

41. Pitt, *Psychogeriatrics*, 108.

42. Lenore A. Kola, Jordan I. Kosberg, and Karen Wegner-Burch, "Perceptions of the Treatment Responsibilities for the Alcoholic Elderly Client," in *Social Work in Health Care* 6, no. 2 (Winter 1980): 71.

43. Monika White, "Case Management: What Is It?" *Discharge Planning Update*, 8, no. 1 (January–February, 1988): 6.

44. Rosalie A. Kane, "Case Management in Long Term Care: Background Analysis for Hospital Social Work," American Hospital Association, 6, (1984).

45. Ibid., 3, 4.

7

SOCIAL WORK
WITH HOSPITALIZED
OLDER ADULTS

Chapters 7 and 8 continue the discussion of illness and debilitating conditions, placing the focus on older adults in hospitals and nursing homes. The effects on the individual of living in an institution, whether it is a temporary stay or long-term, are explored and the functions of social workers in these health-care settings are described. This chapter presents some of the problem situations in hospitals that confront social workers and the ways they go about dealing with them.

Social workers and other professionals from the many disciplines employed in health-care settings are frequently involved with the most disabled of the older population. It is sometimes difficult for them to remember that the majority of older people are not helpless and ill but able to maintain themselves in their communities.

The statistics in relation to illnesses and hospitalization of older people add to this problem, as they are often misleading. In studies of the elderly, the emphasis has usually been placed on measuring the degree of disability in relation to performance of personal care and home management activities. These two categories include bathing, dressing, eating, moving about indoors and outside, managing money, using the telephone, and doing housework. Since experiencing some difficulty in performing these tasks may not indicate that the person requires health services or social services, it has been suggested that the focus should be on whether the degree of disability is great enough for the individual to require assistance to be able to carry out the activity. For example, in a study carried out in 1984, about 23 percent of people 65 and older reported difficulty in performing personal care activities but only 10 percent of them reported receiving help.[1]

It may also be helpful to remember that chronic conditions, such as heart disease and circulatory problems, diseases of the digestive and respiratory systems, and tumors, account for most of the hospital admissions of older men and women.[2] In addition, the debilitating effects of chronic illness vary from one individual to another.

The vast majority of individuals with the diagnosis of arthritis experience few limitations, but a small minority are severely incapacitated by this chronic condition.

Before discussing the process of patient referral and ways in which discharge plans are made, it may be helpful to explore the stressful aspects of hospitalization that may be experienced.

EFFECTS OF HOSPITALIZATION ON OLDER ADULTS

Members of professional staffs in hospitals sometimes place a low priority on providing medical care to the aged. The apparent reasoning is that the older person is no longer productive and, consequently, no longer important. Illness and debilitation may be perceived as inevitable parts of the aging process. In addition, chronic diseases are sometimes judged less "interesting" than other conditions. Most older patients are probably aware when indifference prevails or antagonistic responses occur due to their presence in the hospital. This affects the patient's self-esteem and possibly his or her recuperative powers.

There are other results of hospitalization that may be even more damaging to the older patient who is ill, weak, and in pain: fear of death, disability, or loss of control over events; disorientation because of medication, change of environment, or other causes; and anxiety as a result of pressures exerted on the patient to make critical decisions concerning the patient's life in a relatively short period of time.

Fears of Death, Disability, and Loss of Control over Events

Virtually every person experiences fear to some extent with the realization that hospitalization is necessary. Some may have been hospitalized many times before, but there are many older adults, even in their eighties or nineties, who have never been in the hospital as a patient. Today's older generation grew up in a far different medical world than that of today. When they were children, in the last part of the nineteenth century or the early part of this century, most ill people were cared for at home. If they were fortunate, there was a physician in the area, a family doctor who made home visits. As the house call was made on horseback or in a horse and buggy, since automobiles were not yet common, the family doctor was likely to spend several hours with the patient. Even after automobiles became common, physicians continued to make house calls. This practice continued in rural areas and even in larger towns and cities until World War II. Probably most of today's 70-year-old women and older gave birth to their children in their own homes. Only people who had no relatives to provide care for them, or those who were desperately ill, went to hospitals.

Some older men and women may still associate hospitals with death or abandonment. If they have been denying apprehension, fear, anxiety, and other such feelings, the pressures of hospitalization may release these feelings. In addition to these fears, there may be concern about the spouse of 30, 40, or 50 years or others dependent for support of some kind.

Fear of disability may be even stronger than fear of death. To be disabled and old may mean the loss of independent living to some degree or even complete dependency on others. The specter of life in a nursing home haunts many older individuals.

The feeling of having no control over what is happening is also a frightening and anxiety-provoking experience. Certain procedures are carried out with all patients which are routine to staff but totally new to many of the patients. Older patients, particularly if this is their first hospitalization, are probably more sensitive to many of the dehumanizing processes of hospitalization. However, if they assert themselves, their behavior may be misunderstood. Germain observes that patients who want answers to their questions and insist on their dignity as total human beings are often perceived as problem patients.[3]

Disorientation Because of Environmental Change, Medication, or Other Reversible Causes

Every older patient probably experiences disorientation at some time during hospitalization. Some may experience only a little disorientation, usually on awakening, whereas other patients may respond to hospitalization by becoming extremely disoriented, as in the case example presented in Chapter 4. Explanations must often be given repeatedly in an attempt to orient the patient.

Disorientation is easier to understand when you consider the drastic changes in living arrangements that usually occur very quickly. In many cases the older patient has been living in the same household and community with the same companions and neighbors for many years. Many of the very old are so isolated from the rest of society, by lack of transportation and other reasons discussed in earlier chapters, that they have had little contact with large numbers of people for perhaps years. Those in their eighties and nineties are likely to have established a leisurely routine to which they are well-adjusted. As eyesight and hearing losses have probably been experienced, familiarity with surroundings is of the utmost importance. Furniture is not moved about, and frequently used items are kept in exactly the same places.

Then, as a result of illness, these individuals are suddenly removed from stable, familiar surroundings and thrust into the unfamiliar, fear-provoking hospital. It would be difficult for them to adjust to the new environment if they were healthy and feeling well. Illness, weakness, and pain are added components, as well as medication, that often contribute to a confused mental state.

Physicians and nurses—and social workers—who are not experienced in attending older patients sometimes mistakenly label the older patient's disorientation as either "psychotic" or "senile" behavior and respond accordingly. Even some of the professionals who well understand the nature of the temporary disorientation may have little patience with intractable patients, regardless of reasons for their behavior. They may simply demand compliance of the older disoriented patient.

The majority of older patients gradually become oriented to their surroundings, although many of them, upon first awakening in the morning, or after naps, may continue to be temporarily confused and disoriented. Explanations as to where they are and why they are there may be needed repeatedly throughout the hospitalization.

Anxiety as a Result of Hospital Pressures

Admission to a hospital is traumatic to anyone of any age. During the acute phase of the hospitalization, the patient may be subject to a constant flow of technicians taking blood and urine samples or attaching monitoring equipment to the patients; nurses checking vital signs or giving medication; physicians who are total strangers thumping, feeling, asking questions. There is a never-ceasing bustle of activity taking place, if not in the patient's room, in the corridors and outside, for ambulance sirens blast forth constantly. Older patients become anxious about what is happening. As their responses are slower, the rapid, varied input from the environment may become overwhelming.

Simply adjusting to these activities is enough challenge to the older patient's coping abilities, but illness often signals a long-term change that places even more demands on older patients. Decisions must be made that determine not only where they will live and with whom they will live, but the very kind and quality of life they will lead. These decisions do not wait for convalescence to occur, but often are presented as soon as the patient begins recovery from surgery or illness. Older patients may be able to respond as well, or better, in terms of planning, as someone 50 years younger, but they usually need more time to think, to sort things out, and to evaluate the results of their decisions. The emphasis on haste in making discharges is largely the result of hospital policies related to government health insurance.

Practice Applications

Social workers help their patients deal with the fears that are provoked by hospitalization in a variety of ways. Patients who are experiencing strong fears of death may receive counseling. Pastoral counseling is also provided in institutions and is sometimes the choice of patients who do not accept the social worker's offers of help. Due to the great interest and increased literature on death counseling in the past decade, some hospitals have one or more social workers whose major interest and special skills are in dealing with the terminal patient and family or with other patients needing such help.

Fears of disability are diminished by counseling, which often focuses on the identification and use of the patient's strengths. There is also major emphasis on locating community resources to help the patient meet whatever changes occur. Being supportive and helping the patient to regain as much independent functioning as possible is the major goal.

The fears that most patients experience are intensified by insufficient information or misunderstanding of information. In some settings, members of the health-care staff take the time to explain procedures to patients and describe the after-effects of tests, surgery, and so on. However, this is not always the case. It is not unusual to find older patients who are bewildered and distressed due to their lack of knowledge or misinterpretation of what is happening to them.

In these instances, the social worker locates the appropriate health-care member and shares the concerns of the patient with the physician, nurse, therapist, technologist, or other staff member who is involved. Gaining an understanding of the purpose of the various kinds of tests or treatment helps patients to feel that everything is not out of control and beyond their means of influence. At the very least, they realize that they can refuse tests or request that tests be made when a relative can be in the room on their return.

The anxieties related to haste and the pressure for immediate, life-changing decisions can be alleviated by slowing down the discharge process and allowing the patient to regain the strength needed to deal with these urgent problems. Since there seems to be little hope at the present time for immediate changes in Medicare in relation to making greater time allowances, there seems to be more effort in most hospitals to identify potential discharge problems and make referrals to social services as early as possible. Social workers do the best they can within the limitations of time and do not lose sight of the need for whatever time is feasible to ensure appropriate discharge planning.

These effects of hospitalization—fear of death, disability, and loss of control over events; disorientation resulting from unfamiliar surroundings; and anxiety arising from the pressure to make quick decisions—are easily perceived by social workers and by some, but not all, professional and paraprofessional staff. This lack of knowledge and understanding of older patient's reactions, where it exists, may be mitigated by in-service training or workshops which the social worker may lead. There are also many informal opportunities for social workers to interpret the sometimes bizarre behavior of older patients, which may be incorrectly labeled as "senile," "contrary," or "mean" to physicians, nurses, dieticians, technicians, aides, and others.

REFERRAL OF OLDER PATIENTS TO SOCIAL SERVICES

Although discharge planning is probably the major reason for referral for older adults who can no longer look after themselves without assistance of some kind, patients are referred to the social worker for any one or more of a wide variety of services that are provided to patients of any age. Older adults may require counseling in regard to change of role, rehabilitation, marital problems arising from prolonged hospitalization, and so on. There may be sexual dysfunction due to surgery or illness, which is discussed in Chapter 8. The same areas of dysfunction to which social workers respond by providing counseling or by referral to other agencies applies to the older population as well as the younger.

The referral is usually made as soon as the physician realizes there will be loss of function which may interfere with discharge. The haste to make the referral and proceed at once arises, as stated earlier, from policies related to payment for the hospitalization of older individuals by government insurance programs, Medicare and Medicaid, and recent legislation, the Omnibus Reconciliation Act of 1987 (OBRA 87), which affects discharge planning of mentally ill or mentally retarded patients to nursing homes.

MEDICARE AND MEDICAID

It is beyond the scope of this book to deal with the provisions of these two programs in detail, as they are very complex and are constantly changing. However, it may be helpful to present some information on both programs, as the provision of social work and supportive services are greatly affected by the regulations of these health-care insurance programs.

Medicare is a federal program with provisions applying throughout the United States to people 65 and over and to some disabled people under 65. Medicare consists of two programs: Part A and Part B. Part A helps in paying for medically necessary care in a Medicare approved hospital, skilled nursing facility, or hospice. Part B helps in paying for medically necessary physician's services, outpatient hospital services, home health care, and various medical services and supplies not covered by the hospital insurance part of Medicare. The patient must pay deductibles, as well as pay a monthly premium for Part B of Medicare.

The Medicare Catastrophic Coverage Act, which is to be phased in by 1993, is the most significant expansion of Medicare benefits since its enactment in 1965. The poor elderly are among those who will be helped most, for Medicaid is required to pay their Medicare premiums, deductibles, and coinsurance.

Although service coverage under home health titles of Medicare includes the provision of nursing care, home health aides, social work services, and occupational therapy, eligibility is based on whether the patient is homebound and also needs physical therapy, speech therapy, or skilled nursing care as certified by a physician. Many people who need personal care services do not meet this eligibility standard. An example of this situation is that of the patient with congestive heart failure who receives home health and other services immediately after hospital discharge but becomes ineligible for home health services when skilled nursing care is no longer required, even though other home health services are needed. Another problem in relation to the provision of home health services is the unavailability of these services in some rural areas.

Older men and women are allowed to stay in the hospital under Medicare only when the patient requires an acute level of medical care as defined by Medicare standards. In a move to cut costs of the Medicare program, drastic reforms were made in late 1983 with the creation of a new prospective payment system (PPS). As a result of the PPS, when Medicare patients are admitted to the hospital, they are assigned to one of the diagnostic related groups (DRG's) based on criteria including the patient's diagnosis, age, treatment procedures, sex, and discharge status. Variables that are not taken into consideration at this time, include the stage of the patient's illness, financial resources, and family and community support systems. In addition, the classification system many times is insensitive to cases involving acute care when complications may arise. Each illness, or DRG, has a specific amount of reimbursement which creates a ceiling on the amount that the hospital can receive for each patient's treatment. If the patient is treated for less than the DRG amount, the hospital keeps the profit. If the treatment costs more, the hospital must absorb the loss. As the patient is categorized into a single DRG, this may present problems when an elderly patient has a number of chronic illnesses.

The institution of the PPS and DRG's has had a great impact on hospital administrators, physicians, and social workers. Under this system, there is an economic incentive to shorten hospital stays. Criteria for hospital admission is more strict. The status of discharge planning has been elevated, as meeting the new regulations under Medicare present many more problems in appropriate discharge planning than earlier regulations.

Social workers in hospitals have expanded their roles, becoming involved with preadmission and admission screening. In addition, there are more referrals to social work of discharged patients whose discharge plans have broken down or whose needs for care have changed. Hospital social workers are involved in out-patient and community programs, such as home care, extended care, and patient education. Department hours have been expanded so that many are working evenings and weekends. Social workers are also active in organizing committees in some hospitals and have access to a number of committees that were previously inaccessible.[4]

Medicaid provides medical care for the poor. Medicaid is funded by both the federal government and the state and is available to people of all ages who meet the criteria. Medicaid is administered by the states and eligibility varies to some degree from state to state. States are required to provide Medicaid benefits to all of the individuals who receive federally funded financial assistance, such as Supplementary Security Income (SSI). The states may also provide benefits for other groups of medically needy individuals. However, as it is a program for the *medically needy*, older people who have retirement income in addition to Social Security or possess other financial resources are unlikely to be eligible for Medicaid.

Before the passage of the Medicare Catastrophic Act, older couples were forced to deplete their financial resources before being eligible for nursing home care under Medicaid. The non-institutionalized spouse will now be able to keep more money and a part of the couple's assets, up to a maximum of a designated amount which is presently set at $60,000.

Medicaid does not base eligibility for home health services and other nonmedical services on the need for "skilled nursing care." However, such services are limited by the willingness of the states, as well as their ability, to reimburse for those kinds of services. The states vary in relation to eligibility requirements for home health-care services and the number and kind of services provided, with some states having no home health programs at all.

It is absolutely necessary for social workers who have older clients to have some basic knowledge about Medicare and the Medicaid program of the state in which they are employed and to know whom to call for information. Both are complex programs that pose many difficulties in comprehension. Medicare beneficiaries are often overwhelmed by trying to cope with the procedures required by Medicare. Older people need to be informed about the way Medicare works and about other government resources, as well as the options for private insurance. Education may be provided by social workers themselves and by training volunteers who conduct workshops under their supervision. Speakers may also be obtained from legal services, Social Security offices, state insurance departments, and volunteer groups.[5]

THE OMNIBUS BUDGET RECONCILIATION ACT OF 1987 (OBRA 87)

Sections of OBRA 87 which became effective January 1989 require the State to have a preadmission screening and annual resident review program for individuals with mental illness and mental retardation, using criteria established for this purpose. Medicare and Medicaid-certified nursing facilities must prohibit the admission of any new resident who has mental illness or mental retardation (or a related condition) unless it has been determined by the State Mental Health or State Mental Retardation Authority, that the individual, because of his or her physical or mental condition, needs the level of services provided by a nursing home or another type of facility. If it is determined that nursing home admission is appropriate, a decision must be made as to whether active treatment is required.

OBRA 87 outlines criteria, but not process. There is great concern as to how well the process will be implemented and the quality of care the mentally ill and mentally retarded patients will receive. Major questions that have been raised include how nursing homes must respond to the mental health needs of its residents, who will pay for the care, and what this care should include.

At this time, the regulations of OBRA 87 which affect nursing home admission of mentally ill and mentally retarded patients have been in effect only a few months. Changes in present regulations are likely to occur and new regulations implemented. Social workers in health care need to keep abreast of the regulatory guidelines of this legislation and provide input and support for regulations responding appropriately to patient needs.

DISCHARGE PLANNING PROCESS

Adequate time is needed by the patient and social worker for the assessment and evaluation of the needs of the client, the location of resources, and the involvement of relatives significant to the patient in making plans. There is sometimes a need for delaying discharge in order to obtain a bed in a nursing facility that is most appropriate for the patient, instead of accepting an available bed in a facility that may be far from the patient's friends and family.

Social workers must exercise their judgment in making decisions as to when to demand a postponement of a discharge in instances that involve a loss of revenue by the hospital, in order to have more time to plan or to carry out an appropriate discharge plan; or to yield to pressure and make the best possible plan under the circumstances. Social workers sometimes take a stand alone against a discharge and the postponement is denied. In these instances the social worker may write a note in the chart, if possible alongside the physician's discharge summary, and give the objection to the discharge, stating the reason for the objection. This may result in more care being taken in future discharges. At the very least, the other professional staff members are made aware of the unmet needs of the patient.

In some hospitals discharge teams are designated for each ward or floor and may consist of social worker; physician; nursing supervisor; and possibly physical, occupational, speech therapists, and dietitians. Each team usually meets at a specific time, discusses cases, and plans discharges.

The social worker, or possibly the charge nurse or nurse clinician, is responsible for carrying out the details of the discharge plan and collaborates with the physicians, nurses, dietitians, and others who have knowledge of the patient. Even when there are teams, the nature of a hospital prohibits following an exact routine, as patients' conditions change and staff members must respond to emergencies. Getting all members of the team together for planning becomes impossible at these times.

The social worker considers the totality of needs that the patient has and is usually the most able to perceive the patient as an entity. The social worker coordinates information from each specialized area along with social information in regard to the patient's total environment. This concept of wholeness enables social workers in health-care settings to be keenly aware of the dehumanizing aspects of hospitalization. Consequently, they keep reminding other staff members, often in subtle ways, that the patient is a person, a human being with human needs. Staff members are made conscious of the fact that the social worker is the advocate of the patient.

Mode of Referral

Although the mode of referring patients for social services varies from one hospital to another, there is a growing trend of "open referral" for social work services. In the past social workers usually could work with "charity" patients without a referral, but a referral by the attending physician was required before interviewing private, paying patients. Most hospitals now have policies allowing social work discharge planners to see patients for an initial assessment without a physician's request. They must then consult with the physician about developing and carrying out the discharge plan.

Keeping the attending physician informed of social work action seems a part of ethical practice, as well as being essential in order to maintain an effective working relationship with the medical staff.

In every hospital there are many different individuals who may first perceive a need for social work services, ranging from self-referral to referral by nurses, medical technologists, volunteer workers, ward secretaries, family members, debtors, employers, neighbors of the patient, and ministers, as well as the attending, consulting, or admitting physician.

When the referral is received, the social worker may read selectively in the medical record, check the past social history notes, and have consultations with medical staff before interviewing the patient and family.

Use of the Medical Record

The medical record contains a face sheet that gives vital data about the patient such as name, age, telephone number of nearest relative, employment, and the like.

The admitting physician's notes give the reason for admittance and a medical history which may give social data. Progress notes are written by the physician during the patient's hospitalization. Requests for consultations are noted. Consulting physicians write in their opinions, diagnoses, suggested treatment, and so on. If psychiatric consultation is requested, the psychiatrist may write a brief note in regard to seeing the patient, but a complete psychiatric evaluation will probably be elsewhere. If the patient requires surgery during hospitalization, the details of the operation are transcribed and included in the record. All tests and test results are recorded.

When the social worker examines the chart for medical information, the reason for hospitalization and social information are not the only parts of the record that are carefully read. The patient may have been admitted for minor surgery, but other important aspects of health are noted. This is particularly helpful in the record of the older patient. Is the patient disabled with arthritis? Are there chronic conditions, such as diabetes, that may need to be considered in discharge planning? Is the patient's sight adequate for reading directions? If the patient sees well enough with glasses, does he or she hear well enough to understand the physician's directions or to communicate on the telephone?

Does the patient need or wear dentures? If dentures are needed but not worn, will this interfere with following a prescribed diet?

It is surprising how many times accompanying disabilities are overlooked in discharge planning. Patients may say that they are almost blind without glasses, but not volunteer the information that the glasses are broken. Dentures, glasses, and hearing aids are often lost or misplaced during the flurry of admission or during hospitalization, yet without these basic aids, some patients may be rendered almost helpless when they return home.

Nursing notes are in a separate section in the chart, and these notes are also an important source of information. The patient's nursing needs are recorded in detail; for example, the number of times a patient is incontinent or has uncontrolled bowel movements, refuses to take medication, or requests a sleeping pill. The mental status of the patient is also recorded; this, too, is very helpful. The older patient may be disoriented when the social worker visits, but the nursing notes may identify disorientation "only on waking." When the social worker reflects on the time of the visit, the recollection may be that the patient was awakened from a nap.

Social work notes and summaries are required to be kept in the medical folder. They may be kept on a colored sheet for easy identification and placed at the back of the record. Separate copies may also be kept in the social services office, on file cards in the office, or in the social worker's personal files. In some medical settings, social workers are permitted to write notes in the physician's section. These notes are kept very brief and to the point.

Consultation

If there is a case manager employed by the hospital, the social worker and the case manager may work jointly on discharge planning. If there is no case manager in the hospital and the patient's needs beyond the planned transition are cause for concern, then a referral may be made to a community case manager, if available, for post-hospital planning. However, the patient may have to pay for this service unless he or she has insurance that will cover case management services. The community case manager would be responsible for seeing that the patient's community care is appropriately authorized and in place at time of discharge.

If there is no case manager in the hospital or the community, the social worker usually consults and collaborates primarily with the attending physician and with members of the nursing staff. The physician is relied upon to give medical data about the patient and, more important, to interpret medical data in terms of the amount of disability sustained after discharge. The physician estimates the amount of care that will be needed upon discharge from the hospital and recommends the kind of placement, if the patient is unable to return home. The social worker is responsible for providing information as to available community resources, which also aids the physician in making appropriate recommendations. Social workers are sometimes frustrated by a lack of specificity as to prognosis on the part of the physician, but in some cases specific predictions as to the patient's future capabilities are impossible to make. The amount of recovery from stroke, for example, is difficult to preduct. Even though brain damage from a stroke may appear minimal, the patient may not adapt to the loss. There may be insufficient emotional support and inadequate resources for the patient to become rehabilitated, or the patient may be poorly motivated and may make few gains.

There is sometimes a problem in regard to the physician's interpretation of the patient's family life. All too often, family members will assure the physician that they "have everything worked out," but no concrete plans have been made. They agree to take care of the ailing relative without realizing just what the care entails. Family members may be intimidated by the physician, or they may be eager to have the patient discharged from the hospital for financial or other reasons. Social workers carefully check family information given by the physician or by other medical attendants rather than attempting to make a discharge plan based on secondhand information.

Nurses supply valuable information as to how independently the patient is managing in the hospital. Questions that may be asked by the social worker revolve around what may be expected of the patient after discharge. Can the patient attend without assistance to daily living requirements: eating, walking to and from the bathroom, using the bathroom, dressing and undressing, getting in and out of bed? Does the patient have and wear eyeglasses or dentures? Own and use a hearing aid? Are there other prosthetic devices, such as an artificial limb? If the patient is unable to manage any part of the usual daily activities, do the nurses expect the patient to regain function? The social worker may find a variation of opinion among nursing staff and medical staff about the patient's function in the hospital and expectations of the patient's return of function. When this occurs, the professionals with conflicting views are brought together by the social worker to come to an agreement so appropriate plans may be made.

Consultation with the dietitian is often necessary in planning discharges for older patients, as many of them do not follow the dietary instructions given to them. There are many reasons for their failure to comply. The patient may not understand the details of a prescribed diet but not admit it. The reasons for dietary restrictions may not be clearly understood; consequently, the patient has little incentive to follow the diet. Older adults relying solely on Social Security benefits have so little money that certain diets may be unaffordable without additional financial assistance. They may be reluctant to apply for food stamps or to admit their lack of funds. The failure to stay on a prescribed diet is sometimes due to ill-fitting dentures that prevent the patient from eating anything except soft foods.

If someone other than the patient prepares the patient's food, it is helpful to have that person talk with the dietitian. This does not always necessitate a visit, but may often be handled on the telephone.

The social worker makes use of psychosocial information to ensure that the patient understands and can follow the prescribed diet, as shown in the following brief example:

CASE EXAMPLE: FAILURE TO COMPLY

John Deir is a 68-year-old veteran who has late-onset diabetes which the physician believes can be controlled by diet. The dietitian has spent a great deal of time explaining the diet to Mr. Deir and has given him a number of pamphlets with underscored phrases and notes in the margin to clarify the information. Mr. Deir has assured the dietitian that he fully understands the diet, but the dietitian has some doubts about it and mentions her doubt to the social worker.

Mr. Deir is known to the social worker from previous admissions. He is pleasant, agreeable, and overwhelmingly grateful for the slightest action taken on his behalf. The social worker checks the brief social history which was written at the time of Mr. Deir's first admission and finds that the patient grew up in Appalachia. He had "a little schooling." The social worker wonders whether Mr. Deir can read the pamphlet or the marginal notes given by the dietitian, but would like to avoid confronting him with questions regarding literacy. He asks Mr. Deir about his present living arrangements and learns that the patient lives in a trailer behind his daughter's home. He suggests that Mr. Deir ask his daughter, as she will be the one who prepares his main meal, to come in and talk with the dietitian.

Mr. Deir responds enthusiastically to the suggestion. The social worker suspects there is an element of relief in his response. He later learns from the daughter that Mr. Deir is illiterate and so sensitive about it that she doubts he would have even shown her the pamphlets on his own. Without his daughter's assistance with the pamphlets, Mr. Deir would have experienced great difficulty in remembering and following his diet.

Social workers may collaborate with physical, occupational, and speech therapists when making discharge plans for disabled patients, if these specialists have been involved with the patient's care. Their observations as to the patient's attitude toward therapy and the amount of motivation may be very helpful in detecting emotional difficulties the patient may be having.

Some physical therapists specialize in providing care for older individuals disabled by strokes, arthritis, or loss of limbs. They prescribe exercises to help patients return as much as possible to their previous level of function.

Occupational therapists assist patients in carrying out daily living activities in spite of handicaps. They help arthritic and other patients to obtain the most function possible within their limitations. Occupational therapists are often very creative in making devices that will enable individuals to feed themselves, prepare meals, and so on. They are also effective in helping blind persons function in spite of their handicap.

Speech therapists work extensively with brain-damaged patients who are trying to learn again to communicate. They train families and friends so that they may continue to help the patient after discharge.

Each of these therapists makes valuable contributions to discharge planning when information is needed as a guide to future functions of the patient. Social workers find they have a much better understanding of the patient's limitations if they visit the patient, even briefly, in physical, occupational, or speech therapy.

The therapists in these specialties are also usually aware of resources in their fields—for example, places in the community where the older person can carry out exercises, such as walking. They may be knowledgeable about community resources for aids not covered by insurance.

Possibly one of the greatest difficulties experienced by all those involved in hospital discharge planning is that of determining whether there are sufficient supports in the home and/or community so that the patient will be able to function safely. The social worker is usually the team member who is expected not only to know the resources but to be able to evaluate the quality of the resources in relation to whether the patient's needs will be sufficiently met. This is a matter of judgment, as the social worker cannot be absolutely certain. One way to lessen anxiety about discharges is to involve all of the appropriate health-care providers during the planning and decision making so that there is a clear understanding of the patient's needs and capabilities.

Discharge Planning with the Patient

The social worker may interview the patient before or after consultation with other professionals. The interview is held as privately as possible, although hospitals do not espouse privacy. Many social worker-patient interviews are conducted with several interruptions. In wards, curtains may be drawn around the bed to create some feeling of privacy.

Patients express many fears. Even though they may be eager to return home, they may also be fearful of leaving the hospital. In the hospital there are nurses within easy reach and regular visits by their own physician, as well as by other physicians. Many convalescing patients feel very secure in the hospital and are uneasy about returning home. They may not put their fears into words. The social worker may recognize the fear when responding to the emotions and feelings behind the words. These patients need assurance that they are well enough to leave the hospital and that this is the first step to recovery.

The social worker may be unable to plan the discharge with the patient if the patient is too ill to participate. In those cases, planning is conducted with a relative. However, even then the social worker does not omit the patient. Patients who are going to be discharged into a nursing home are told as far ahead as is feasible so they will not be taken by surprise by an abrupt transfer to another facility.

Pressure on the worker to hasten discharge, and the often-sudden availability of a bed at nursing homes, combine to make discharge planning at times a whirlwind effort that is more involved with paperwork than with human feelings.

On those occasions that the patient is able to plan, his or her choice of discharge alternatives is sought. The patients who have been admitted to the hospital from their own homes usually want to return to their homes, regardless of post-hospital needs. The patient's home may be inadequate, poorly heated, or isolated, and meals may consist of cold food and snacks, but it is familiar and known and therefore better than any unknown.

There are alternatives to home discharge in some communities that older patients might prefer, if they were familiar with them. Some older individuals do familiarize themselves with the various kinds of long-term-care facilities in their communities that offer a protected environment, before the need for them arises. It is more likely that most patients are not aware of all choices in their communities. The social worker may arrange with the hospital for the patient to visit a facility that may meet the patient's needs. If this is impossible, a resident or staff member of the facility may be able to come and talk with the patient. Brochures and pamphlets may be shown to the patient.

If there is a possibility for a discharge to the patient's home, the social worker seeks information about the physical environment. Questions such as the following may be asked: Does the patient live alone? Are there steps inside the house? Outside the house? If the patient is now confined to a wheelchair, are the doorways wide enough to accommodate a wheelchair? Are there ramps to provide entry into the house? The social worker asks questions to determine the demands that will be made on the patient. Does the patient own or drive an automobile? Will the patient have to prepare meals and clean house? In rural areas, the patient may be asked about the availability of indoor toilets and running water.

The social worker asks about significant people who may provide emotional support, as well as assist the patient in practical ways upon the return home. How close is the nearest relative, friendly neighbor, or good friend? Is this individual at home during the day and evening? Can the client be checked upon from time to time? Does the older person belong to a church, or a civic, fraternal, or social organization that may provide recreation, transportation, or financial help, if needed? Family relationships are explored. There is usually at least one family member identified by the patient as being willing to assume responsibility.

Occasionally the patient will say there is nobody—no relative, or friend—that would help. Most social workers agree that continuing to press for a suggestion, tactfully and gently, will eventually result in being given the name of a friend or relative.

Older adults who are hospitalized for the first time are often extremely disappointed to learn that Medicare insurance will not cover all hospital costs fully. The patient is sometimes overwhelmed by the realization that there are gaps in both Medicare and Medicaid coverage. Depression and anxiety may occur over financial problems, adding to the other problems they are experiencing.

Discharge Planning with Family Members

Social workers are accustomed to hearing medical staff complain that families do not take care of their aging parents as they should. These complaints are especially vocal when nursing home beds are full and discharges slow. These complaints are not based on fact. Most older people live close to a family member and rely on relatives for help. A nationwide survey of a population of people aged 65 or older revealed that four out of five in the survey had one or more surviving children and that three quarters of this group had one child living in the same household or within a half hour's travel time. In addition, three-quarters of the group had seen at least one child in the previous week.[6]

Most families try to avoid institutionalizing their parents and assume a great many responsibilities for their care. According to data from the Health Care Financing Administration's 1982 Long Time Care Survey of disabled elderly living in the community, relatives accounted for 84 percent of all caregivers for males and provided 89 percent of the required care. Relatives represented 79 percent of caregivers for older disabled women and provided 79 percent of care.[7]

The concern felt by families for their parents or other older members is evidenced in these studies. However, interviews with family members in regard to discharge planning can be very difficult. Many emotions may be present that influence decision making. Guilt feelings are probably the most prevalent. Family members may blame themselves for the parent or close relative's illness or feel guilt about events that occurred long before the relative became ill. They may feel inordinately responsible for assuming care. Consequently, patients needing around-the-clock care are sometimes discharged into an insistent son or daughter's home and are cared for at the expense of the caregiver's physical and emotional health.

Another emotion that can make discharge planning difficult is that of anger. Families sometimes align themselves into two camps: one side desiring discharge into a nursing home or other facility and the other opting for home care. There may be a dispute over which relative will provide care. Too often, the sons in the family are willing to pay for services but are unwilling to provide any services themselves, leaving this to the women in the family. Old feelings of sibling rivalry erupt as one child accuses another of being unfeeling or unsympathetic, selfish, or noncaring. Hostility may become open, and wounding statements made that add to difficulties in planning appropriately for the patient.

Overprotection by family members is another factor that often comes into play. The health-care discharge team may believe the patient should be returned home, provided there are some supports arranged for the patient. The family may disagree. One or more relatives may think the home cannot be made sufficiently safe. There is a tendency to imagine dangers that are unlikely to happen and to exaggerate the older relative's inability to meet difficulties that may arise. A frequently mentioned fear is fear of fire from leaving cigarettes or pipes on furniture or as a result of leaving a pan on the stove. With some patients these may be realistic fears, but with others such incidences are no more likely to occur than with a younger individual. Some of the commonsense safety steps that may be taken include the following: making certain the telephone is conveniently located for the patient's use, which may require a longer cord or a new extension; removing the knobs from the stove so the stove cannot be lit unless there is a responsible adult in the home; removing car keys; placing in a locked box or removing from the home medication, matches, and poisonous substances such as cleaning materials and alcohol. Many precautions related to falling were given in Chapter 3.

Physicians sometimes give a prognosis for the aged patient in terms of days or a few weeks. Family members who are unable to assume long-term care for the patient will strain their resources to provide care on a short-term basis and then find that the patient who was to die in six weeks is still alive six months later. The caregiver may by then be in a state of ill health, or the family may have become completely disorganized. Such diagnoses happen frequently enough to suggest that social workers warn family members about the possibility of the prognosis being inaccurate. Families unable to provide care beyond a few days or a few weeks need to plan for this eventuality.

Families may view the patient as being more ill and disabled than is the case. When they visit, they see the patient dressed in a hospital gown, usually lying in bed. Nurses may be assisting the patient with eating, dressing, bathing, and in other ways. Feelings of anxiety may be further aroused by the appearance of fragility that often accompanies illness. This may be the first time that the middle-aged child has allowed himself/herself to face the fact of the parent's aging and eventual death.

The social worker deals with the emotions and fears of the family as they appear. It may be necessary to counsel certain family members, such as those who insist on assuming care at whatever cost to their own well-being. Reconciling angry family members may be required in order to conduct a planning session. The social worker continually reminds the family members that the patient is an *adult* whose wishes and desires cannot be ignored. It is rare, when considering long-term care, that the patient is too incapacitated to participate in the planning process. If the patient wants to return home, understands the risks that are involved, has been fully informed of viable alternatives, and is deemed well and capable enough by staff to attempt it, then the patient's decision must be treated as an adult decision.

The social worker helps the family to explore whatever resources they are able to provide and acquaints the family with community resources. Family members may be asked to be specific about tasks they can perform for the patient, or times they will be available for attending to banking, providing transportation to and from the clinic or physician's office, and so on. The social worker strives to help family members find this planning time rewarding in terms of enriching family relationships and providing unity by identifying family strengths and overcoming weaknesses.

DISCHARGE ALTERNATIVES

The usual procedure in hospitals is to discharge patients when they no longer need medical care by physicians. The older patient, depending on the physical condition and resources, may be discharged to return to the previous living arrangement, to live with relatives, to a boarding home or similar arrangement, to a nursing home, or to hospice care.

Discharge to Previous Living Arrangements

The first discharge possibility that may be considered is whether the patient can return to the previous living arrangement. If the admission to the hospital is due in part to unhealthful housing or a failure to use available community supports, then these conditions must be altered before the patient can return home. At times, only a simple step must be taken during the discharge planning to permit the patient to return home; for example, the discharge of a patient with a diagnosis of bronchial pneumonia who has been living in a poorly heated basement apartment. The social worker may contact the landlord and request an apartment for the client that is dry and appropriately heated, elsewhere in the building. The social worker may also warn the landlord to install better heating in the basement apartment or risk being reported to the city for violation of codes.

The problems that arise in regard to sending patients to their previous homes may revolve around meeting daily living needs. The older patient may be "functionally dependent," needing help in bathing, dressing, getting to and from the bathroom, and preparing meals on a temporary basis. Transportation to the physician's office or to a clinic for hospital care may be a problem.

Social workers assess the patient's needs and seek supportive help from friends, neighbors, volunteer groups, church groups, and any other community resources. As Chapter 12 describes supportive resources, such as home health-care and day-care services, that may be helpful to an older adult in order to maintain independent living in the community, they will not be reviewed here. Social workers in hospitals rarely have the time to provide case management services after discharge. They attempt to locate another professional person in the community to coordinate follow-up services so that any dysfunction in the support system will be quickly detected.

Discharge to a Relative's Home

The discharge plan that places the patient into a relative's home must receive careful consideration. Although abuse does not occur in the majority of families who provide care, the social worker is aware of the potential for abuse when an older person becomes dependent on family members for a great deal of care. The willingness on the part of the relatives and their husbands or wives to provide care of the patient, the health of the caregiver, the amount of disruption that may occur in the household, the sacrifices that may be made by the one who provides the care, and the financial cost that may be involved must be carefully assessed.

There must be adequate space for the addition of the relative and the financial means to provide adequate clothing and food. The caregiver must be fully informed as to the details of the care needed. Caregivers are often taught by members of the nursing staff to give injections, apply medication to wounds, apply dressings, and so on, prior to the patient's discharge.

One of the older person's daughters often assumes this care. She is usually middle-aged and may be a grandmother. She may be guilt-ridden because she feels some resentment but believes it is her duty to assume care. She may have a very satisfying, loving relationship with her father or mother and may wholeheartedly accept any sacrifices in order to provide care. In either case, marital relationships may become strained. In addition, her children may resent the intrusion of the grandparent for this may interfere with their relationship with their mother.

Adding another member to the household may also be an added financial burden. Some daughters retire from full- or part-time employment, or give up volunteer activities that have been a source of socializing and other satisfactions so that they may provide care for the aged parent.

The contrary is also true. The social worker is conscious of the temptation, in a household with very limited means, for a family member to offer care to the ill, older person in order to obtain the Social Security check. It is sometimes difficult to believe that a person may be added to the household to obtain a check for as little as $200 or $300. However, in some households there is no steadily employed worker, no reliable monthly income. Financial resources are so limited that the meager check appears inordinately desirable. The decision to take the older individual into the home is only in response to the added income and not out of concern for the aging relative. Society's devaluing of the older person reinforces this noncaring attitude.

Social workers carefully evaluate the relative's home in regard to income and to past treatment of the older person. Every effort is made to determine whether there will be a caring, warm acceptance of the older individual into the home.

Discharge to a Nursing Home

Some social workers may be concerned about discharging patients into nursing homes, fearing the patients will not receive adequate care. A great many stories are told to social workers by angry relatives about filthy rooms, patients lying for hours in urine and feces, poorly educated aides who humiliate patients, and so on. Unfortunately, there is ample documentation for such abuses which occur in some nursing homes. However, there are also nursing homes with qualified, caring staff members who work very hard to provide good care for the residents.

Concerned social workers feel more comfortable about nursing-home discharges by visiting nursing homes used by patients in their area and by noting the conditions of patients who are discharged to nursing homes and later readmitted to the hospital. In addition to the patient's actual physical condition in terms of illness, the general appearance of the patient, nourishment, condition of skin and hair, length of fingernails and toenails, and the patient's expressed opinion contribute to assessing the kind of medical and nursing care the patient has received and the way in which care was administered. The social worker may also request the opinion of the nursing staff and physicians in regard to their evaluation of care. Nursing homes from which patients are admitted to the hospital with decubiti, fecal impactions, and the like are suspect. Evaluation on readmission to the hospital is one way that nursing-home abuses, or home-care abuses, are identified and brought to the attention of the appropriate authorities. Abuse is discussed more fully in Chapter 11.

When planning discharge, most patients strongly resist consideration of nursing-home placement. The nursing home represents "the last move." Even though the patient may be very ill and may require a great deal of nursing care, there may be resistance. If the patient primarily needs custodial care and there is no relative able or willing to provide it, the patient may have deep feelings of bitterness, frustration, and anger. Allowing the patient to ventilate these feelings may enable him or her to move past these feelings and start to consider ways in which life in the nursing home may be made more palatable. The social worker in the hospital often alerts the social worker in the nursing home to ways of helping the patient adjust to new surroundings. If the nursing home allows the patient's own furniture and personal belongings to be used, arrangements are made to send those belongings so they will be there when the patient arrives.

Family members may also initially reject nursing home care, even for a seriously ill relative. There are usually guilty feelings, no matter how ill the parent may be. Some older patients considered for nursing-home placement are bedfast and lack bladder and bowel control. If the patient is not kept clean and dry and the body position changed every few hours, the skin may break down and decubitus ulcers appear. This may not seem to be a major problem until the health and physical condition of the "children" are taken into consideration. The 50-, 60-, or possibly even 70-plus "child" may earnestly wish to keep the patient at home but simply be physically unable to do the lifting and turning of the patient and the changing and laundering of linens necessary to prevent decubiti. It is sometimes very difficult for older, ill parents to accept the fact that the inability to lift and turn them is a valid reason for their children not caring for them at home, for they still perceive their children as being young or ageless.

Social workers are sometimes tempted to become judgmental about family members who appear able to care for their aging parent or other close relative but resolutely refuse to do so. Careful questioning may bring forth old resentments and anger toward the parent for happenings in the past. Some relatives openly express their hostility toward a parent whom they view as having been neglectful, abusive, noncaring, and unresponsive to their childhood needs. Others remain silent as to their reasons about refusing to assume a more active role in their aging relative's care. It is important to remember that the vast majority of "children" do want their parents to be comfortable and secure and that a great many undergo enormous personal and financial hardship to provide care for their aging parents.

When patients are discharged into nursing homes, family members are encouraged to visit them and to bring them home on weekends or holidays, if this is possible. This reduces feelings of abandonment, assuages family members' guilt feelings, and acts as a stimulant to nursing-home staff to provide good service. Social workers remind relatives that being alert to nursing-home conditions and making complaints or giving praise may have great effects on the quality of care provided.

Discharge to Other Living Arrangements in the Community

Social workers make use of all of the options available in a given community. These include congregate housing, resident hotels, boarding homes, and, for emergencies, missions that provide short-term housing. As these facilities are discussed in Chapter 12, they will not be reviewed here.

Discharge to Hospice Care

The time may come when hospice care is available in all parts of the country, and discharge to hospice care will be an option for every terminal patient. Although hospices are sometimes thought of as institutions occupying separate buildings, hospice is a *concept* of care rather than a place.

The concept of hospice care originated in Ireland in the nineteenth century and spread to England and other countries. The first modern hospice, St. Christopher's, was opened in a London suburb in 1967 and has most influenced Americans. There the patients find an informal, homelike setting. Staff members are unhurried and have time to engage in friendly conversation with the patients. A play school for young children of the staff is situated behind the main building in a garden area. Volunteers who first come in experience difficulty in determining which person is the physician, social worker, secretary, and so on. Even on the wards, it is sometimes hard to tell the well from the sick. Patients who can do so pursue their hobbies with family members, including children. The rooms are airy and cheerful and filled with lively activity which belies the fact that most of the patients are terminally ill.[8]

The concept of hospice care includes forms other than that of separate institutions. Some hospice programs are called "scattered bed" programs, as hospice patients are scattered throughout the hospital in various wards or departments, and a hospice team makes daily rounds to visit each patient. In other hospitals a wing or floor may be set aside for hospice care. Hospice home care is available in some areas. In this form of care, hospice home-care teams visit patients in their homes and provide support services through team members and volunteers. The team is often available on a 24-hour basis.

A basic tenet of the hospice concept is that all terminal patients who need this type of care be provided care whether they are able to pay for it or not. Medicare hospital insurance can help pay for hospice care if a doctor certifies that a patient is terminally ill and care is provided by a Medicare-certified hospice program. Hospice care is also being paid by some insurance companies. The funding of many hospice programs is aided by contributions.

In the United States in 1984 there were 935 operational hospices and 410 additional programs that intended to initiate services in the "near future." Information on these programs is provided in *The 1984 Guide to the Nation's Hospices.*[9] The hospice-care team is a multidisciplinary unit usually composed of physicians, nurses, social workers, physical therapists, dietitians, possibly speech and hearing therapists, and volunteers.

The purpose of hospice care is to alleviate pain and meet the psychological, spiritual, and social needs of the patient and family during the final stage of illness and to provide bereavement counseling after the person's death. Hospice care must be available on a 24-hour basis. As only terminal patients (3 to 6 months to live) are eligible, the emphasis is on care rather than cure, on symptom control instead of tumor control.

Palliative measures, reducing and alleviating pain, and making the patient physically comfortable are major goals. Freeing the patient from pain as much as possible permits the patient to enjoy and make use of whatever time remains. Individuals who are in chronic pain simply do not have the energy to cope with anything outside pain. Analgesics (pain-killing medication) are given at a level that will control pain without reducing awareness and alertness. Although addiction to drugs is not a consideration, for the patient is near death, hospice care teams sometimes find that patients and families are fearful of using strong medication and need counseling prior to its use.

In hospitals, terminal patients are usually given drugs only when the patient requests them; usually the pain has become severe and the medication is given by nurses at intervals. When effects of medication begin to diminish, more is administered. This practice results in the patient's becoming anxious and apprehensive of the pain that will return. In hospice care the appropriate dosage is determined and a level of medication maintained so that the patient can be free of pain without intermittent suffering between times of medication. Physical suffering and its debilitating effects on both patient and family are thereby avoided. In hospice care, the drug is self-administered or given by a family member.

It is part of the hospice-care concept that a physician be on the team, providing care and arranging for whatever medical consultations are needed. Volunteers are a vital asset and provide many services. They are not expected to provide counseling, but to be like friends or neighbors to patient and family.

Relief of pain is not the only consideration in making the patient comfortable. The dietitian studies the patient's dietary needs, likes, and dislikes, and attempts to provide tasty special dishes. The physical therapist places emphasis on helping the patient make maximum use of the abilities that can still be used and strives to help the patient maintain these functions as long as possible. Pastoral services are provided to meet spiritual needs of the patients, but religion is not thrust upon them.

Family members feel freer to ask questions that they may hesitate to ask in traditional medical settings. In hospice care, questions are encouraged to determine how much the patient knows about the illness and to learn about the concerns of the patient.

Family members who are caring for the terminally ill member at home are often frightened by the elements of care. Many older patients are discharged from the hospital with the statement that there is nothing else that can be done. The patient may be in such a fragile condition that loving family members are justifiably terrified. If a crisis occurs, what are they to do? If the patient begins to bleed, has labored breathing, appears to be dying, whom should they call? As hospice care embraces the concept of 24-hour, on-call service, this can alleviate some of the anxiety of such families.

Dying patients may have "unfinished business"—a debt they wish to pay, a quarrel to reconcile, an old friend they would like to see. Hospice team members, often with the use of volunteers, assist the patient in fulfilling these wishes. Family members are also involved in caring for the patient. Performing even small tasks may help them later when dealing with their grief, which often includes guilt feelings.

For some patients, the very word *hospice* may be threatening, for it is associated with death. The patient or family member may think of a hospice facility as a "death house." Both patient and family may be denying the imminence of death or may feel that anyone outside the family is intruding into their private grief. It may be necessary, as the hospice concept is relatively new in this country, to explain the concept. If there is a hospice institution nearby, a visit may be arranged to dispel fears of gloomy surroundings. Most families who are taking a patient home during their final days realize that help will be needed and welcome assistance from the hospice home-care team.

If the decision is made to discharge the patient into a hospice facility or for hospice home care, the medical social worker contacts the hospice social worker, who then is likely to visit the patient in the hospital. The patient is involved in planning the discharge and making the choice.

Social Worker as Member of Hospice Team

The social worker on the hospice home health team may make the initial visit to a referred patient. The needs of the patient are assessed and questions answered as to the hospice program. The social worker may help the older patient by making use of the community resources discussed in Chapter 12, as well as by providing volunteers from the hospice program. The patient is also interviewed for psychosocial information that will aid the team in planning appropriately for the patient. Wills, pensions, and other financial matters are also discussed. Questions the social worker may ask are given by one source as follows:

- the patient's understanding of his or her condition,
- problems raised by terminal illness and their possible solutions,
- the patient's emotional situation, whether anxious—angry, depressed,
- the patient's relationship to family and friends,
- the patient's life-style prior to illness,
- the patient's strengths,
- future plans of the patient and family,
- what special services are needed.[10]

Social workers in the hospice setting have many of the functions of the hospital social worker, such as identifying community resources and acting as the resource person on the team. They also conduct workshops with volunteers in regard to death and grief reactions. Follow-up with the surviving family members and the provision of bereavement counseling may also be part of the functions of the hospice social worker.

FAMILY RESPONSES TO DISCHARGE PLANNING

Families respond in a variety of ways to the suggestions regarding discharge that are given them by physicians, social workers, and the patients themselves. There are probably as many responses as there are combinations of personalities involved. The following case example demonstrates one kind of family response and the ways the social worker may deal with each member of the family while trying to work out the best possible plan.

CASE EXAMPLE: STRENGTHENING FAMILY RELATIONSHIPS

Joe Galt is a retired 87-year-old manager of a dry cleaning business who is admitted to the hospital following a fall. His left hip is fractured and requires surgery. Mr. Galt has had arthritis in his knees for many years. A flare-up of arthritis in his right knee is considered the cause of his fall. The patient also has high blood pressure and mild emphysema, with the latter causing difficulty in breathing at night.

The patient is referred to the social worker by the orthopedic surgeon shortly after surgery for discharge planning. The surgeon notes that he expects Mr. Galt to remain in the hospital approximately two weeks. He believes he will be able to use a walker in that length of time and may return home.

Upon receiving the referral, the social worker first reads the medical record. The patient has been hospitalized several times during middle age for minor surgery and for diagnostic tests. There is no social information. She notes that this is the first contact the orthopedic surgeon has had with the patient. There are medical notes by the rheumatologist, but they also indicate few contacts with the patient. Mr. Galt seems to have had a few flare-ups of arthritis, but in general has not been hampered by it. The nursing notes are discouragingly sparse. Mr. Galt seems to be complaining quite a bit about pain in his knees. The physical therapist has a guarded comment as to the patient's prognosis.

The social worker visits Mr. Galt in his room. She asks him to tell her about his fall. She listens and empathizes as he describes in detail the way he turned to enter a doorway to a concrete patio and felt his knee throb with pain. He tells of his fear as he realized he was going to fall, and the sickening thud as his body struck the concrete. He relates the excruciating pain he felt in his hip and, a little later, his panic when he remembered that he was alone in the house and might be for hours, as his daughter had just left for the evening. Fortunately, she had forgotten to take a sweater and had returned only minutes after his fall.

When the story is told, Mr. Galt looks sharply at the social worker and makes the comment that nobody else has asked just how it all happened, but he has gone over and over it in his mind. Mr. Galt admits he is very anxious about falling again. The social worker responds that she hopes talking about it and expressing his feelings will help him to be able to stop thinking so much about the experience and think instead about working toward getting better.

Mr. Galt appears to take it for granted that he will return to his daughter's home where he has lived since his wife died after a long bout with cancer two years earlier. He comments that his wife and his 67-year-old daughter's husband died within a month of each other. He sold his home, but it was so heavily mortgaged and in need of repair that he made very little on the transaction. He then moved into his daughter's home. He has been able to help her with some of the work in the yard, and he is "still a good fixer," especially with home repairs. His Social Security check is also helpful, as her Social Security check is small. He has some stocks and bonds that he bought from the sale of the house. They pay a few dividends and that helps, too.

The social worker agrees that he has probably been very helpful to his daughter. She then tells the patient that she will be visiting him in physical therapy to see how he is getting along. Mr. Galt seems pleased but expresses concern about his progress. He wishes his knees were less painful.

Later in the day the social worker receives another referral, this one from the rheumatologist who attends Mr. Galt. The physician notes in the referral that he expects Mr. Galt will need temporary nursing-home care, for the arthritis in his knees will probably prevent him from using a walker. He believes the flare-up of arthritis will subside and that physical therapy in the nursing home will probably strengthen Mr. Galt so that he will be able to return to his previous living arrangement in a matter of weeks.

The conflicting opinions of the orthopedist and the rheumatologist are disturbing to the social worker. It is difficult to plan discharges when the physicians have different expectations. At least both doctors believe the patient will be able to return home; only the time estimate is different.

The social worker decides to check with two nursing homes that provide physical therapy and are near the patient's home as to the possibility of a bed in about eight days. She receives a "maybe" from one of the nursing homes and an "impossible" from the other.

On the same day the physician sets the discharge date. Mr. Galt is eligible for nursing-home care under Medicare, since he needs physical therapy.

The following morning a very slight, fragile-appearing gray-haired woman who identifies herself as Frances Hart, Mr. Galt's daughter, visits the social worker. She appears very troubled and speaks at some length of her concern for her father's health and welfare. She wants him to have the best of care while he is in the hospital, and she wants him to be discharged to her home. The surgeon told her he will be dismissed in about a week.

The social worker asks whether Mrs. Hart has talked to the rheumatologist. Mrs. Hart looks away and remarks that the rheumatologist doesn't really know much about her father. The surgeon is "the main doctor" and is the one to say where her father should go.

The social worker comments that Mr. Galt has expressed the wish to return to her home, but that the rheumatologist believes he may need a few weeks or so of physical therapy in order to use the walker. This can be provided in a nursing home under Medicare.

Mrs. Hart quickly responds that it doesn't matter whether or not he uses a walker. She is strong enough to push him in a wheelchair, or even look after him in bed, if necessary. She adds that the nursing home staff would not care about her father, but that she does care and would look after him properly.

The social worker explains that the main concern of the hospital staff is to help Mr. Galt to become as independent as possible. Although it is kind of Mrs. Hart to want her father to come home and to look after him herself, the best discharge may be to a facility providing physical therapy in order to help him become as healthy, able, and independent as possible. The physicians will make their recommendations, but the decision will rest with Mr. Galt, as he is capable of deciding what he should do.

Mrs. Hart, in a hostile tone of voice, asks whether the social worker has talked to her sister and brother. It sounds to her as if the social worker is "siding" with them. The social worker responds that she has talked to neither of them. Before she can say more, Mrs. Hart abruptly leaves the office and slams the door behind her.

The social worker wonders whether Mrs. Hart wants her father to come home in order to have the money he puts into the household. She hopes that is not the only reason. She wonders how well Mrs. Hart has been looking after him.

The social worker talks again with Mr. Galt in an effort to determine the kinds of physical hazards he may encounter in the home environment and what his life is like at his daughter's home. She learns that Mr. Galt enjoys tinkering around in his deceased son-in-law's workshop, which is in the garage. There is no automobile, as it was sold when Frances's husband died. The house is one story and there are only two steps up to the front porch. His daughter seldom leaves the house in the daytime, but she does play bingo twice a week in the evening at a service organization her husband had joined. The patient thinks she could stay home those nights, too. He gets tired of looking at television alone when she is gone. There is nothing else to do. He has survived most of his old friends, but occasionally visits a friend or receives a visit. He misses his wife, Ida, who was lively and "a big talker." Frances is quiet and never has much to say.

The social worker observes that both he and his daughter probably need the companionship of other people and suggests he might enjoy going to the bingo game with her. Mr. Galt appears surprised by the question and replies that he hates bingo. He doesn't really mind Frances going, but he can't see that it's necessary, either. She talks on the phone enough that she shouldn't need anything else.

Before the social worker leaves the patient, she reminds him that it will be up to him to make the decision as to where he will go from the hospital. The physicians will recommend the kind of care he will need to become as independent as possible. She will provide whatever information he needs for the decision in regard to nursing homes, Medicare coverage, and so on.

Mr. Galt responds that he doesn't want to go to a nursing home. He knows he will never leave it, if he ever has to go. He has seen many friends go to the nursing home and die.

The social worker assures him that many people older than he go to nursing homes for physical therapy and leave when they are strong. Both physicians believe that he will do the same. She observes that the patient's anxiety seems to lessen, although he does not respond verbally.

The social worker visits the physical therapy department daily to encourage and check the progress of the patients who have been referred to her. The physical therapist confides that he believes some of Mr. Galt's difficulty in walking is rooted in fear of falling. Many patients react this way, but usually overcome it much more quickly. He wonders whether Mr. Galt is too worried about nursing-home placement to concentrate on physical therapy.

It is at this point that Mr. Galt's unmarried daughter, Grace, and married son, Frank, make their appearance. Frank is accompanied by his wife, who is meeting her father-in-law for the first time. Frank has been divorced for a great many years but remarried in the past year. Frank and Grace live in the same city in a distant state. They had learned from Frances that their father was in the hospital, and that there was "some talk of nursing home." The three of them had driven one-and-a-half days to visit Mr. Galt. They have not yet seen their sister, but will be staying in her home.

Frank and Grace appear very concerned about their father. They are distressed by his appearance. They cannot recall ever having seen him in bed in the middle of the day. Both had offered to have him "take turns" staying in their homes when their mother died. They are now here to make certain that he goes to a good nursing home. Frances is the oldest in the family but they believe, with her husband deceased, that she needs some help in making the decision as to which one to select. It's a shame, they say, that they have had so little contact with Frances over the past 20 years. The three of them had been so close before Frances married so late in life, but her husband had not welcomed their visits and had not allowed Frances to visit them. The social worker hears the anger underlying their words and comments that Frances may have been as unhappy about this as they but may not have known how to handle it.

They do not respond to this, but tell the social worker that their father has an entire floor of antiques in Frances's house. These antiques are rightfully as much theirs as Frances's. Then there are the stocks and bonds. They must be protected or the nursing home will get everything he owns. It would be really unfair for his money to go to strangers instead of to his own flesh and blood, although it's not a lot of money. On the other hand, their father needs to be safe and secure. They suppose Frances has been doing her best, but their father is so old that he really needs constant care. He might fall and break his other hip. The nursing home may be the best choice; besides, Medicare would pay for it.

The social worker quietly comments that Mr. Galt is in full command of his senses and that he is the one to make the decision as to where he will go from the hospital. Her statement is met with astonishment. They cannot believe that she thinks an 87-year-old sick man can "think straight."

At first the social worker is angry over all that has been said. She struggles to maintain a nonjudgmental view. As she continues to listen and they talk about wanting to do the best thing, she begins to believe they are speaking sincerely. She reflects on the hostile tone that Frances used in reference to her brother and sister and the anger they barely concealed that was directed toward their sister. In spite of this, she detects a sense of deep caring and concern. She believes the statement may be true that was made earlier in reference to their having been a very close family before Frances's marriage late in life. There seems to be an honest good will in wanting to help their father. There also seems to be genuine sorrow over having lost the closeness they had once shared with Frances.

The social worker thinks they have rationalized their selfishness until they believe their father really would be distressed if the little he had worked so hard to save should be "wasted" on a nursing home. They are also clearly unaware, just as their sister is, of their father's ability and privilege to make his own decisions. This is the area the social worker believes must be examined with all three of the "children."

She talks with the son and the two women in this regard and believes they are giving her comments consideration. She explains that advanced years do not reduce intelligence. Mr. Galt, like the majority of people his age, is alert, oriented, aware of everything that is happening in his environment. He shares the normal concerns that all patients have: to get well and regain his independence.

The social worker adds that Frances seems to have tried very hard to make her father satisfied and comfortable. She expects that Frances misses the close relationship they have described as much as they do. She suggests that this visit they are going to have together can provide a time for them to renew old bonds and settle their grievances, if they are willing to try to achieve that goal.

The social worker believes enough has been said at this point. She hopes she has helped them to look at the whole situation from a new perspective. She then sets a time for a meeting with the four family members in a few days, explaining that she needs to have some agreement from staff as to their recommendations. She wishes there were more time, but the discharge date has been set. A discharge plan must be settled upon.

They nod in agreement. Four days will give them time. As they leave with sober, thoughtful expressions, the social worker believes there is also an air of resolution about them.

The social worker turns her attention to finding a time that she and the two physicians, the physical therapist, and the nursing supervisor can meet together to discuss Mr. Galt's discharge within the next day or so. Members of the staff and attending physicians are accustomed to the social worker acting as coordinator and calling them together when difficulties arise in the discharge.

When they meet, there is some difference in opinion between the two physicians as to the patient's recuperative powers. The orthopedic surgeon believes a few weeks of physical therapy will be sufficient; the rheumatologist thinks it will take more time than that. The physical therapist believes the patient's fear of falling is holding him back more than the pain in his knees.

The nurse reports that Mr. Galt needs to be turned in bed, as he claims his knees are too painful for him to turn himself, but that he is doing a little better each day. He can manage his eating without help, but needs assistance with bathing and dressing. He has stopped asking for pain medication during the night. The nurse is inclined to agree with the physical therapist that the patient's fear of falling is seriously interfering with his rehabilitation.

All four have met the son and his wife and the two daughters. Although they would like to discharge the patient home, they believe Mrs. Hart is too frail to care for her father at home until he can at least be on a walker. They express annoyance over Mrs. Hart's insistence on taking him home to try to care for him alone in his present condition and the other two children's urging to have him sent to a nursing home.

The social worker shares some of the information about the family. The daughter wants her father to return to her home, and this is the patient's choice, if this is at all possible. The visiting son and daughter seem to be overprotective and believe he will be safer in a nursing home. She believes they are a genuinely caring family and will be helpful in carrying out a plan.

After much discussion, there is agreement that the patient, for whatever reason, is progressing very slowly in physical therapy, although he is healing in every other respect. The most desirable plan would be to have him remain in the hospital for further physical therapy, but the family resources are not large enough to foot the bill. The second best choice would be to have him remain in the home and continue physical therapy in outpatient clinic; the third is a nursing-home setting with the expectation that he will improve so that he may return to his daughter's home.

The social worker has an appointment with the four family members the following day. She has located a nursing-home bed, if no other plan can be worked out.

As soon as the two sisters, their brother, and his wife join the social worker in her office, she realizes there are different feelings toward each other. There is a relaxed, easy air about the group.

The first comment is made by Frank who says very warmly that they have had three "great" days together. He adds that his two sisters have always spoiled him, as he was the only boy, and he has enjoyed being spoiled during this visit all over again. Before the social worker can respond, Frank begins to thank her for helping them to realize their father was the one who would suffer or benefit from a decision and therefore should be the one to make it. They agree they simply hadn't thought things through. They don't want their father to go to a nursing home. They believe they've worked things out, but haven't mentioned it to their father, in case the physicians don't agree.

At that point, Frances speaks for the first time in the meeting. She is glad to say that her brother, his wife, and her sister are staying for a couple of weeks. If their father isn't on the walker by then, her "kid sister" will stay on for a while and use Frank's car to take Mr. Galt to physical therapy. She and Grace can manage alone once her father improves.

Frank interrupts to add that they're all pitching in, just like they used to when their mother was alive, to help out. They will have their father walking in two weeks. If not, Frank is giving up his car for at least a month. His wife is willing to ride the bus with him all the way back home if that becomes necessary. Now that none of them are "spring chickens" any more, they've got to help each other out. It's too late in life to get upset over a few pieces of old furniture that their mom would have thrown away if she could have afforded new furniture. His wife and two sisters laugh with him over the last remark.

The social worker is relieved. She congratulates them on their ability to work together and come up with a plan that will allow Mr. Galt to return home. Their plan sounds feasible, and she can supplement their care with some supports in the community. She adds that there is an outpatient social worker who may be able to help them in various ways while Mr. Galt is attending physical therapy on an outpatient basis. The social worker then suggests they discuss their idea with Mr. Galt and see what he thinks of it, even though they are certain he will be delighted.

She makes the referral to the outpatient social worker. She explains that Frank and his wife will leave in a few weeks if all goes well; Frances and her father will probably need supportive services of some kind. Frances may need counseling to enable her to avoid making unnecessary sacrifices to provide more care than her father really needs.

The social worker in this case is working with two groups of people: the discharge planning team and the family group. The problem-solving process is used with both groups. In the former, the problem (the patient's illness and need for rehabilitation) is readily identified. Each specialist makes an assessment of the patient's capabilities and they are discussed. Rehabilitation goals for the patient are set. Alternative solutions in regard to how the patient will be maintained away from the hospital are considered and evaluated. However, at this point the discharge team is dependent on the other group with which the social worker is planning, the patient and his family, for the selection and implementation of the solution.

The social worker is involved to some extent with the family members individually and with them as a group. She uses counseling skills as well as other skills as she helps the family identify the problem, consider solutions, and set goals. Their needs, in terms of the resolution of problems, include much more than meeting the specific discharge need of the patient. They are able to use their limited time together constructively, so that they can settle their differences and strengthen their family ties in the process. They are then ready to join the first group, the discharge planning team, to implement the solution. Follow-up is provided for the patient and caregiver that may help to accomplish the goals that were set.

The social worker has many roles in this example. She is an *enabler*, enhancing the problem-solving, coping, and developmental capacities of the family. She is a *broker*, as she links the patient with a number of systems, including the family system, rehabilitation services, and social systems in the community. She is the patient's *advocate* throughout the process, never losing sight of the patient's decision-making rights, making certain that these rights are protected.

NOTES

1. *Aging America: Trends and Projections*, 1987–88 edition. Prepared by the U.S. Senate Special Committee on Aging, in conjunction with the U.S. Administration on Aging, and the American Association of Retired Persons, 106.

2. Ibid., 114.

3. Carel B. Germain, "An Ecological Perspective on Social Work Practice in Health Care," *Social Work in Health Care 3*, no. 1 (Fall 1977): 70.

4. Evelyn Bonander, "Summary and Recommendations". Paper presented during the Proceedings of the National White House Briefing on Prospective Pricing of Medicare for Social Work Administrators, November 3–5, 1983, Washington, D.C.

5. Shirley H. Wattenberg and Leona McGann, "Medicare or 'Medigap'? Dilemma for the Elderly," *Health and Social Work* 9, no. 3 (Summer 1984): 236.

6. Ethel Shanas, "Myth as Hypothesis: The Case of the Family Relations of Older People," *Gerontologist* 19, no. 1 (February 1979): 6, 7.

7. *Aging America: Trends and Projections*, 121.

8. Sandol Stoddard, *The Hospice Movement: A Better Way of Caring for the Dying* (New York: Stein and Day, Publishers, 1978), 70.

9. *The 1984 Guide to the Nation's Hospices*. Published by the National Hospice Organization, Suite 402, 1901 Fort Myer Drive, Arlington, Virginia, (Copyright 1984).

10. Parker Rossman, *Hospice: Creating New Models of Care for the Terminally Ill* (New York: Association Press, 1977), 166, 167.

8

SOCIAL WORK SERVICES IN NURSING HOMES

Various aspects of discharge planning, including the responses of patients and family members to nursing-home placement, were examined in the previous chapter. Chapter 8 continues the discussion, following the patient and family through the process of adjustment to a nursing home. Other responsibilities and functions of social workers in nursing homes are explored.

The term *nursing home* is one that is fraught with emotion, possibly the chief emotion being distaste to the point of dread. Employment in a nursing home is sometimes avoided by health-care workers. Some of the factors that influence the reluctance to work with the ill aged in long-term-care facilities may be the image of a nursing home as a place for old, ill men and women to go to die; the fear of working with a population composed, as a whole, of those closer to death; and, possibly the greatest negative influence, the aura of hopelessness that tends to pervade our thinking in regard to nursing homes.

Fortunately, the growing awareness of the needs of the older population is extending to the nursing-home population. More efforts are being made to improve the lives of nursing home residents. Instead of accepting the stereotyped image of aged individuals as hopeless, helpless, and sick, there is more consciousness of individuality and the potential for continued growth until death. To help older people fulfill this potential, the need for a broad range of social work skills in nursing homes is being recognized. Many social workers are becoming sharply aware that the nursing home is a setting in which they can "make a difference."

It is beyond the scope of this book to include every aspect of social work services in nursing homes. An in-depth discussion of the nursing-home social worker's involvement with Medicare and Medicaid is omitted, largely because the social worker's responsibilities vary widely in this respect from one institution to the next.

A major purpose of Chapter 8 is to point out some of the many opportunities for social work intervention that can improve services provided by nursing homes. However, before entering into a discussion of social work services in nursing homes, it may be helpful to consider some pertinent aspects of nursing homes and characteristics of nursing home populations.

CHARACTERISTICS AND UTILIZATION OF NURSING HOMES

There was a rapid growth in nursing home utilization following the introduction of Medicare and Medicaid in 1966 and deinstitutionalization in the 1960's. By 1985, an estimated 1.3 million older people lived in nursing homes. About 1 percent of the elderly population age 65 to 74 were residents, as compared to about 6 percent of those age 75 to 84 and about 22 percent of those age 85 and over.[1]

Nursing facilities vary in the size of population served, administration, funding, and level of care provided. The sizes of nursing homes range from 25 or fewer beds to institutions with over 500 beds. In 1982 approximately 65 percent of all nursing homes contained less than 75 beds. Slightly over 4 percent had 200 beds or over. The small facilities (under 25 beds) represented two of five nursing homes.[2]

Homes may be managed by a person, couple, or family, sometimes referred to as mom-and-pop operations, or by one or more administrators. Certification of administrators varies from state to state and may require only nursing-home experience, with less than four years of college. However, there seems to be a trend toward strengthening education requirements in many states.

About four-fifths of all nursing homes in 1982 were operated on a profit basis, with 14% voluntary nonprofit and 4% government-operated.[3]

The disciplines represented by the staff vary according to the size of the facility and the level of care provided. The staff of skilled rehabilitation facilities may include occupational, physical, and speech therapists; an audiologist; recreation director; crafts teacher; and others. Nursing homes employ one or more social workers or none, but may have a consultant to assist the person designated to provide social services. Trained social workers may have a bachelor's or master's degree.

As Brody points out, although all members of the nursing-home staff, as well as family members, are aware of and meet social needs of the resident, the skills of the professional social worker are needed to identify social/emotional needs and modes of treatment. The professional social worker should provide and direct social services.[4]

Levels of Care

In order to meet Medicare and Medicaid specifications, nursing homes provide levels of care as specified by those two programs. There are three primary levels of care: skilled nursing care, intermediate care, and custodial care. Nursing facilities can be certified as a skilled nursing facility (SNF), an intermediate care facility (ICF), or both.

In 1984 approximately one-fourth of all nursing homes in the United States were certified as SNF. The typical skilled nursing facility contained 90 beds.[5] All states have standards and regulations that must be met by extended-care facilities, whether certified or not by Medicaid and Medicare. Licensing is usually accomplished through the Department of Public Health and the Department of Mental Health and Retardation of the state in which the nursing home is located.

POPULATION OF NURSING HOMES

Although the majority of nursing-home residents are over 65, there are also younger residents. Some younger individuals who have conditions such as paralysis after stroke, crippling arthritis, early-onset Alzheimer's disease, or other dementing illness receive care in nursing homes.

The typical nursing home resident is about 81 years old and a widow. Nearly 84 percent of nursing-home residents are widowed, as compared to 45 percent of the elderly who are not institutionalized. Only 63 percent of older residents have children, compared to 81 percent of the elderly residing in the community.[6] These figures indicate that many of these very old individuals may be in nursing homes because they have outlived their spouses. They may also have outlived their children, or their children may be disabled or financially unable to assist them. Children of individuals in their eighties and nineties are often in their sixties and seventies and are coping with retirement, bereavement, and other issues discussed in later chapters.

There are about 4 to 5 million older adults who are functionally dependent. About 1.2 million of the functionally dependent, disabled, and impaired persons who cannot cope with all the basic functions of everyday living without assistance are cared for in nursing homes and other institutions.[7] About 70 percent require assistance in walking or are chairbound or bedfast.[8]

A large number of nursing-home residents are psychiatrically impaired. Teeter reported that 85 percent of a sample of 74 nursing-home residents had significant psychiatric disorders, along with multiple physical problems. Nearly two-thirds of the psychiatric problems had been undiagnosed. Some of these patients had organic brain disease.[9]

Many nursing home residents display some type of behavior problem. Depression, withdrawing from others, hyperactivity, abusiveness of staff and other patients, and wandering are frequently observed behaviors. However, the prevalence of psychiatric and behavior problems among institutionalized older people is understandable when the environment of many institutions is considered. The lack of stimulation and meaningful recreation, the use of untrained or poorly trained aides for much of the personal contact with patients, and numerous other aspects of institutional life contribute to poor mental health—to say nothing of the individual circumstances that bring the older person to the long-term-care facility.

ROLE OF THE SOCIAL WORKER

Social work services are described in the *NASW Standards for Social Work Services in Long Term Care Facilities.*[10]

    This chapter is primarily concerned with Standard 4 which is as follows:

> The functions of the social work program should include but not be limited to direct services to individuals, families, and significant others; health education for residents and families; advocacy; discharge planning; community liaison and services; participation in policy and program planning; quality assurance; development of a therapeutic environment in the facility; and consultation to other members of the long-term care team.

    The discussions of social work functions, including those services described in Standard 4, are not organized as stated in the NASW standard. The functions are grouped as follows, in the order discussed: providing social services to residents and family members, social worker as team member, social worker in the consultant role, and social worker as advocate. When reading this section, it is important to remember that all of these roles are overlapping and, in actuality, cannot be separated into separate entities.

PROVIDING SOCIAL SERVICES TO RESIDENTS
AND THEIR FAMILIES

Services to residents often begin prior to the actual time of admittance. As stated in the previous chapter, if the person is being transferred from a hospital, a hospital social worker may alert the social worker at the nursing home and provide information about patient and family, as well as make suggestions for care. Older adults living in the community may be accompanied by family members on a visit prior to admittance unless they are too ill or disabled to visit before admission is made.

    Social workers discuss the ways in which the new resident can be made to feel more comfortable in new surroundings. Family members are encouraged to provide the relative with familiar items from home that the institution allows. Residents sometimes use their own pillows, linens, nightclothes, and so on.

Some institutions permit residents to bring bedroom furniture, with the exception of beds. New residents who weave, knit, or have other hobbies are encouraged to bring these materials.

The social worker's ability to empathize is an especially important skill at this point. Regardless of the number of times the social worker has interviewed new residents, the ability to recognize the incoming resident's feelings must remain fresh and uncalloused to ameliorate the problems arising from relocation. A brief case example may help to demonstrate the kinds of changes encountered by the new resident.

CASE EXAMPLE: NEW ADMISSION

Fred Marks is an 85-year-old widower who has lived alone in a small rented house since his wife's death 15 years earlier. He is admitted to the nursing home following hospitalization from a fall resulting in a fractured hip. It is unlikely that he will be able to return home, as he has no living relatives and the community has a weak support system for the elderly. Mr. Marks is bewildered by the sheer number of people he encounters the morning of his admission. The administrator welcomes him absent-mindedly and quickly reads aloud to him a booklet entitled *The Legal Rights of Nursing Home Residents*. He is then wheeled to his bedroom, where he is distressed to find a roommate who is disoriented, confused, and bursts unaccountably into laughter or profanity at intervals.

An aide then escorts Mr. Marks in his wheelchair to an "activity room," which seems a mile from his room. The aide disappears and a kind-appearing woman tries to engage him in working a puzzle. He does not express his feeling of being insulted, but as soon as her back is turned, wheels himself into the corridor. He has no idea which way to go until an aide passes and gives directions so loudly that he is embarrassed, for his hearing is unimpaired.

The new resident toys with the food on his plate at lunch. He is accustomed to having lunch, usually a peanut butter sandwich and milk, in front of the television while he looks at the noon news show. Sitting at a table with six other people is a new and unenjoyable experience. Even if he felt like eating, the clamor of trays is giving him a headache. The lady across from him is having trouble chewing. Seeing the food dribble over her chin makes Mr. Marks feel a little queasy. He looks at his watch and sighs, for he is going to miss nearly all of the noon news.

The afternoon is slow. Even the veterans' hospital had more interesting afternoons. He had enjoyed swapping stories with the other veterans. When he was at home he took a walk every afternoon, rain or shine. In nice weather he walked to a park about two miles away. Sometimes he sat on a bench with a couple of old cronies, if they were well enough to be outside. Other times he watched the children. He often took bread to toss to the birds. That seems a long time ago.

A nurse taps his shoulder and announces that it is time for the evening meal. He realizes he had dropped off to sleep, sitting in his chair. He looks closely at the nurse; he has not seen her before, which means the second shift has arrived. He looks at his watch. Dinner at five o'clock. He has been eating his evening meal at seven o'clock ever since he can remember. He isn't hungry, but there is really nothing else to do. Clattering dishes, so many voices, somebody's angry voice. The food looks all right but it tastes so different he can hardly swallow it. He takes a few bites, then quits. He keeps getting lost when he tries to find his way back to his room.

It's now 5:30. Mr. Marks wonders what he will do until 11, his usual bedtime. When he is at home and it's summertime, he weeds the garden in the cool evening air. He smiles, thinking about his neighbor's cat, a feisty gray tom that was forever prowling in his garden, but never did any harm.

The evening seems interminable. He doesn't want to go to the activity room, but the aide insists, saying the "able-bodied" are "supposed" to be in the activity room. He wonders why he is considered able-bodied, until he compares himself to the inert bodies lying in bed in the rooms he has passed. He is introduced to a large number of people who seem to take little interest in him, with the exception of one woman. She believes she lived next door to him in Louisville. Even though he explains he has never even visited that city, she is not convinced and keeps asking him whether he remembers the corner grocer, the neighborhood soda shop, and so on.

He lies awake that first night for what seems like hours. His roommate wakes up, goes to the bathroom, and then tries to crawl in Mr. Marks's bed. Even though this does not happen again, Mr. Marks finds himself waiting, each time there is a noise on the other side of the room, for the stranger to return. Other noises are also disturbing: rubber soles padding against the floor, doors slamming, a sudden scream, a wail of abandonment. He finally drifts into an uneasy sleep.

The experiences of Mr. Marks are not unusual. The new resident is placed in a bedroom which is now "home." The belongings of a lifetime are condensed into a size that can be packed into a small closet. Possibly for the first time in many years, someone shares the bedroom—a complete stranger sleeping in the same room.

The person newly admitted to a nursing home must also undergo an immediate change in the accustomed pattern of living. Meals are usually served on a rigid schedule and may consist of food that is unfamiliar or prepared differently. Bedtime may be earlier or later than the accustomed time, and there may be very little to do between one meal and the next. Contacts with old friends are difficult to maintain, for many of the new resident's friends may be disabled or lack transportation to visit. In addition to all this, it may be very difficult to adjust to the noise of other residents and staff members as they go about their routines.

Finding the way around the building may pose problems for newly admitted, sight-impaired, or forgetful individuals. Being lost is a fearful experience and may appear demeaning to the person new to the nursing home who is initially feeling insecure.

Staff members, even social workers, may become so accustomed to admitting new residents that the admitting procedure becomes automatic.

Consideration of feelings of the patient may be overlooked due to the pressures involved in completing the paperwork and attending to the mechanical details of admission.

It may be helpful to look again at Mr. Marks's admission when the social worker and other staff members are involved in planning for the new resident.

CASE EXAMPLE: PREPARATION FOR NEW RESIDENT

Prior to Mr. Marks's arrival, the social worker consults with the social worker at the VA hospital. She learns that Mr. Marks has no family, but does have a few old friends still surviving in his community who are not quite as disabled as he is. She finds that Mr. Marks likes to play cards and enjoys gardening. She also learns that he prizes his physical independence and wants to do everything possible for himself. In the hospital, he was constantly trying to help others even though they were less helpless than he.

The morning of Mr. Marks's arrival, the social worker places several plants in his room that were left by a recently discharged patient. She asks a resident to make an identification sign for Mr. Marks's room and suggests using playing cards in the design.

The social worker is concerned about Mr. Marks being moved initially into a room with a disoriented person, Mr. Harris, a resident who has also just been admitted. Mr. Harris was transferred from an understaffed nursing home. His confusion and disorientation had been accepted without attempts to help him. She is hopeful that Mr. Harris will become more oriented and that his behavior will become less agitated as a result of their programs and personal attention. Mr. Marks may accept Mr. Harris as a roommate when he learns more about the confused patients and finds them less alarming. The social worker will tell him, as soon as possible after his arrival, that in two days he will be joining a well-oriented, pleasant person whose present roommate will be discharged during the weekend.

As she returns to her office, she notes that all the corridor signs are in order, with arrows giving directions to the dining room, visiting area, activity room, nursing station, and so on. The doors to these rooms are labeled in large print, and each resident's room has a name or identifying symbol of some kind. A clock and calendar are at the end of each corridor with a separate page giving the date and day. She believes the patients seem more confident since the staff added these orienting signs and is glad the new resident will have them for guides.

The social worker stops at the nursing station. The staff has been alerted to the new admission and has received medical information from the hospital. The social worker has shared relevant social information with the staff. In addition, members of this staff have had many in-service training programs and are sensitive to issues surrounding new arrivals. She feels confident they will be alert to any problems in adjustment that the new resident may experience.

The social worker reminds a nursing assistant, Frank, that he is to keep an eye on Mr. Marks today. With his cooperation, she has structured Mr. Marks's day. Frank has an easy, quiet way with new residents that seems to make them feel comfortable with him. He is to introduce Mr. Marks to his replacement at 3 o'clock, another aide who seems to have a talent to create comfort.

When Mr. Marks arrives, the social worker gives him some information about the nursing home but does not overwhelm him with too many facts. She emphasizes that she is available to talk with him about his concerns. There is plenty of time to talk together; it is not necessary to try to cover everything this first morning. Her office door is open to residents, and she visits them as well. She expresses her hope that he will feel free to ask for her help when needed. She encourages him to ask questions about his main concerns. Plans for the day are discussed in relation to Mr. Marks's interests and wishes. She explains that Frank, whom he has met, will be on his ward that day and available to answer questions. A resident volunteer is to accompany Mr. Marks on a leisurely tour of the facility. Staff members are accustomed to this "first-day tour" and will be welcoming the new resident individually. She warns him not to expect to remember so many names and faces. They will "come together" after a while.

As they converse, she notes his tension receding. She observes his relief when told that he will soon have a new roommate. She lays the ground for future conversations about the residents who are confused and disoriented, as she remarks on the disoriented resident's past career and achievements. She then comments that she was told by the VA social worker about Mr. Marks's helpfulness to other patients while hospitalized. She is hopeful, when he becomes accustomed to the surroundings, to enlist his help with some of the less-able residents.

The social worker then discusses some aspects of the nursing home. She stresses the choices that are his to make as she discusses the routine. He may select his meals from a menu. He is free to talk with a dietitian at a time convenient for both about menu changes he would like. Mr. Marks is told about the group that plays cards every afternoon and encouraged to join them whenever he wishes. The activity room belongs to the residents and they use it when they like. He may decide to have meals alone in front of his own television set, if he finds this enjoyable, or have meals in the dining room. The social worker emphasizes that although all residents are subject to some rules and regulations, every effort is made for residents to have personal freedom and freedom of choice. Life in the nursing facility may not be ideal, but she and the rest of staff, with the help of residents, are constantly trying to improve conditions. She talks with him briefly about the legal rights of nursing-home residents, the ombudsman program, and about the residents' council. She promises they will discuss these subjects in more depth in the next day or so.

Before Mr. Marks leaves, the social worker explains that another resident is available to be a "buddy" for a few days, helping to answer questions or just supply companionship. The buddy will introduce Mr. Marks to other residents when he is ready. She adds that transportation can be arranged for his neighborhood friends whenever he would like to have them visit.

She makes an appointment with him for the following morning, so that he knows he will be seeing her soon again. The social worker is pleased to see that Mr. Marks seems much more relaxed when he leaves. His last comment is heartening: "This place may not turn out to be nearly as bad as I thought it would be."

As demonstrated in this case, staff members work together as a team. The social worker individualizes the residents and coordinates services to help the client adjust to the new living situation as comfortably as possible. The relationship is established so the resident is not reluctant to continue calling on the social worker for assistance when needed. The social worker also takes the initiative in keeping in contact with the residents and with family members.

FAMILY RESPONSES TO ADMISSION TO NURSING HOME

In earlier chapters, counseling family members has been discussed in detail in relation to family feelings in response to debilitating mental or physical illness and to decisions concerning parental care. Guilt feelings, sibling rivalries, overprotective attitudes, feelings arising as a result of role reversal, and the like were explored. In the previous chapter, nursing home placement directly from the hospital was discussed. The next step is to examine the effects on the family during intake procedures at the nursing home.

This point in time is extremely stressful for both family members and resident. In some instances the admission comes about very suddenly, as the result of a nursing-home bed unexpectedly becoming vacant. The admission of the resident may constitute the first visit of the family to the institution.

Family members are interviewed and are important contributors of information, particularly in the event that the new resident is very ill or disoriented. It is important for the social worker to be aware that family relationships may have been strained or that the family may have little emotional investment in the newly admitted resident. Family attitudes and actions, in regard to visiting the resident and participating in care, range from complete neglect and disinterest to all-encompassing care and concern.

Emphasis is placed on the family as members of the team providing care. Unfortunately, many relatives are physically exhausted and emotionally drained by the time the decision is made for nursing-home placement. Often they have had little respite from care for months or even years.

There is frequently a readiness to assume that the relative is now in good hands with a nursing staff and a physician on call. Some family members tend to believe that their attention is no longer vital for the welfare of the aging relative.

This assumption is often shared by administrators and nursing-home personnel. They may encourage families to visit and give lip service to families about being "partners in care," but may be unresponsive to the family's observations and requests. In those instances in which the individual is not a private paying patient but supported by Medicare and Medicaid, there may be an unspoken opinion that the resident and family have little right to complain about care.

However, as noted in the previous section, residents do have legal rights, which include voicing grievances and recommending changes in policies.

Social workers encourage family members to visit as frequently as they can, not only to provide emotional support to the resident, but to pay attention to the kind of care the resident is receiving. This includes attention to the content and quality of meals; the cleanliness of the institution and the individual's bedroom and bathroom; the hygiene of the patient, particularly the condition of hair, scalp, fingernails, feet, and toenails; the presence of decubiti on the pressure points of the body; notice of bruises, abrasions, or scratches; and the attitudes and behavior of staff, including administrators and aides. Relatives are reminded that any problems that are identified should be reported to the director of nursing staff or to the administrators so they can be appropriately addressed.

In addition to noting the physical care of the resident, visitors are asked to help plan activities with and for the resident that will make life meaningful. If it is at all possible, family members are urged from the beginning to continue to have their relatives visit in their homes, to take them on outings, and to try to maintain any community ties the resident may have. There may be some staff resistance if special preparation of the resident is needed for trips outside the nursing home, but this usually can be overcome by careful planning.

When family members object to rules that interfere with a resident's adjustment to the nursing home, they receive support from social workers. An example of this is the ambulatory older individual who has always been a loner and who wishes to dine alone. Instead of forcing such persons to have lunch in the dining room, the social worker attempts to work out arrangements for meals with some degree of privacy.

Relatives sometimes find the older person so changed by the illness that they experience difficulty in relating to this individual. The older person may be experiencing delirium, dementia, depression, or other severe illness. Relatives have difficulty in accepting the lack of response or responses that differ from those they customarily received from these older adults who have figured so prominently in their lives. They may comment that the person is being "indifferent" or "doesn't seem to care."

Added to this is the change in physical appearance that so often occurs. Attempts by staff to groom the patient may tend to be minimal. This may be due to understaffing, so that cosmetic efforts have a low priority; indifference of staff; or the belief that the person is too ill to undergo the discomfort of hair dryers and hair curling, or close shaving, mustache trimming, and so on. The hair is combed back from the face. Dentures are removed to prevent choking, in the event they become loose. The changes in appearance are often drastic and tend to make the residents look very much alike. The visible sameness makes it easier to forget the invisible differences that comprise the uniqueness of each individual.

If the older resident fails to recognize the relative or confuses identities, even more feelings of distress and distance are created. Reactions of family members to the change in the resident range on a continuum from a reluctance to visit to overinvolvement in the individual's care.

It is vital for social workers to be alert to the reactions of family members. In most instances there are vestiges of the personality and character that were once whole. The social worker may need to prod the concerned relative to identify the familiar characteristics and qualities that remain. Involving families in reality orientation programs and helping family members to reminisce with the patient when possible may aid them in recognizing traits and habits that still remain. They may be reminded of earlier, closer times, and perhaps a link between past and present can be forged.

No one can say with certainty that the brain-dead patient or the individual in the end stage of Alzheimer's disease is aware of the presence of loved ones. However, many experienced health-care workers believe that such patients sense the presence and touch of close relatives and friends. even though there may not be an overt response.

Family members may become overinvolved with patient care and spend so much time at the nursing home that difficulties arise in other areas of their lives. Over-solicitousness may also interfere with nursing care. The ill resident may be distressed because the relatives are spending so much time at the nursing home. The social worker may direct their attention to other needs that are not being met, such as needs of other family members and their own health needs. Social workers provide other services to residents and family members, directly and indirectly, which are discussed throughout the remainder of the chapter.

SOCIAL WORKER AS TEAM MEMBER

Social workers usually attempt to work with all staff, including administrative staff, toward providing a "therapeutic community" in which all members of staff are mutually supportive and hold positive attitudes toward the residents. This concept also requires creating an atmosphere of lively optimism and enthusiasm. This is a difficult concept to achieve, but one well worth pursuing.

Although procedures may differ in various nursing homes, an overall care and treatment plan is made for each patient upon entrance to the nursing home. Goals, problems, needs, target dates for change, and treatment approaches are given. As goals are met or changed, progress notes are placed in the chart reflecting these changes.

The nursing staff, rehabilitation therapists, and social worker meet on a regular basis to discuss each resident's treatment plan and progress. There is often no physician present. Some nursing homes have house physicians who practice in the community but make rounds at the nursing home and coordinate medical care. The house physician may take over the care of the resident from a referring physician, but will continue to consult with the referring physician. Some patients have physicians of their own who are summoned by the nursing-home staff or by family members when they have concerns about the institutionalized resident. It is important to note that social workers in nursing homes do not usually have the frequent opportunities for consultation with physicians as does the hospital social worker.

The social worker's written contribution to staff is the social history that is completed on each resident, even though a social history may accompany the resident on admission. Medical information, reports from the speech therapist, physical and occupational therapists, dietitian, and any other disciplines, in addition to the psychosocial history, are used to assess the patient much the same as in hospital social work. As medication may affect behavior in such a variety of ways, the social worker may record this for future reference.

A goal-oriented approach is often used by social workers in nursing homes. Long- and short-term goals are stated clearly in the social work plan. The treatment approach is described, and problems experienced by the patient are presented in the social service plan.

Progress notes are written, just as the title suggests, to describe the resident's condition and to note any change that may have taken place. The progress note describes the kind of change that occurs, the efforts made by the social worker, and whether they worked. Treatment plans or approaches are rechecked and revised on a regular basis as needed.

The progress notes and other records are vitally important, for government survey teams visit nursing homes and use medical charts as primary documentation in the certification process for Medicare and Medicaid. Progress notes furnish accountability by describing the ways in which social workers provide services.

In addition to planning treatment for new admissions, discharge planning is also a team effort. Those who are unfamiliar with nursing-home work are often surprised to find that a number of discharges are made. Residents are often discharged from one nursing home to another to be closer to relatives or because they need a different kind of care. They may be discharged to the hospital for emergency or other services. If they are admitted to the nursing home for rehabilitation services, such as physical therapy following stroke, they are discharged when they have become rehabilitated. The location of additional resources sometimes makes it possible for them to return to the community. The responsibilities of the social worker in regard to discharge planning are the same in general, including community linkages, as those involved in working out discharges for hospitalized patients, discussed in the previous chapter.

THE CONSULTANT ROLE
IN REGRESSIVE BEHAVIOR PROBLEMS

The social worker is often consulted in relation to the interpretation of resident behavior. Overdependency, incontinence, overt sexual behavior, and wandering behavior are some of the chief causes of frustration.

Social workers help staff and family to attempt to locate the cause of the regressive behavior instead of viewing it as behavior that is purposefully chosen by the resident to irritate and annoy others.

Many health-care workers, including well-meaning volunteers and family members, may not be aware of ways they may be contributing to the development of attitudes of dependency and displays of regressive behavior. Tarbox refers to "benign neglect," in which the neglect of the older person is totally unconscious and nonmalicious. The perpetrators may even believe they are being attentive.[11] This type of neglect underscores the need for more or better training of nursing-home personnel.

Dependency and Overdependency

Nursing-home residents are dependent on the nursing-home staff in various ways and in varying degrees, according to the individual. Some who need help resist efforts of the nursing staff to provide assistance and others, who could function reasonably well, sometimes need a great deal of encouragement to do so. Members of the nursing home staff need to take the time to differentiate between the patients, in terms of their needs and abilities, while keeping in mind that *all* of the residents need an environment that is accepting, loving, and nourishing. There is a balance that must be kept which involves meeting the dependency needs of sick residents without creating overdependency and helping residents to maintain as much independent thought and action as they can without neglecting their dependency needs.

Overdependency may be encouraged by overworked or indifferent aides and visiting relatives who push residents in wheelchairs instead of taking the more time-consuming route of assisting them by walking slowly and carefully. To save time, the staff may feed stroke and arthritic patients who may be able to relearn basic skills or who could learn to eat with the provision of special aides. Bathing and dressing patients may be performed hurriedly without waiting for the residents to do as much as they are able. Preferences in regard to activities, meals, visits, and excursions may be completely ignored. The fact that preferences exist may not be acknowledged.

In addition to assuming most of the daily functional tasks of the residents, some staff and family members often talk to residents as if they were children. Scolding, speaking in a patronizing way, addressing the residents as "Mama," and assuming a parental role without realizing it are common practices demeaning to the older person.

An anecdotal report included in a survey on nursing homes mentions the observation in several nursing homes of aged women with dolls which the women and staff referred to as their "babies." It was noted that this is a psychologically destructive kind of care.[12]

Family members of the resident may relate to the resident differently now that the move to the nursing home is completed. Dependency may be further encouraged and infantile actions accepted as appropriate behavior for someone old and "senile."

Residents may respond to this kind of treatment by feeling even more helpless and dependent. They may feel as if they are losing control over their environment and losing their identity. The result may be an aggressive acting out in opposition to these feelings. Fecal incontinence may be an unconscious response. Feelings of frustration and rage may be forcefully expressed. Other individuals may become increasingly passive and dependent and may exhibit signs of depression, such as withdrawal and apathy.

A major role of the social worker is to help staff examine regressive behavior in an effort to determine the kinds of problems that may be underlying the behavior, instead of focusing only on the behavior. Scrutinizing ways that care is being provided and considering alternative practices to help the resident acquire more autonomy may prove helpful. Each staff member may be encouraged to set personal goals to improve one-to-one relationships with residents. Those who work well with specific individuals may be agreeable to changing schedules to be with those residents more frequently.

Incontinence

Incontinence is a cause of great distress to relatives and staff. It is probable that incontinence is a major factor in making the decision for nursing-home placement, as this condition places heavy demands on the caregiver who may also be old and disabled to some degree.

Incontinence refers to fecal incontinence as well as urinary incontinence. Research indicates that there is a correlation between the two, since the majority of older people who have urinary incontinence also have bowel incontinence. Incontinence is more prevalent in women than in men. Reasons given include confusion, which is twice as prevalent in women as in men, longevity, and physiological differences. *Stress incontinence* is a common disorder in women. The cause is often a rectocele (hernial protrusion of the rectum into the vagina) or cystocele (hernial protrusion of the urinary bladder through the vaginal wall), which may occur after childbearing. Exercises to retrain the pelvic-floor muscles have been proved helpful in restoring continence. Surgery is also sometimes used to correct the problem.[13]

According to Forbes and Fitzsimons, urinary and bowel incontinence may be managed through nursing intervention and a therapeutic bowel and bladder program. Key factors for success are the understanding and support of the nurses for the incontinent patient and the interest of the individual in participating.[14]

Studies have shown a direct correlation between nursing staff morale and the incidence of incontinence; also, that individuals who received nursing care from a professional nursing staff have less incontinence than those cared for by ancillary staff.[15] These and other studies indicate that there are psychological factors in the incidence of incontinence.

Although psychological factors may account for some instances of incontinence and medical problems may account for others, there are still other causes which social workers may aid in identifying. These include such things as the positioning of the switch to summon the aide for assistance; the height of the nursing-home bed, which may interfere with the person's slipping easily out of bed; night-time confusion, which requires someone to take the individual to the bathroom at set times both night and day, establishing a pattern; changing the timing for medication taken with a full glass of water; reducing fluid intake in the evening; and prescribing diuretics for daytime hours.

Another possible factor in incontinence which is overlooked is the habitual use by many older people of a chamberpot. The difficulties in getting in and out of bed and getting to the bathroom may have been solved by use of a receptacle. When admitted to the nursing home, they are unlikely to mention it unless asked. These patients can be provided with a utensil which they can keep out of sight, if it is a cause of embarrassment.

Many residents do not want a commode chair placed in their room. It is a highly visible indicator of problems relating to incontinence. It also symbolizes helplessness and increasing disability that is very threatening to self-esteem. Before resorting to the use of a commode chair, every effort must be made to determine and remedy the cause of incontinence.

Overt Sexual Behavior

The continued interest in sexual activity on the part of older people is discussed in detail in Chapter 10. Although the same needs for intimacy and physical sharing holds true for nursing-home residents, there is often little acknowledgment of a need for or interest in the warmth and comfort of bodily contact. Conjugal visiting is not encouraged, and the need for privacy of married couples, much less single adults, receives little attention. The only mention of sex in many nursing homes may be limited to references made to passes by "dirty old men."

In a study conducted in a nursing-home population in Wisconsin, the findings indicated that the aged interviewees (63 men and women) "enthusiastically supported" sexual activity for many older persons in their homes, but they personally were not involved. The main cause was given as a lack of opportunity. Most of the subjects admitted that they had sexual thoughts and feelings.[16]

One section of the interviews referred to factual knowledge. There was, overall, a general lack of knowledge in the area of sex, with women scoring lower than men. Almost 20 percent of the men, but only 3 percent of the women, had a score of 75 percent correct.[17]

In a survey conducted among 90 members of the nursing staff of a 400-bed extended-care unit for older men, three types of behavior were identified as causes of problems to staff. They were sex talk (use of foul language, reports of past and present sexual experiences, etc.); sexual acts (touching or grabbing, masturbating openly, or exposing genitalia); and implied sexual behavior, such as openly reading pornographic material. The sexual behavior perceived by staff as positive and acceptable included limited physical contact between staff and patient and masturbation in privacy.[18]

Suggestions by staff in regard to kinds of behavior to be encouraged were verbal expressions to patients of kindness and love, hugging, hand-holding, and kissing on the cheek or forehead. It was recommended that genital care be provided men by male staff when there was a likelihood that a sexual incident might be provoked.[19]

These and other studies point up the need to bring discussion about sexuality in the nursing home into the open, for the sake of employees as well as residents. In-service sex education in relation to old age may be helpful. Staff may be able to accept sexual feelings and desires as a natural part of the older personality, and residents may be helped to accept their own feelings without shame or self-blame.

Coping with overt sexual behavior in nursing homes is a relatively new area of inquiry, so that there is little research to use as a basis for action. The staff may find that open discussion of their concerns in regard to specific incidents, and sharing successful ways of dealing with residents' overt sexual behavior, may provide solutions. The eventual outcome may be a workable solution in regard to providing privacy for desired sexual activity and protection for residents who are distressed by sexual advances and behavior.

Wandering

Older adults may wander away at night and be found by the police walking aimlessly at a great distance from home. The wanderer may be dressed in pajamas and may even be in a wheelchair. Older people who wander away from the nursing home, hospital, or their own homes are a cause of great concern to caregivers. There is anxiety in regard to the person's falling, being run over, or mugged, or suffering from exposure. Out of concern for the person's safety, physical restraints and drugs are sometimes used to prevent wandering.

Wandering behavior has been sparsely researched in the past but has recently begun to receive more attention. There are some conjectures as to why older people may wander: a need for exercise, an attempt to escape boredom, ard a desire to return to a place the person remembers.

Some older people have been very active prior to moving to an institution and suddenly find themselves confined to surroundings that require them to do very little. Even everyday chores are performed by others. Sitting or napping all day is boring. Pacing the floor, restlessness, and, finally, wandering may replace the former useful activity the person enjoyed.

The person who experiences some confusion may remember a place that would be pleasant to visit. Unable to locate the place exactly and equipped with only vague memories, the person wanders about, seeking this place.

"Wandering" may be a misnomer. The person identified as a wanderer may not be wandering, but may have a very definite idea as to where and why the journey is taking place. Lack of transportation may be the only reascn the journey is being undertaken on foot. The lack of a clear understanding as to how to reach the destination may account for the aspect of "wandering."

In a study exploring the life-style of wanderers and nonwanderers in long-term care, Monsour and Robb found that wanderers had engaged in a higher level of social and leisure activities and had been more busily occupied in earlier years than nonwanderers. They suggest that caregivers need to select and implement activities that do not block the release of the random energy of wanderers, but direct this activity into constructive channels. Decreasing stressful environmental factors is also recommended. The kinds of programs can be determined from the wanderer's preferences during the person's more able-bodied years.[20]

When a resident has been identified as a wanderer, the social worker may enlist the aid of staff to determine whether the label is warranted. Studying the person's current behavior and past history may provide clues as to prevention. Providing more recreation and opportunities for exercise, as well as taking residents on short trips and excursions, may be preventive measures.

Burnside raises three questions for consideration in relation to intervention in "wandering" situations:

> To whom is the behavior unacceptable? Why is the behavior unacceptable? What needs of the intervenor are being met?[21]

These questions may help in knowing when, how, and, perhaps, in some nonthreatening situations, whether to intervene, not only in the case of wandering, but with other kinds of behavior that are a cause for concern.

SOCIAL WORKER IN ADVOCACY ROLE

Nursing homes offer many avenues of intervention for the social worker in the role of advocate. The social worker may sometimes represent the conscience of the institution in the role of patient advocate. Staff members may need to be reminded of the legal rights of patients and the need to uphold those rights, even when it may be inconvenient to do so.

The social worker may identify rules, regulations, practices, and policies that are inconsistent with the rights of nursing-home residents, or with the provision of care for the residents, and to work toward their change. The latter may be a slow process, requiring a number of social work strategies and a great deal of patience. The residents' council, ombudsmen, or other community resources may be brought into play in order to effect needed change.

Some nursing-home practices that affect patient care negatively include the following: hiring practices, such as employing untrained personnel and not being amenable to the provision of any type of education; understaffing and failing to seek the cause of, or provide the remedy for, high rate of staff turnover; inadequate staffing, such as failing to provide persons to plan meaningful activities for residents; making rules for the convenience of staff instead of for the welfare of the patient. Failure to provide policies also causes problems; for example, not having a policy to allow for privacy for conjugal visitors, even though this is a legal right.

It is important for the social worker not to assume that the administration is an adversary, for many of the goals of social worker and administrator are the same. It is to the administrators' advantage to have satisfied residents and relatives who are not complaining about care or the conditions of the nursing home. It is also financially sound to have a contented nursing and rehabilitative staff who take pride in what they are doing, as this may decrease employee turnover.

Advocacy in the Community

The advocacy role extends from the nursing home into the community. Members of an informed community are more likely to be alert to the quality of care being offered and to be willing to contribute time and services to nursing-home residents. Establishing a community advisory board for the nursing home may be a means to increase community participation in the nursing facility's activities and programs. Keeping the community aware of innovative programs fostered by the nursing home and inviting members of the community to events in the nursing home can be a marketing device as well as a means to monitor services.

Social workers and other nursing-home staff members may plan and provide educational kinds of programs for the community, such as programs giving practical suggestions in caring for stroke patients or patients with brain damage. Information about the nursing home's programs and needs for volunteers can be shared with church groups, fraternal organizations, and schools. Reaching out to varied groups and making efforts to involve them in some way with the nursing home may have many unforeseen benefits.

Advocacy for Appropriate Care

Nursing care is the responsibility of the nursing staff and, ultimately, the director of nursing. However, nursing homes are often understaffed. Many of them have few registered nurses on duty and must rely on less-educated nursing personnel. Social workers, as members of the health-care team, should be careful observers of the kind of care that is provided and report lapses in care provision.

Two common concerns of attending physicians and patients' families are oversedation of the patient and failure to follow physicians' directions in regard to exercising the patient. Both of these problems are discussed in the paragraphs that follow.

Oversedation.   According to a report in 1974 by the Senate Commission on Aging, 75 percent of nursing-home patients were receiving at least one standard psychotropic drug at any given time. The committee estimated that nursing homes annually bought $60 million dollars worth of chlorpromazine and thioroidazine.[22] As noted earlier, tranquilizers can mask symptoms and add to the confusion of already disoriented individuals.

Social workers should be aware of the possibility of oversedation. If a formerly alert resident suddenly appears drowsy or is constantly napping, oversedation is one of the possibilities.

Social workers do not prescribe or make recommendations in regard to medication, but they do raise questions, giving the reasons for their concern about the patient. They may ask the attending physician or head of nursing staff to reevaluate the patient's medication and physical condition.

Failure to Exercise the Patient.   Social workers should also pay close attention to the individual who must lie in bed for prolonged intervals and be alert to any departure from the treatment plan of the patient. Complications that may develop include the following:

1. Decubitus ulcers
2. Stagnation of blood in the feet and legs
3. Softening of bone
4. Kidney stones
5. Bending contractures of the limbs
6. Formation of blood clots in the legs
7. Muscle weakness
8. Sputum plugs in the lungs with development of lung infections
9. Emotional regression of the patient until he is concerned only with his physical needs for food, water, bowel movements, and constant attention[23]

To avoid these complications, physicians often prescribe passive exercise for patients who cannot exercise themselves. They may also leave orders for bed patients, such as being assisted in walking a certain number of times each day, or to be gotten into chairs, or, for the very ill, to be turned frequently in bed. The attending physicians may be unaware that their orders are not being carried out until they find that the patient's condition has worsened.

As lack of exercise has such extremely debilitating effects on weak and ill residents and on even the more able-bodied, it seems within the realm of social work responsibility to be observant of whether residents are exercising.

There is also the need to report lapses in following physicians' orders to the charge nurse if they occur.

Programs Promoting Advocacy

Social workers have at least four tools to utilize in providing advocacy in nursing homes: the National Ombudsman Program, the National Citizens' Coalition of Nursing Home Reform, residents' councils, and the Legal Rights of Nursing Home Residents.

Ombudsman Program.   A long-term-care ombudsman program was mandated by 1978 amendments to the Older Americans Act.
The federally mandated ombudsman's functions are as follows:

1. Investigate and resolve complaints made by or for older individuals residing in long term care facilities relating to administrative actions that may adversely affect their health, safety, welfare, and rights;
2. Monitor the development and implementation of federal, state, and local laws, regulations, and policies with respect to long-term-care facilities in the state;
3. Provide information to public agencies about the problems of older individuals in long-term-care facilities;
4. Train volunteers and promote the development of citizen organizations to participate in the Ombudsman program; and
5. Carry out other activities consistent with the requirements of this section which the commissioner determines appropriate.[24]

States vary in the ways in which the mandates have been carried out. Some have one ombudsman; others have several. Volunteers are used widely in these programs.

Ombudsman programs are required to prepare annual reports which are available to interested parties. Social workers in nursing homes should find these annual reports helpful in evaluating the homes in which they work, as well as pinpointing current long term care issues and possible solutions in their individual states.

National Citizens' Coalition for Nursing Home Reform.   This organization was formed in 1975. It seeks to improve the long-term-care system and the quality of life for nursing-home residents. There are presently over 100 local groups. Information about the coalition may be obtained from the national office, located at 1424 16th NW, Suite 204, Washington, D.C. 20036.

Residents' Council.   Newly admitted residents are informed about the council, its activities and purpose, and they are urged to participate. If a residents' council has not been established, the social worker may work with the residents toward forming this council. Administrators and staff members, dietitians, nurses, aides, and others are usually urged to attend. Involving staff members and encouraging their participation, as well as their attendance, helps to ensure a viable program.

The formation of a residents' council may provide the potential for greatly improving institutional life for some or all of the residents. In addition to providing input in regard to health-care policies, the council may plan activities for the more able-bodied members and programs for those who can do very little. Picnics, "wheelchair Olympics," or trips to a shopping center, play, or movie may be arranged.

Legal Rights of Nursing Home Residents. Regulations have been issued by the Department of Health and Human Services which give nursing-home residents certain rights. Skilled nursing facilities and intermediate-care facilities have separate rights. In order for nursing homes to participate in Medicare and Medicaid programs, they must establish patients' rights policies. Full information on the rights and responsibilities and all rules governing conduct must be given to each resident before or at the time of admission. A brochure that explains the legal rights of nursing-home residents may be given to each resident.

Since Medicaid differs from state to state, certain rights may differ from one state to the next, but federal rights are the same throughout the country. As they are too lengthy to be given in their entirety, they will be briefly presented. In general the federal rights include the following: full information in regard to residents' rights must be given to the resident at or before admission and this must be acknowledged in writing; residents must be informed about services available in the facility and the charges for these services; information must be provided about his or her medical condition unless this is medically contraindicated by an attending physician on the medical record; residents are encouraged and assisted to exercise their rights as patient and citizen, voicing grievances and recommending change without fear of reprisal; the resident has the right to manage his or her own financial affairs, but if the facility is given written responsibility for this for any given period of time in conformance with state law, the facility must give the resident a written accounting of all transactions made on behalf of the patient; a resident may be discharged only for medical reasons, his or her welfare or that of other residents, or for non-payment of care; residents must be free from mental and physical abuse and from chemical and physical restraints (except in emergencies or for other certain specified reasons); residents must receive confidential treatment of personal and medical records and accorded considerate, respectful treatment; residents are assured private written and oral communication and freedom of participation in social, religious, and community groups, unless medically contra-indicated; residents retain personal clothing and possessions as space permits; residents have privacy for conjugal visits and permission to share a room with spouse unless medically contraindicated by the attending physician in the medical record.[25]

Most or all states have composed brochures which are given to the nursing-home resident. The brochure interprets the rights and gives the names, addresses, and telephone numbers of persons or agencies that can supply assistance and legal aid.

It must be pointed out that each social work setting provides a limited amount of tolerance for social work advocacy. Totally losing the social work position, or disrupting services as a result of being perceived as overstepping boundaries, is likely to accomplish very little. Each social worker must exercise careful judgment as to which issues can be targeted for action and plan carefully as to how they will be approached. When positive results are observed following advocacy, there are likely to be more opportunities and more support to bring about even greater change. In cases of abuse or mismanagement, social workers must respond according to their professional ethical responsibilities.

The preceding sections have dealt with the consulting and advocacy roles of social workers in nursing homes and with providing direct services to patients and families. There are also some special techniques that are sometimes used. These techniques are discussed in the following section, along with brief descriptions of innovative programs that are being used in various nursing homes located throughout the United States.

SPECIAL THERAPEUTIC TECHNIQUES
AND INNOVATIVE PROGRAMS

Group Work

Many kinds of groups are formed in nursing homes for purposes of stimulation, socialization, and other therapeutic goals. Oberleder observes that activity is therapy for older adults; allowing too much time for introspection can be harmful. Older people often have fewer inner resources, and these resources must be "exercised and stimulated." Daydreaming may prevent the patient from receiving the stimulation needed.[26]

Two kinds of groups currently being used with apparent success in nursing homes are reality orientation and reminiscence groups. There are also other kinds of groups that have not been led in nursing homes but could be adapted to nursing facilities.

Reality Orientation. The concept of reality orientation is based on the premise that there is a correlation between the ability to function adequately in an environment and the degree of orientation to the environment. It is also based on the theory that even severely brain-damaged persons retain a usable portion of the brain.[27]

Reality therapy may be conducted on a 24-hour basis, with the entire staff involved in helping patients to maintain their orientation. Any staff member may reorient a patient at any time that confusion appears. Repetition and consistency are the main components of the reality orientation program.

Classes for disoriented patients are usually held daily for a half hour and may consist of small groups of five or six patients. Brightly colored clocks, calendars, pictures, bulletin boards, blocks, maps, games, and so on are used. Photographs of the participants may be used to aid them in identifying themselves and others in the group.

Some institutions do not attempt 24-hour orientation, but have group meetings regularly with the purpose of aiding residents to maintain contact with reality. Some of the staff continue to reinforce throughout the day the teaching that occurs in the groups.

Reports of reality orientation programs are often enthusiastic as formerly apathetic patients appear to respond. There does appear to be some question as to how long the patient retains orientation.

Reminiscence Groups. Reminiscence as a therapeutic technique was discussed in an earlier chapter. Group work using reminiscence as a focus also appears to be a viable technique in nursing homes. In addition to the benefits provided by socialization with others, Ebersole points out that convening to discuss the past helps older adults to identify the contributions they have made to society, which in turn may help them develop a sense of pride in their accomplishments.[28]

According to a report on a pilot project using group reminiscence as a means of interrupting excessive isolation and mental decline in confused nursing-home residents, positive effects were observed. All the residents in the group initially exhibited difficulty in most or all of the following: orientation, recollection of recent and immediate incidents, ability to express thoughts in sequence, and consistently giving attention and responding appropriately to staff. Changes that were observed include more alertness, increase in length of verbal contributions and spontaneity, more frequent sharing of humor and laughter, a gradual but dramatic increase in the length of time spent in socializing prior to and after the group meeting, more attentiveness and increased responsiveness to others in the group.[29]

Innovative Programs

Pet Programs. Among the programs that have been integrated into nursing institutions in recent years are programs involving pets and children.

Many of the laws that did not allow pets in government housing have been repealed. It is now possible in some states to have pet programs which may include keeping pets in the nursing home or having pets visit residents. As pet lovers have long known, animals freely give their affection and offer an opportunity to cuddle, hold, and embrace an animate object. Animals are also a source of entertainment and provide stimulation to patients who are weary of sitting or walking aimlessly.

Pet programs may involve having professional trainers or representatives from the humane shelter bring unusual animals or fowl and explain their habits or have them perform. Scout troops and other children's groups may participate in the programs.

Nursery and Day-Care Programs. Day care for children has been combined with nursing-home services in some areas. Low-cost child care for the staff is sometimes provided in one part of the building. This type of arrangement may encourage staff members to remain at their jobs, which in turn can provide more lasting relationships with nursing-home residents. Another arrangement is to operate a day-care center for the community within walking distance of a nursing home. Children visit the residents, who may tell them stories, teach crafts, or engage in other activities which help to build warm and loving relationships between members of both generations.

Social workers and other staff in nursing homes are constantly seeking ways in which the self-esteem of residents, particularly the confused and disoriented, can be increased. Family members are also often aware of this need for increased self-esteem but feel helpless in trying to meet it. Families and staff joined together to develop the project described below.

Project to Raise Self-Esteem. A project to raise the self-esteem of mentally impaired patients in a nursing home in Washington, D.C. was developed by two social workers following a meeting with a visitor who expressed regret about knowing nothing about the residents' past lives.[30] He felt this knowledge would enrich his relationships with them. He suggested a display of information about their lives so that others, also, would have this information.

Photographs of residents as they were in the past and brief biographies were obtained and given to the art therapist at the nursing home. Posters were created which conveyed special information. Volunteers and family members also became involved in the project and prepared eye-catching posters. Before displaying the posters, residents were asked for their consent.

There were many good results, the most important being the positive effect on the morale of the staff and the enhanced pride of the residents. Residents who had been kept at a distance by staff and visitors were more warmly received, and the residents sensed that they had gained esteem in the eyes of others.

NOTES

1. *Aging America: Trends and Projections,* 1987–88 edition. Prepared by the U.S. Senate Special Committee on Aging in conjunction with the American Association of Retired Persons, the Federal Council on the Aging, and the U.S. Administration on Aging, 118.
2. U.S. Bureau of the Census, *Statistical Abstract of the United States: 1987* 107th edition, (Washington, D.C., 1986), 99.
3. Ibid., p. 93.

4. Elaine M. Brody, *Long Term Care of Older People: A Practical Guide* (New York: Human Sciences Press, 1977), 100, 101.

5. U. S. Bureau of the Census, 98.

6. *Aging America: Trends and Projections*, 118.

7. U.S. Department of Health and Human Services, Pub. No. (OHDS) 81-20157, *Long Term Care in Home and Community*, 1981.

8. U.S. Department of Health and Human Services, Pub. No. (OHDSI) 8120704, *The Need for Long Term Care, Information and Issues*, 42.

9. Ruth B. Teeter et al., "Psychiatric Disturbances of Aged Patients in Skilled Nursing Homes," *American Journal of Psychiatry* 133, no. 12 (December 1976), 1430–1434.

10. NASW Standards for Social Work Services in Long-Term Care Facilities, Long Term Care Facilities Standards Task Force of the NASW Committee on Aging, June 20, 1981, National Association of Social Workers, Inc., 1425 H St., N.W., Washington, D.C.

11. Arthur R. Tarbox, "The Elderly in Nursing Homes," *Clinical Gerontologist* 1, no. 4 (Summer 1983): 46.

12. D. Bragg, *Report on Texas Nursing Homes to John L. Hill, Attorney General of Texas* (Austin, Tex.: Nursing Home Task Force, 1978). Cited in Tarbox, "Elderly in Nursing Homes," 43.

13. Elizabeth Jane Forbes and Virginia Macken Fitzsimmons, *The Older Adult: A Process for Wellness* (St. Louis: The C.V. Mosby Co., 1981), 207, 208.

14. Ibid.

15. Ibid.

16. Mona Wasow and Martin B. Loeb, "Sexuality in Nursing Homes," *Journal of the American Geriatrics Society* 27, no. 2 (February 1979): 73.

17. Ibid.

18. George Szasz, "Sexual Incidents in an Extended Care Unit for Aged Men," *Journal of the American Geriatric Society* 31, no. 7 (July 1983): 407–411.

19. Ibid.

20. Noel Monsour and Susanne S. Robb, "Wandering Behavior in Old Age: A Psychosocial Study" *Social Work* 27, no. 5 (September 1980): 415.

21. Irene Mortenson Burnside, "Symptomatic Behaviors in the Elderly," in *Handbook of Mental Health and Aging*, ed. James E. Birren and R. Bruce Sloan (Englewood Cliffs, N.J.: Prentice-Hall, Inc., 1980), 740.

22. Panzetta, A., Senate Special Committee on Aging. (Washington, D.C.: U.S. Government Printing Office, 1974). Cited by Philip Bobrove et al., "A Partial Hospitalization Program for Nursing Home Residents," *Hospital & Community Psychiatry* 34, no. 6 (June 1983): 554.

23. Gertrude D. Cherescavich, *A Textbook for Nursing Assistants*, 3rd. ed. (Saint Louis: C.V. Mosby Co., 1973), 105.

24. Public Law 95-478, October 18, 1978. 42 USC 3927, Section 307.

25. *The Legal Rights of Nursing Home Residents*. Booklet prepared by Long Term Care Ombudsman, 325 W. Walnut St., Johnson City, Tenn.

26. Muriel Oberleder, "Emotional Breakdowns in Elderly People," *Hospital & Community Psychiatry* 20, no. 7 (July 1969): 26.

27. Sylvester Kohut, Jr., Jeraldine Joanne Kohut, and Joseph J. Fleishman, *Reality Orientation for the Elderly* (Oradell, N.J.: Medical Economics Co., 1979), 59, 60.

28. Priscilla Ebersole, "Problems of Group Reminiscing with the Institutionalized Aged," *Journal of Gerontological Nursing* 2, no. 6 (November–December 1976): 25.

29. Jacqueline B. Cook, "Reminiscing: How It Can Help Confused Nursing Home Residents," *Social Casework* 65, no. 2 (February 1984): 90, 92, 93.

30. Judy Weisberg, "Raising the Self-Esteem of Mentally Impaired Nursing Home Residents," *Social Work*, 28, no. 2 (March–April 1983): 163, 164. Copyright 1983, National Association of Social Workers, Inc.

9

MAINTAINING VITALITY IN OLD AGE

Chapters 9 through 12 are concerned with the kinds of services that can enable older men and women to remain as active and involved with the community as possible. There is an emphasis on maintaining wellness and making use of community supports that heavily influence the quality of life of older adults.

A major trend has been developing in regard to health maintenance. Physicians are placing more emphasis on individual responsibility in monitoring health and maintaining good health practices. Information on diet, exercise, sleeping patterns, and medication is appearing in professional and lay journals and is presented on radio and television. Much of this information is also disseminated to the public in pamphlets made available in health-care settings. However, every individual does not receive this information; even those who do receive it may misunderstand or forget it. This is particularly true of older people. Impaired hearing, a reluctance to admit a lack of understanding, and the slower retrieval from memory may combine to prevent the assimilation of needed information.

Social workers, in the many fields in which they work, are making daily contact with men and women who can benefit from the reinforcement of patient education. They are also often in the position of being able to identify its misuse.

This chapter is concerned with sleep disorders, medication, exercise, nutrition, and ways of using this material in social work practice with older adults. As sleep complaints are often presented by older individuals, this topic will be the starting point for this chapter. Discussions of medication, nutrition, and exercise follow, in that order.

SLEEP DISORDERS

The diagnosis and treatment of sleep disorders is a relatively new field which is rapidly expanding. The work of Nathaniel Kleitman, a physiologist, during the 1920s, 1930s, and 1940s established sleep research as a legitimate field of study.[1]

The development of the electroencephalogram and other polygraphic techniques made many discoveries possible, such as the discovery of rapid eye movements (REM) in sleep. Due to the interest in this field, Project Sleep: The National Program on Insomnia and Sleep Disorders was established in 1979. This is a major educational and research effort to increase the level of knowledge of physicians and patients in regard to sleep disorders.[2] The development of sleep disorder clinics throughout the United States for diagnostic and treatment purposes is another result of the increased interest and research in sleep disorders.

A number of studies has been made to determine the incidence rates for insomnia in the United States. Although the exact percentages vary, depending on the population sample and phrasing of the questions, the results indicate that the problem of initiating and maintaining sleep is widespread.[3] Sleep complaints have probably received more attention from physicians since the recent discovery of the association of extreme daytime sleepiness with potentially life-threatening conditions.

Many people have not regarded excessive sleeping or excessive sleepiness as symptomatic of any vital problem. Many physicians have prescribed sleeping pills and dismissed difficulties in sleeping as inconsequential complaints. Many mental health workers have assumed that anxiety and depression were the underlying causes of troubled sleeping and planned therapy accordingly. Before discussing the findings of recent sleep research that are affecting these responses to sleep complaints, it may be helpful to describe the normal stages of sleep and the ways in which they change with age.

Sleep Patterns

Sleep consists of a series of stages which are regulated by neural mechanisms. There are five stages in the sleep pattern: rapid eye movement (REM) and four separate stages of non-rapid eye movement (NREM). Although cognitive changes occur during all five stages, vivid dreams usually occur in REM sleep.

In stage 1 sleep (the lightest sleep), the person begins to relax and awareness of the environment is reduced. In stage 2 the body temperature drops and breathing is slower and more regular, as heart rate and blood pressure reach their lowest level, and there is further loss of awareness. Stage 3 is a deeper sleep; stage 4 (delta or D-sleep) is the deepest level of sleep.

Kellerman notes that a major difference between each of these stages is in reference to the state of physiological arousal that characterizes them. During deep delta sleep, both respiration and heart rate are slow, and a state of deep relaxation characterizes vital signs. Respiration, heart rate, and other physiological processes are heightened during REM sleep.[4]

Changes with Age

REM sleep and total sleep time are high throughout childhood, but the percentage of time spent in REM sleep gradually declines. Stage 4 sleep is highest in infancy and decreases with age. During the prepubertal period and puberty, total sleep declines from about ten hours to about seven-and-a-half hours.[5]

There is a fairly stable sleep pattern during the adult years, between ages 20 and 60. The total percentage of time spent in REM sleep is about 25 percent, a percentage that remains fairly stable until about age 70.[6]

The aging process produces insomnia-like wakefulness experiences. The very old experience little of the restful stage 4 delta sleep. Kellerman observes that it is possible that very old individuals may not experience any delta sleep.[7] No significant major changes have been observed for sleep stages 1, 2, and 3.[8]

Around age 50, the percentage of time spent in bed while awake increases. Frequent interruptions of prolonged duration are occurring by age 70. Consequently, there is less nighttime sleep. However, total sleep throughout a 24-hour period remains about 7-and-a-half hours, the same amount of time as that which occurs before 40 years of age. This sleeping time includes daytime naps, although many older people may deny napping. EEG monitoring over 24 hours has revealed that short periods of sleep (microsleeps) occur. These brief periods of sleep are of only 1- to 10-seconds' duration and coincide with the lowering of the eyelids. Although the amount of REM sleep falls slightly, the relative percentage of sleep that is REM remains the same until extreme old age.[9] Increased wakefulness and decreased slow-wave sleep are experienced by the individual as being less sound sleep.

Some older adults adjust to these changes in sleep patterns and do not appear distressed by the curtailment of sleep. Others appear to suffer. Worries are often expressed by older men and women as to whether they are getting "enough" sleep, even though they may not complain about ill effects from lack of sleep. They may observe that everyone sleeps less after age 60, but they are concerned as to whether the amount they are getting is "normal."

This concern may be due to the idea ingrained in most of us that eight hours of sleep is necessary for one to feel truly rested and to be able to perform capably during the day. Many investigations have proved this is not true. However, older adults who believe they need more hours of sleep sometimes request sleeping pills and may become dependent upon them.

Excessive wakefulness may be due, at least in part, to this anxiety about not sleeping. Excessive napping during the day and little or no exercise may contribute to sleeplessness. Using the bedroom and the bed for activities other than sleeping may result in associating both with wakefulness; for example, habitually reading in bed leads to the association of the bed with reading instead of sleeping.

In addition to the age-related changes in sleep patterns, older people are also subject to the same medical and psychiatric causes of sleep disturbances that are experienced by younger men and women. These are discussed in the following sections.

Insomnia

Insomnia refers to the inability to sleep and may be a symptom of a number of different conditions. *Transient insomnia* refers to insomnia resulting from minor situational stress, such as hospitalization for elective surgery. *Short term insomnia* is usually associated with stress from work and family life. *Long-term insomnia* may be associated with a specific sleep disturbance, or medical or mental disorder. Each type of insomnia is treated differently. It is recommended that physicians start the treatment of insomnia with the assessment and correction of sleep hygiene and habits. Psychotherapy, behavioral approaches, and drug therapy, alone, or combined should be considered in the overall treatment plan. When drug therapy is indicated, patients should receive the smallest effective amount for the shortest clinically necessary time; this recommendation is especially applicable to the elderly.[10]

Organic Causes of Sleep Disturbances

Organic causes of sleep disturbances include sleep apnea, narcolepsy, and nocturnal myoclonus.

Sleep apnea.   There have been recent discoveries of profound changes in respiratory functions during sleep. These findings have led to the discovery of one of the major causes of sleep disorders, a condition which can be life-threatening, called *sleep apnea. Apnea* is defined as "a cessation of air exchange at the nose and mouth lasting at least ten seconds."[11] There are three types of sleep apnea: *central apnea, upper airway (obstructive) apnea*, and *mixed apnea*. The form most commonly seen is obstructive sleep apnea and is more prevalent in men than in women.[12] Snoring is caused by an obstruction in breathing. The primary symptom is extremely loud snoring, which may be accompanied by excessive daytime sleepiness. The individual with sleep apnea stops breathing while asleep and comes suddenly awake, usually with a snorting aspiration, in order to continue breathing. The patient is usually not aware of the stop in breathing. The spouse may notice it but, unaware of its significance, will fail to mention it to the physician unless asked directly about it.

Serious cardiopulmonary abnormalities can be associated with sleep apnea. Orr notes that some patients who have been seen many times with unexplained congestive heart failure have been diagnosed as having obstructive sleep apnea as the underlying pathology.[13]

Complaints made to physicians about loud snoring were largely ignored prior to the recognition of this sleep-related disorder. However, it is important to remember that the majority of those who are heavy snorers probably do not suffer from sleep apnea and do not have any serious health effects related to snoring.

Treatment for sleep apnea depends on the type of sleep apnea and may consist of diet and weight-reduction programs, medications, and surgery to correct the obstruction to airflow.

Narcolepsy. It is estimated that there are more narcoleptic individuals in the United States than those with muscular dystrophy or Parkinson's disease. Individuals with narcolepsy have been mistakenly diagnosed and treated for hypoglycemia, schizophrenia, depression, hypothyroidism, and other conditions, and have been viewed as lazy or unmotivated.[14]

Excessive daytime sleepiness is characteristic of an individual with narcolepsy as well as one with sleep apnea. Individuals with narcolepsy experience an irresistible desire to sleep, even though conditions are highly unfavorable to sleeping; for example, while conducting business or engaging in athletic activities, which is not only embarrassing but dangerous.

Cataplexy, a sudden and reversible loss of skeletal-muscle tonus which lasts between a few seconds and 30 minutes, occurs in a great number of narcoleptic patients. Other symptoms that are less frequent but may occur are hypnagogic hallucinations (vivid dreamlike experiences at onset of sleep) and sleep paralysis, a feeling of being totally paralyzed, usually as the individual falls asleep or on awakening from sleep.[15]

Narcolepsy usually begins between the ages of 15 and 30.[16] A major difference between narcolepsy and sleep apnea is the age of onset, as sleep apnea nearly always occurs after age 40, with a history of experiencing sleepiness during the previous five to seven years.

Since the discovery of the condition of sleep apnea, it has been found that some older people with sleep apnea were mistakenly diagnosed in previous years as having narcolepsy. With a change in diagnosis, appropriate treatment may be administered.

Individuals with narcolepsy must make adaptations in their lifestyles. Sitting still and monotonous activities are avoided. Unless the disease is well controlled with medication, driving a car is discouraged. Various medications are used to stimulate the nervous system and reduce sleepiness, and the individual's life-style must sometimes be altered to avoid hazards in occupation or recreation.

Nocturnal myoclonus. *Myoclonus* is a term that refers to rapid muscular jerks. Nocturnal myoclonus is characterized by leg jerks that occur regularly, approximately every 20 seconds. The individual often does not fully awaken and may be unaware of the twitching, but the spouse is conscious of it. The disturbances interfere with the sleep pattern, producing daytime sleepiness. Some cases of nocturnal myoclonus may be helped with medication.[17]

Sleep interference due to other medical conditions. There are other medical problems that interfere with sleep. These include endocrine and metabolic disorders, such as diabetes and Addison's disease, pulmonary problems, nutritional disturbances, renal problems, infections, cardiovascular disorders, and itching.

Arthritis may be painful and disturb sleep when the individual changes sleeping positions. There may be great difficulty in obtaining a comfortable sleeping position.

Sleeplessness is associated with delirium. The agitated state that accompanies delirium interferes with nighttime sleeping and daytime naps.

Medication and Sleep

Many kinds of medication prescribed to remedy various conditions can also cause insomnia. Unfortunately, physicians sometimes fail to tell the patient that the medication prescribed for an illness may interfere with sleep. Many older individuals do not make their sleep complaints known to their physicians, but buy over-the-counter drugs without reading the fine print. The patient may experience a change in sleeping patterns but not associate it with medication.

The effects of sleeping medication on sleep were not precisely documented until polysomnographic studies were made in the sixties and seventies. Sleep medications were found to be of little benefit after about two weeks. Increasing the amount of medication extends their usefulness only for a short time, but adds risks of increased hangovers, tolerance, and dependence. Although restful sleep is induced in the early phase of use, REM sleep is suppressed and reduced by virtually all sleeping medication.[18]

Withdrawal from some drugs can cause depression. Reliance on drugs to relieve the symptoms of depression can occur when the patient is taking relatively small doses. When withdrawal occurs, depression accompanied by insomnia may result.

Diuretics administered near bedtime interfere with sleeping. The patient awakens frequently to urinate and may have difficulty in going back to sleep.

Alcohol as a Sleep-Inducing Agent

It is important to be aware that some older people, in an effort to induce sleep, will depend on alcohol for initial relaxation, but then waken later, unrested and more tense than before. Alcohol taken in moderate single doses has been shown to cause an early onset of sleep, but to increase wakefulness in the last half of the night. The interrelationship of alcohol with sleep is a matter of widespread concern. Both sedatives and alcohol are abused in attempts to obtain sleep. More definitive research is needed in this area.[19]

Psychiatric Problems Resulting in Altered Sleeping Patterns

The frequency and prevalence of depression increases with age and should be considered a possible cause for sleep disorders. Older people who are depressed have the same complaints as younger persons in regard to experiencing difficulties in falling asleep and awakening early in the morning. Sleep studies have shown that older depressed individuals have a different EEG pattern from normal older adults. These include a shortening in REM latency, decreased sleep time, and an increase in the number of shifts and arousals during the night.[20] These findings support the use of EEG sleep recordings as a diagnostic aid in evaluating sleep problems of older individuals.

As discussed in Chapter 6, reactive depressions often occur with the loss of the spouse or a series of losses. Insomnia frequently accompanies this kind of depression. If the depression does not improve over time, insomnia is likely to become the main complaint.

Individuals with endogenous depression, more or less a lifelong depression, usually develop periods of insomnia. If they are prolonged, it is possible the individual is seriously engaged in suicidal ruminations.

Practice Applications

The physical and emotional results of sleep deprivation have been well documented. Although sleep patterns change with aging, extreme daytime sleepiness and fatigue indicate problems of some kind that warrant the attention of a physician to determine cause and treatment. Throughout the literature on sleep disorders, there is an emphasis on the necessity of obtaining a careful and complete history of the disorder in order to make a diagnosis. Social workers can provide information in relation to the patient's complaints to aid the physician in making a diagnosis.

Social workers can also contribute to prevention of the development of some conditions by being aware of danger signals that indicate medical attention is needed. In many instances, such as sleep apnea and nocturnal myoclonus, the individuals are not aware of their sleep behavior. Information is needed from the spouse or other individuals close to the patient. When a physical problem is suspected, urging the client to seek a medical evaluation and providing resources such as transportation, name of a specific clinic, and so on may lead to amelioration of the problem or even be life-saving.

The kinds of information that may be useful to the physician to determine the basis of the problem involve not only the psychosocial history but physical data. The data must be obtained from the individual with the complaint and from the spouse. This includes a description of the client's 24-hour sleep pattern: whether there are difficulties in falling asleep, awakening extremely early, or both; periods of wakefulness throughout the night; occurrence of snoring or stoppage of breathing; frequency and duration of daytime napping; and extent of daytime sleepiness.

The area of daytime sleepiness must bear careful scrutiny. It is vital, for the physician's diagnostic purposes, to learn whether the individual is sleepy all the time (irresistibly sleepy), or at specific times, such as early afternoon after lunch or while reading, whether there is alertness or sleepiness during a normally exciting pastime, and so on.

Other areas to explore include presence of symptoms of cataplexy, hypnagogic hallucinations, and sleep paralysis; the amount of exercise or activity during waking hours; feelings of fatigue or the presence of an irresistible urge to sleep; the use of drugs or alcohol to induce sleep; the kind and amount of medication currently being taken, or whether there has recently been a discontinuation of medication.

Physicians find that having the client keep a record of nighttime and daytime sleeping often reveals that more time is spent sleeping than was realized. A detailed description of the onset of the sleep disorder in terms of age of occurrence, the specific time that the sleep pattern changed, and the events that occurred at the time is of the utmost importance in the identification of depression as a possible cause. In addition to careful history taking, social workers can reinforce the recommendations made by physicians to their patients in regard to medication, weight reduction, exercise, and so on.

The psychosocial problems that may arise from excessive sleepiness may be eased by social work intervention. Marital problems or other problems in interrelationships may ensue from a condition causing excessive daytime sleepiness.

Some older people may have been diagnosed years ago as having narcolepsy. They now may need a medical reevaluation in regard to the possibility of obstructive sleep apnea.

Being alert to the possibility that clients may turn to alcohol as an aid to falling asleep and urging them to seek medical attention may prevent a major problem. Referring chronic alcoholics and their family members to appropriate resources for assistance may be the first step toward their recovery.

If it is noted that the client has become less physically active and is napping frequently during the day, a more stimulating environment may be needed. Boredom and loneliness may be the greatest barriers to restful sleeping, as well as the basis of many other problems associated with old age.

MEDICATION

More than half the drugs currently being used were not even on the market a dozen or so years ago.[21] It is largely due to the appropriate prescription and administration of drugs that a great many older men and women continue to live independently in their communities.

Difficulties arise when medication is not prescribed as it should be and when it is not administered as prescribed. As a wide variety of medications consist of over-the-counter drugs, many of which are of dubious value, their misuse is a recurring problem.

Drug interaction is of great concern to physicians who may unintentionally overprescribe for a patient. Whenever the physician does not know about all the drugs that a patient is taking, whether prescribed or over-the-counter, the danger of harmful drug interaction exists.

Another problem arises from the habit many older people have of exchanging medication. Although the drug may help the person for whom it was prescribed, it may be harmful for the friend, if for no other reason than that it may interact undesirably with another medication.

Older people all too frequently harm themselves by taking too much medication. In a study conducted by the New York-Cornell Medical Center, one out of every four patients made errors in self-medication. All patients taking 5 or 6 medications daily consistently made at least one error.[22]

Many older clients freely admit that they have trouble remembering to take their medication. As the number of tablets and capsules for one individual may range from 5 to 20 or more in one day, mistakes in medication are understandable. A contributing factor may also be the number of tranquilizing drugs taken. Four psychotropic substances (chlordiazepoxide, glutethimide, phenobarbital, and diazepam) are among the ten most-prescribed drugs for persons aged 65 and older.[23]

As noted earlier, a number of older people are not aware that marked changes in physiologic functioning occur with aging that cause drugs to affect older people differently. Changes in the cardiovascular system, renal and central nervous system, and general changes in body composition are significant areas of concern in relation to drug management, as they lead to altered distribution of drugs.[24]

Practice Applications

As overmedication appears to be a major problem, the social worker may need to stress the importance of understanding the amount to be taken and the intervals between dosage. Clients may be helped to work out a daily medication plan. Some older people place their medication in the same place each day, measured out for the day, with a card stating times. There are also many devices in drugstores that may be purchased which keep medication in order with little effort.

Social workers should also be aware that older clients sometimes skimp on medication because they are unable to buy all that has been prescribed. They may take lesser amounts or wait longer intervals between dosage than has been prescribed in an effort to obtain at least some help from the medication.

Older individuals may need reminding that they must keep their physicians, if there is more than one, informed about every medication they are taking, including all over-the-counter medication, such as aspirin and laxatives. This includes medication prescribed by dentists and oral surgeons.

Social workers might suggest that their older clients ask their pharmacists to keep a file of their prescription medication and include over-the-counter purchases. The individual could then take a copy of the list on visits to the physician. In communities with large concentrations of older people, the social worker may suggest this to the pharmacists with the observation that this practice would provide a public service and a means of creating goodwill among their older patrons.

Resources may be located for education about specific drugs, drug usage, and the importance of avoiding under- or over-medication. Arranging talks about medication presented by pharmacists, physicians, or nurses to patient groups or community groups may be helpful.

Finally, being alerted to the medication that an older client is using—the kind, amount, and purpose of the medication; and how, when, and where the medication is being administered—may help in preventing the misuse of drugs and the possible ensuing detrimental effects.

The following brief case example may provide some idea of how a social worker may be alert to misuse of medication.

CASE EXAMPLE: MISUSE OF MEDICATION

The intake social worker at a community mental health center is taking the psychosocial history of a 70-year-old woman, Miss Hanes. She has been brought to the clinic by her niece. The niece has infrequent contact with Miss Hanes, who is her deceased mother's sister. However, once or twice a year she takes food and clothing to her, as she seems to be barely surviving on Social Security. The niece believes her aunt has "gone crazy" since she last saw her. She can give little background information except that she has never seen her aunt act irrationally until the occasion of her visit the day before. Her aunt seemed confused and "out of her head," but not physically ill. The niece had considered taking her directly to the "asylum" but had decided to drop by the mental health clinic first.

The social worker gains the attention of the client and asks her questions to ascertain her orientation. Miss Hanes does not know where she is or how she arrived. She answers questions about her health but contradicts herself, saying that she has both high and low blood pressure, a cardiac condition, arthritis, insomnia, and tuberculosis.

To the social worker, Miss Hanes appears intoxicated or possibly impaired by a stroke, rather than mentally ill. Her eyes are glazed and she speaks with difficulty. The social worker asks her about medication she is taking. Miss Hanes, at that point, suddenly empties her handbag on the desk. Dozens of pills, of various sizes and colors, roll out and fall on the floor, along with partially empty bottles and boxes.

The social worker refers the client to a neighboring hospital emergency room and suggests the niece talk with the social worker at the hospital after her aunt is evaluated. Later she calls the social worker at the hospital and finds that Miss Hanes has been taking an assortment of drugs prescribed by a variety of physicians. It is believed that Miss Hanes had become confused as a result of taking a mixture of drugs and made mistakes in dosages which, if continued, could have become fatal.

Miss Hanes is treated at the city hospital and her medication carefully examined and greatly reduced. Social work services are provided and additional financial assistance is obtained through the city's welfare program. Miss Hanes is able to return home in a much better state of health and the likelihood of more careful attention to her health and medication needs by the city hospital staff.

In this case, the social worker did not assume that the client was a mental patient and concentrate only on the psychodynamics of the client. Since the social worker knew that a health condition or the misuse of medication could also cause behavior that appeared psychotic, she explored that possibility. Assessing only the mental status would have resulted in failure to detect the source of the problem.

NUTRITION

There are a number of concerns in relation to aging and nutrition that continue to be expressed by physicians, health-care workers, and those most involved: the older population. Misunderstandings in relation to the United States Recommended Daily Allowances, the need for and difficulties encountered in research, general guidelines for good nutrition, vulnerability to dietary deficiencies, and resources for older people are discussed in this section.

The RDA (United States Recommended Daily Allowances)

The RDA originally were developed as a guide for planning and obtaining food supplies for national defense. They were first published in 1943 to provide standards to serve as a goal for good nutrition, but were not considered permanent. The report has been revised a number of times, at approximately five-year intervals, as more data became available. The purposes of RDA have become much broader and include establishment of guides for public food assistance programs, the development of new food products by industry, and establishment of guidelines for nutritional labeling of foods.[25]

Although many individuals refer to RDA in order to check the nutritional quality of their diets, the RDA are not intended as requirements for a specific individual but are established for population groups composed of healthy people. Special needs for nutrients that arise from conditions such as inherited metabolic disorders, chronic disease, and so on are not covered by the RDA.[26] There is also an underlying assumption that food will be selected from a wide variety of choices so that individuals will consume an adequate amount of the nutrients known to be needed, but for which no allowance has been set.[27]

RDA are estimated in such a way that the daily nutritional requirements would be met for most healthy individuals, yet one who eats less than the amount recommended for such nutrients may not have an inadequate diet for those nutrients. However, since the requirements for a specific individual are unknown, the more often an individual's intake drops below the RDA and the longer it continues, the greater the risk of deficiency for that person.[28]

Need for Research

The need for systematic, well-controlled nutrition research in relation to aging is an area of great concern, but there are many problems presented by this population. Shock points out that nutritionists and gerontologists have related problems. The gerontologist does not have a clear index for an older person's functional age, and the nutritionist is still trying to work out an index of nutritional status for older people; both nutrition and aging are processes that are the net result of many individual events; and in both fields, there are also a number of "faddists and charlatans with ready 'cures' for aging."[29]

Two major difficulties in developing information in regard to nutritional requirements of older adults are described by Calloway: the differences in work patterns, which suggest that changes in men may not occur in the same way as in women; and the small number of older people who may be termed 'healthy older people'.[30] In traditional families, women continue to follow their usual homemaking activities, whereas many men leave an occupation that required activity for a more sedentary life in their later years, although the opposite may occur. Studies of 'healthy older people' may include a number who have subclinical diabetes, mild hypertension, arthritis, or some other problem. They may be taking medication that would affect their nutritional status when it is compared with others who are not on medication. If older individuals who have such conditions are excluded from study, there remains a very small population of 'healthy older people'.[31]

Nutritionists are concerned about changes that accompany aging and the ways they may interfere with nutrition. These changes include the following:

1. There is a decline with age in the basal metabolism rate. Starting in the third decade of life, lean body mass, or muscle, decreases at a rate of 1 percent per year. There is less need for calories, but they must be high-quality calories.[32]

2. Changes occur in the senses of taste and smell. This often results in a tendency to select saltier foods or use larger amounts of salt, which consists of 40 percent sodium and 60 percent chloride. Overuse of sodium is a factor associated with high blood pressure.

3. The loss of teeth and use of dentures may reduce the consumption of fibrous foods. A great many older people are edentulous. When they were children, the benefits of fluoridation were unknown, and the primary remedy for aching teeth was extraction. About 60 percent of all men and women between 65 and 74 have untreated dental problems.[33]

4. There is reduced motility and enzyme activity in the gastrointestinal tract, associated with aging. Certain foods, such as dairy products, may be avoided by some older people because these foods cause digestive problems.[34]

5. There is a decrease in the ability of the stomach to absorb Vitamin B12, due to less secretion of acid and another factor necessary for its absorption. Consequently, iron, which needs the acid to be well absorbed by the body, and vitamin B12 are two potential deficiency problems in older people.[35]

6. Kidney function is also changed by aging. An enzyme is provided by the kidney that converts vitamin D from an inactive form, the way it is taken in the diet, to an active form that works in the body. This conversion is not as ably done by the older kidney. As vitamin D is the most important mechanism for absorbing calcium and putting it into the bones, many experimental trials are being made in relation to the use of vitamin D in the treatment of osteoporosis.[36]

Because of these and other physiological changes, in addition to the effects of chronic diseases which prevail among older people, many nutritionists believe that the dietary needs of the older population may be significantly different from those of young and middle-aged adults. However, until further guidelines are developed based on more research, the U.S. Department of Agriculture and the U.S. Department of Health and Human Services provide some general guidelines.

General Guidelines for Good Nutrition

- Eat a variety of foods.
- Maintain ideal weight.
- Avoid too much fat, saturated fat, and cholesterol.
- Eat foods with adequate starch and fiber.
- Avoid too much sodium.
- If you drink alcohol, do so in moderation.[37]

A "variety of foods" refers to a well-balanced diet including foods from the four major food groups: fruits and vegetables; whole-grain and enriched breads, cereals, and grain products, such as rice or pasta; fish, poultry, meat, eggs, dry peas and beans; and milk, cheese, and yogurt.[38]

Nutritionists have other suggestions for older people in relation to dairy products, phosphates, fiber, alcohol, and salt. Instead of avoiding dairy products completely, because they may be difficult to digest, ingesting smaller amounts many times during the day make it possible to obtain calcium. As there is some evidence pointing to an increase of calcium loss through the urine as a result of a diet high in phosophorous and protein, decreasing the intake of the amount of phosphorous (contained in many carbonated drinks) and protein is important.[39] As mentioned in an earlier chapter, there is some evidence linking osteoporosis with a decrease in calcium intake.

Colon cancer and diverticulosis have been associated with the lack of fiber in the diet in this country. Simply increasing the intake of fiber is not considered a solution, for many older people have difficulty in chewing and digesting some kinds of fibrous foods. There are some common soft foods, such as cooked carrots, which provide fiber.[40] A few tablespoons of unprocessed bran added to cereal and other foods is acceptable; however, excessive intake of bran can decrease the body's absorption of minerals such as iron and calcium.[41]

As excess weight is a factor in diabetes, heart disease, and high blood pressure, the intake of fatty foods, sweets, salty snacks, high-calorie drinks, and alcohol should be limited. They are high in calories but low in nutrients.[42]

Since the amount of sodium may be a problem due to its role in water retention and hypertension, older people with mild hypertension may be advised not to add salt, but those with severe hypertension should have a progressively decreased sodium intake. As 1–2 grams daily (1000–2000 milligrams) is the suggested goal, foods that are unprocessed or have been minimally processed should be used. Seasonings such as oregano, garlic, and basil may be used to enhance flavor.[43]

Nutritionists are also concerned with the question as to whether the aging process can be delayed or changed by altering eating patterns early in life. Artherosclerosis, cancer of the colon, and osteoporosis are among the diseases associated with long-term eating patterns. Changing the diet may prevent further progression of some conditions and may even improve the conditions in some cases.[44]

Vulnerability to Deficiencies

Shock points out that dietary deficiencies are seldom found among normal people living in the community, but that deficiencies in specific nutritional elements are found among poor and disadvantaged older adults. He observes that older people are more vulnerable to dietary deficiencies due to their reduced food intake and sameness of diet.[45]

There are other factors associated with aging that often prevent older people from obtaining adequate nutrition. Many older adults have their meals alone due to widowhood, physical or mental disabilities, or lack of transportation. Solitary dining does not whet the appetite, for food is associated with special events and with socializing with others.

Poor vision interferes with meal preparation. There may be difficulty in measuring ingredients, reading recipes, and judging doneness of food. In these circumstances, cooking may be perceived as too much of a chore, and snacking may replace balanced meals. Decreases in vision, along with sensory losses of taste and smell, interfere with the aesthetic appeal of food.

Illness of the wife may make it necessary for the husband to assume responsibility for meal preparation. In some households the husband has rarely undertaken any domestic responsibilities and is unable or unwilling to shop for groceries or prepare meals.

Older people who are disabled from arthritis or other conditions may abstain from food preparation to avoid the strain on their painful muscles and joints.

Search for "Eternal Youth"

Some older individuals are less concerned about dietary deficiencies than they are about the effects of aging; they purchase vitamin supplements in the hope of ameliorating the effects. Large doses of Vitamin E are sometimes taken in the expectation that this substance will delay aging. There are no controlled studies to support theories attributing maintenance of youth by using vitamin E.[46] Some vitamins taken in large amounts can be dangerous. Too much vitamin A can eventually cause liver and bone damage. Kidney damage in adults can be caused by high doses of vitamin D.[47]

It is important to note that dietary supplements are helpful to some older people who have dietary deficiencies due to causes such as digestive difficulties which interfere with their obtaining required nutrients. Consulting with a physician or dietitian before taking a supplement is recommended to those who believe they need vitamins of some kind. The individual's health status and diet can then be examined in the event that other steps need to be taken to improve nutrition.[48]

Butler points out that pharmacologic guidelines are also needed in relation to diet. As the intake of drugs, both prescribed and over-the-counter, increases with age, there is increased risk of an unfavorable reaction between drugs and food.[49]

Government Role in Nutrition

The U.S. government addressed the nutritional needs of older people with the appropriation of nearly $100 million in 1973 to establish the Nutritional Program for Older Americans (NPOA), as mandated by the 1972 Title VII amendment to the Older Americans Act of 1965. Funding has increased steadily each year. The legislative mandate of the Title VII program called for the development of a nationwide nutritional program to provide meals in community settings with easy access by the older population. Health goals and supportive components were also part of this mandate, but they have not received the emphasis needed to provide implementation. Emphasis has been on the provision and serving of meals.

According to an estimate by the AoA (Administration on Aging) at the end of the first-quarter fiscal year 1978, over one-fifth of those who participated in the program were minority older people, and 66 percent were low-income.[50] Most studies of the Title VII program reveal that the major effects of the program have been on financial savings, improved socialization, and enhanced morale and life satisfaction. In other significant areas—improved health, nutrition, and diet-related behavior—the program has had a more variable impact. The reasons for this are believed to lie in the low overall frequency of program participation, the high annual rate of participant dropout, the underserving of the elderly in relation to their concentration in the population, low supportive service delivery in relation to meal delivery, difficulties in peer interaction, variable quality and appropriateness of meals, and competing activities which interfere with participation.[51]

Social workers need to familiarize themselves with the nutritional program (which is now under Title III of the Older Americans Act) in their communities in order to bring about change in the areas discussed in the preceding paragraphs.

Practice Applications

The client's eating habits must be taken into consideration when evaluating the home condition and life-style. Inquiry as to where and with whom meals are eaten, how and where meals are purchased and prepared, and the dietary content are within the realm of social work concern. The social worker in the community setting may refer the client who has dietary questions to a dietitian, home economist, or nutritionist in the public health services, medical clinics or hospitals, senior citizens center, county extension office in rural communities, and to local heart and diabetic association offices.

The social worker in health-care settings, as a member of the health-care team, has the opportunity to provide input in the development of nutrition programs for older patients attending outpatient clinics. In nursing homes or other boarding institutions, the amount and quality of food can at least be noted and recommendations made.

A resource available in most communities in addition to the government food-site program is that of Meals on Wheels programs. These are usually provided by religious or civic organizations or senior citizen centers. In some communities, Human Services Departments may authorize and pay for the meals served to individuals who receive old-age assistance or have a very small income. A hot luncheon meal is delivered once a day, usually five days a week. A cold supper is also sometimes provided. There may be a small fee, but, in most paying programs, there are many who are unable to pay, and they are not required to do so.

The following brief case example emphasizes social work intervention in providing nutritional needs.

CASE EXAMPLE: IDENTIFYING NUTRITIONAL NEEDS

A social worker from protective services visits the apartment of Mr. and Mrs. James, a frail-appearing couple in their eighties who have been referred by a neighbor. The neighbor is concerned about the apartment being a "fire trap" and causing the entire building to burn down.

The social worker finds a number of newspapers and cardboard boxes, but no other fire hazards. He also notices that there is almost nothing in the kitchen to eat. As he talks with the couple, he learns that they are receiving a noon meal from a Meals on Wheels service which is provided only once a day and not at all on weekends. They order pizzas on week-ends and sometimes during the week, as they can have them delivered, but the result is gastric distress for both of them.

The social worker learns that neither of them is able to shop for groceries, although they have money to pay for whatever food they need. Mr. James receives a pension which is more than ample to meet their needs. Mrs. James has crippling arthritis in her hands, wrists, and ankles. Mr. James has congestive heart disease and has been advised not to try to shop for or carry groceries.

The social worker suggests they pay a neighbor to do the shopping. Mrs. James nods, but her husband stridently objects to "forking out money" for this service. The social worker discusses the possibility of one or both of them becoming ill from a lack of proper nutrients and the additional costs that would ensue. Finally, with some reluctance, the husband agrees. Mrs. James delightedly announces that she knows the person who will shop for them.

They immediately start making a grocery list, and the social worker realizes that the items do not comprise the elements of a balanced, nutritious diet. Thinking quickly, he comments that he knows of a way for the Jameses to have assistance in deciding what to buy and possibly save some money: by making use of a dietitian service offered by the health department to older people.

Mr. James agrees to this suggestion. The social worker leaves the apartment with a feeling of relief.

In this case, the social worker noticed the lack of food in the apartment and explored the reason for it. He made an effort to learn about the eating habits of the older couple and knew enough about nutrition to recognize their inability to plan appropriately for their food needs. He knew of a suitable resource and is able to help the couple make use of it by appealing to the client's concern about money, instead of stressing other factors that might have alienated the client.

EXERCISE

The interest in physical fitness that has swept the nation has had its effects on older and chronically ill men and women who formerly thought they were too old to exercise. As more research is reported, attitudes are changing. Regular physical activity or exercise is thought to slow the aging process, and there is some evidence that exercise may even reverse some parts of the aging process. Many individuals whose health conditions were once considered too risky for exercise are now encouraged to exercise, within certain restrictions.

There are some differences in the physiological responses of older adults to exercise. However, there is no longer any doubt that the health benefits from exercise are similar to those obtained by young and middle-aged adults.[52]

There are losses in functional capacity that are reported in the scientific literature as age changes, but which may be the result of other causes. Both maximum cardiac output and maximum ventilation decrease. There is a gradual decrease in the strength of skeletal muscles and a loss of some capacity for muscular endurance. An actual loss of muscle occurs: 3–5 percent of total muscle tissue is lost per decade with old age. The combined effect of these losses is loss of ability to transport oxygen from the air around us to the cells and to make optimum use of oxygen at the cell level. In turn, there is a loss of vigor; about 50 percent of this loss occurs in men by the time they are 75, and women have similar losses. De Vries suggests that these functional losses may be hypothesized as resulting from at least three contributing factors: an increasingly sedentary life-style, unrecognized incipient disease processes, and true aging phenomena. He observes that the first factor can be reversed easily, as physical conditioning can slow down the agewise losses in the functional capacities of older people.[53]

Potential benefits that occur with an increase in physical activity include improvements in the cardiovascular and pulmonary systems: lower heart rate, better air passage and lung function, lower rate and depth of breathing, and greater efficiency of the total body. Vulnerability to rhythm disturbances in the heart is decreased. Physical activity helps the body adapt to hot and cold temperature. There is also less perceived effort with every task if functional reserves are maintained.[54]

It has been found that bone mass can be increased by exercise, strengthening bones, and thereby decreasing chances of fractures, and improving flexibility, which can reduce arthritic pain.[55] In a study of 40 older people—20 in an experimental group (mean age 71.8 years) who exercised three times a week for one hour over a 12-week period and 20 in a control group (mean age 73) who did not participate in organized exercise during that time—there was an average increase in flexibility of 22.6 percent in the experimental group and an average decline of 3.75 percent in the control group.[56]

Although we tend to think of exercise as vigorous, bouncing, and jumping about, chair exercises can also be beneficial. A study using chair exercises indicated that physical activity can have favorable effects on bone mass. In the study, 30 older women, 18 of whom acted as controls and 12 as participants, were in an exercise group for 40 to 45 minutes three days a week for three years. The exercise was done from a sitting position in straight-backed chairs. The kinds of exercise selected were based on a treadmill test taken by the participants. Bone mineral measurements were obtained ten times during the three years. A 3.2 percent loss occurred in the control group, whereas a 2.29 percent increase was obtained by the physical activity group, indicating that bone will respond to stress placed upon it despite age.[57]

Although only a limited amount of research has been done, some of it contradictory, there appears to be general acceptance of the idea that exercise is beneficial to *emotional* well-being. This may be due in part to the physiological improvements that result from exercise. Wisner observes that there also may be a change of emotionality due to changes in body image and/or availability of more positive psychosocial stimuli.[58]

Practice Applications

Many older people are fearful of exercising and sometimes refrain from all types of exercise. It is probable that some older women and some older men would participate in organized exercise programs but feel self-conscious about their appearance. Having separate classes for men and women may be helpful to some extent, although there may be resistance to this also. The physical therapist, nurse, or other health professional may need to design an individual exercise program that the person can follow at home alone.

Social workers do not prescribe exercises, as the client may have underlying conditions that contraindicate certain kinds of exercise. They may suggest that the older client seek advice from the physician as to appropriate exercise. Health fairs are often conducted in senior citizen centers and other designated places in the community which may provide an opportunity for older people to inquire about the amount and kind of exercise that is safe for them to attempt.

Older clients may require help in locating an exercise class or a place to carry out exercise. Senior citizen centers usually have exercise classes not only for the well person, but for individuals with disabling conditions. Adult education programs sponsored by local school systems often provide a class for older people, as do church groups and Y groups. Shopping malls in many cities open early every day to allow walkers to use the malls. Some churches have gymnasiums and indoor tracks for their members, but invite nonmembers to use them.

Social workers may also find the following resources helpful:

1. The National Association of Governors' Councils on Physical Fitness and Sports. This was organized to complement the President's Council on Physical Fitness and Sports. At least 32 states are affiliated with these autonomous programs. In addition to sponsoring programs in schools in regard to life-style activities, many councils are beginning daily fitness programs at nutritional sites, senior citizen centers, and homes for the elderly.

2. Senior olympics are competitive events conducted in many states through the Governors' Council, corporations such as Blue Cross/Blue Shield, teachers' organizations, and other volunteer organizations.

Olympic activities include swimming, freethrow, bike races, race walking, sprinting, and golf. The olympic programs offer many opportunities for socializing, in addition to the competitive events. They are sometimes held on college campuses, which provide inexpensive lodging and meals. Some local Blue Cross/Blue Shield organizations provide information in regard to initiating senior olympic competitions.

NOTES

1. William C. Dement, *Foreword*, *Sleeping and Waking Disorders: Indications and Techniques*, ed. Christian Guilleminault (Menlo Park, Calif.: Addison-Wesley Publishing Co., 1982), xiii.

2. Ibid., xiv.

3. Peter Hauri, "Evaluating Disorders of Initiating and Maintaining Sleep (DIMS)," *Sleeping and Waking Disorders*, 226.

4. Henry Kellerman, *Sleep Disorders: Insomnia and Narcolepsy* (New York: Brunner/Mazel, Publishers, 1981), 136.

5. William C. Orr, Kenneth Z. Altshuler, and Monte L. Stahl, *Managing Sleep Complaints* (Chicago: Year Book Medical Publishers, Inc., 1982), 16.

6. Ibid., 17.

7. Kellerman, *Sleep Disorders*, 145.

8. Patricia N. Prinz and Murray Raskind, "Aging and Sleep Disorders," *Sleep Disorders: Diagnosis and Treatment*, ed. Robert L. Williams, Ismet Karacan, and Shervert H. Frazier (New York: John Wiley & Sons, 1978), 306.

9. Orr, Altshuler, and Stahl, *Sleep Complaints*, 17, 18.

10. *Consensus Conference.* "Drugs and Insomnia," *Journal of the American Medical Association*, 251, no. 18 (May 1984): 2410–2414.

11. Christian Guilleminault and William C. Dement, "Sleep Apnea Syndromes and Related Sleep Disorders" in *Sleep Disorders*, 9.

12. Ibid., 11.

13. Orr, Altshuler, and Stahl, *Managing Sleep Complaints*, 86.

14. Kellerman, *Sleep Disorders*, vi.

15. Ismet Karacan, Constance A. Moore, and Robert L. Williams, "The Narcoleptic Syndrome," *Psychiatric Annals* 9, no. 7 (July 1979): 377, 378.

16. Ibid., 380.

17. Orr, Altshuler, and Stahl, *Managing Sleep Complaints*, 144.

18. Ibid., 33.

19. Alex D. Pokorny, "Sleep Disturbances, Alcohol, and Alcoholism: A Review," in *Sleep Disorders: Diagnosis and Treatment*, 255, 256.

20. David J. Kupfer et al., "Electroencephalographic Sleep Recordings and Depression in the Elderly," *Journal of the American Geriatrics Society* 26, no. 2 (February 1978): 53–57.

21. *Using Your Medicines Wisely: A Guide for the Elderly*, U.S. Government Publication, Washington, D.C., 1981.

22. Joanne Olson and Judith Johnson, "Drug Misuse Among the Elderly," *Journal of Gerontological Nursing*, 4, no. 6 (Nov.–Dec. 1978): 13.

23. Alexander Simon, "The Neuroses, Personality Disorders, Alcoholism, Drug Use and Misuse, and Crime in the Aged," in *Handbook of Mental Health and Aging*, ed. James E. Birren and R. Bruce Sloan (Englewood Cliffs, N.J.: Prentice-Hall, Inc., 1980), 664.

24. Matthew E. Ochs, Janice T. Callaway, Thomas C. Shank, "Physiologic & Pharmacokinetic Alterations in Aging," *American Association for Clinical Chemistry* 8, no. 10 (March 1984): 8.

25. National Academy of Sciences/National Research Council, *United States Recommended Dietary Allowances*, 9th ed., rev. (Washington, D.C.: National Academy of Sciences, 1980), v.

26. Ibid., 1.

27. Ibid., 6.

28. Ibid., 10.

29. Nathan W. Shock, "The Role of Nutrition in Aging," *Journal of the American College of Nutrition* 1;3–9 (1982): 8.

30. Doris H. Calloway, "Nutrition and Aging," in *Summary of Minutes*, 24. The Fifteenth Meeting of the National Advisory Council on Aging, January 28–30, 1980.

31. Ibid., 208.

32. Robert N. Butler, "Nutrition and the Physiology of Aging," in *Nutrition in the 1980's: Constraints on Our Knowledge* (New York: Alan R. Liss, Inc., 1981): 208.

33. Carole Allen and Herman Brotman, comps., *Chartbook on Aging in America, the 1981 White House Conference on Aging*, (Washington, D.C.: Superintendent of Documents, n.d.): 82.

34. S. Jaime Rozovski, "Nutrition for Older Americans," *Nutrition and Health* 5, no. 3 (1983): 1.

35. Myron Winick, "Nutritional Considerations for the Active Senior," in *A Synopsis of the National Conference on Fitness and Aging*, September 10–11, 1981, Shoreham Hotel, Washington, D.C., 26.

36. Ibid.

37. *Nutrition and Your Health: Dietary Guidelines for Americans*, (Washington, D.C.: Government Printing Office, 1980).

38. Ibid.

39. Rozovski, "Nutrition for Americans," 1, 2.

40. Ibid.

41. "Nutrition: A Lifelong Concern", *Age Page*, September 1984, (Washington, D.C.: U.S. Government Printing Office.

42. Ibid.

43. Maudene Nelson, "Dietary Guidelines," *Nutrition and Health*, 5, no. 3 (1983): 4.

44. Myron Winick, "Nutrition for the Elderly," *Nutrition and Health* 1, no. 6 (1979): 1.

45. Shock, "The Role of Nutrition in Aging," 3.

46. "Questions and Answers," *Nutrition and Health* 1, no. 6 (1979): 6.

47. U.S. Department of Health and Human Services, *Age Page*, (Washington, D.C.: U.S. Government Printing Office, 1983).

48. Ibid.

49. Butler, "Nutrition and Aging", 1.

50. Barbara Posner, *Nutrition, Planning, and the Elderly: Policy Development, Program Planning, and Evaluation* (Lexington, Massachusetts: Lexington Books, 1979), xix.

51. Ibid., 173.

52. Henry de Vries, "Functional Fitness for Older Americans," in *National Conference on Fitness and Aging*, 27.

53. Ibid.

54. Samuel M. Fox, III, "Health and Heart Enhancement," in *National Conference on Fitness and Aging*, 18, 19.

55. "Exercise for Older Americans," *Healthfinder*, National Health Information Clearinghouse, Washington, D.C.

56. Everett L. Smith, "Physical Activity: The Foundation of Youth in Aging" in *National Conference on Fitness and Aging*, 30.

57. Ibid., 31.

58. Robert A. Wiswell, "Relaxation, Exercise, and Aging" in *Handbook of Mental Health*, 943.

10

PRESERVING SEXUAL VIGOR THROUGHOUT LIFE

Sexual expression as a vital part of each person's identity and a major part of life force is a familiar concept, but social attitudes have denied the existence of a sexual component in the lives of older men and women. Only recently has there been an emphasis on sexual expression continuing through life, helping the individual to maintain a sense of self and satisfying the need for physical closeness to another human being.

The association of sexuality with old age is frequently viewed with distaste, disgust, disbelief, or derision. Reluctance to consider older adults as sexual objects may be due in part to the incest taboo. It is very difficult for most people to think of sex in connection with parental figures.

Sexual activity has traditionally been associated with youth. Sex is viewed as important and "natural" for the young, but depraved and immoral for the old. It is "natural" to think of a young man approaching a young woman in search of sex, but "unnatural" to think of a 75-year-old man interested in a 70-year-old woman for the same reason. These strong negative societal attitudes affect older people's attitudes about themselves. There are accounts by clinicians of couples in their seventies and eighties who have considered themselves immoral or depraved, because they continued to be sexually active.

Sexuality is also sometimes considered in a very limited way as involving only passion. Sexuality also includes intimacy and closeness, the sharing of private thoughts and feelings. The need for tenderness, affection, touching, and being touched are needs that do not disappear with age. Each of us needs to have close physical contact with other human beings. Ignoring, disclaiming, or deriding the sexual component of aged individuals tends to push the older adult out of the mainstream of life.

ATTITUDES TOWARD OLDER MEN

The words "dirty old man" have become a common derogatory phrase. Although often used in a joking manner, the underlying idea attributes lechery to older men. The association of old men with the commitment of sexual offenses against children is made, although sexual offenses do not appear to be a frequent occurrence. In one study of 141 patients committed as "sexually dangerous," only 11—between 7 and 8 percent—were over 60 years old.[1]

In a survey of 796 college students, 19.2 percent of the women and 8.6 percent of the men had been sexually victimized as children. However, men over 50 years old comprised "only a tiny fraction" of the offenders.[2]

When sexual offenses do occur, exhibitionism or pedophilic activities which involve caressing without physically harming or injuring are the more likely forms of offenses made by older persons. Whiskin observes that older people long for the warmth and comfort of youthful contact. Although it is considered natural for older women to hug and fondle children, older men are confined to a "salutory pat." He points out that there may be an element, in pedophilia and exhibitionism, of attempting to prove maleness along with an effort to obtain a more passive kind of sexual gratification.[3]

EARLY SEXUAL ATTITUDES OF TODAY'S OLDER GENERATION

It is difficult for today's younger generation to understand the earlier attitudes toward sex and sexual expression that existed when members of today's older population were young. As observed in Chapter 1, during the formative years of most of today's older men and women, sex was an unmentioned and unmentionable word. Only the reproductive aspect of sex was considered, and many myths prevailed that are still believed by a great many older people. As an example, in a study conducted with 100 women from 60 to 94 years of age, 61 percent believed masturbation causes mental illness.[4]

In recent years there have been studies in regard to sex and aging that have received attention. Unfortunately the studies have been few and the samples small. More studies with larger samples are needed. However, reports of the studies that have been conducted, as well as articles in popular magazines about the continuation of sexuality throughout life, seem to be helping to dispel some of the negative thinking about sexual activity and age.

There are physiological changes with aging that affect the reproductive organs and functions of the sexual response cycle in both men and women. The changes are not abrupt, but occur gradually over a number of years. There are also many other factors that contribute to loss of libido. However, it is essential to keep in mind that sexual activity is possible well into old age.

Many older (and younger) men and women have a confused or incomplete understanding of the changes in the reproductive system that occur with aging. The following section deals with these changes, which may affect sexual attitudes and performance.

CHANGES IN THE REPRODUCTIVE SYSTEM

Estrogen and progesterone secretions begin to decline in women when they are in their forties and proceed to decrease rapidly when they are in their fifties and sixties. If removal of the ovaries by surgery becomes necessary, the symptoms of menopause occur suddenly. In men, the production of the male hormone, testosterone, occurs throughout the life span, but gradually decreases with age.

In a review of the three major studies on the physiologic ability to maintain sexual functioning in old age, Berman and Lief give the following findings.

In men, these are the most consistent findings: (1) although erective ability is maintained consistently in the absence of illness, there is a need for greater direct general stimulation to achieve erection, and erection is slower; (2) there is often absence of preejaculatory 'seeping'; (3) the stage of ejaculatory inevitability is briefer (and may be absent in cases of testosterone deficiency, or if ejaculation has been long delayed in order to stimulate the partner); (4) the amount of seminal fluid is decreased, and (5) there is a rapid loss of erection following ejaculation, with a longer refractory period; (6) most crucially, the need and ability for ejaculation at each sexual contact is markedly reduced. Sensations become less genital, but more sensuous and diffused. It is crucial for both male and female to know that orgasmic return in the sense of an obvious ejaculation is not necessary or desirable at each coital connection.

In the aging female: (1) lubrication is slower, and more direct stimulation is needed; (2) the orgasmic phase may be shorter; (3) particularly with low levels of estrogen, there may be irritability of vaginal tissues, pain on clitoral stimulation, or painful uterine spasms during orgasm. These are easily treated with estrogen replacement. The capacity to have orgasm, including multiple orgasm, remains unimpaired.[5]

For many years, estrogen therapy was prescribed to alleviate problems resulting from hormone deprivation. However, in more recent times, since the adverse effects of hormone replacement therapy became known, physicians and their women patients very carefully weigh the risks against the advantages of hormone replacement. As many women do not receive hormone replacement therapy during menopause or after surgery, sexual activities of older people may be more affected by the absence of this type of therapy than is generally acknowledged.

Prolapse of the uterus, rectoceles (hernial protrusion of the rectum into the vagina), and cystoceles (hernial protrusion of the urinary bladder through the vaginal wall) may occur in women who have had children. These conditions interfere with sexual activity. Prescribed exercise may be helpful in some cases, or surgery may be required to correct these conditions.

Masters and Johnson emphasize that aging does not cause loss of the facility to achieve erection.[6] For both men and women, reasonably good health and the availability of an interested and interesting sexual partner are necessary for continued sexual functioning.[7]

The physiological changes that occur with age may be alarming to men and their sexual partners, if they do not understand that they are normal and that sexual capability is not at an end. In women the onset of menopause is a specific change that signifies the end of the reproductive cycle and makes women aware that significant changes are taking place in their bodies. Since men do not have such an identifiable event, they may not be as aware of changes that are occurring until there is a difference in their sexual responses. There is a need for both sexes to have information about the way their bodies have changed and the effects on sexual functioning. The provision of knowledge and reassurances may help older people to maintain their sexual proficiency.

CONTINUANCE OF SEXUAL ACTIVITY

According to research, older men are more interested in continuing sexual activity and continue being more sexually active than older women. One such study, a longitudinal study of aging and human development, began at Duke University in 1954. Data have been obtained on past and present sexual behavior as part of the study concerned with somatic, psychological, and social changes associated with old age. The study began with 254 subjects ranging in age from 60 to 94, with about the same number of men and women. The number gradually lessened as subjects died, became ill or disabled, or left the study for other reasons.[8]

The opportunity to cross-validate some of the information was provided by 31 intact married couples. At the start of the study, of the men whose health, intellectual status, and social functioning were not significantly impaired, 80 percent reported sexual interest and 70 percent reported regular sexual activity. Ten years later, the proportion of those who were sexually interested had not declined, but the proportion of sexually active had declined to 25 percent.

About one-third of the sample of women whose health, intellectual status, and sexual functioning were not significantly impaired at the start of the study reported sexual interest, with one-fifth stating sexual activity. Ten years later, this proportion did not decline in regard to sexual interest or activity.[9]

The differences between the women and men in regard to sexual interest and activity may be due to the disproportionate number of older women to older men, which enables older men to have more opportunities for sexual activity. In addition, there is little or no social stigma attached to older men having relationships with younger women. Women are more likely to be widowed and are less likely to seek younger men as sexual partners. Men may overreport sexual activity in order to maintain a traditional attitude of appropriate masculine interest. Women may underreport sexual interest and activity as a result of being socialized to believe they "shouldn't" have such feelings or activities.

ATTITUDES ASSOCIATED WITH LOSS OF LIBIDO

Libido does not depend wholly on hormonal secretions. Older women may avoid sexual relations. Because they feel unattractive and undesirable, they may fear rejection.

Impotence in men may be caused by fear of failure. Male *fear* of impotence is often noted as a powerful threat to potency; the presence of morning erections is considered a good indication of psychogenic impotence.

Older adults may feel they "shouldn't" have sexual feelings or desires, reflecting societal attitudes, and repress them. Negative feelings, such as resentment and anger, toward the spouse may interfere with libido. Older people who did not enjoy sexual activity in their younger years may consider themselves no longer obliged to continue sexual performance.

PHYSICAL CONDITIONS THAT MAY INTERFERE
WITH SEXUAL ACTIVITY

The majority of older men and women have at least one chronic medical condition; some have several. The physical disabilities that accompany some diseases may interfere with sexual expression, and fear of the effects of sexual activity may also present obstacles. A few of the conditions that may be major causes of disrupting sexual expression are cerebrovascular accidents and myocardial infarctions, severe arthritis, prostatectomy, vaginal infection, Parkinson's disease, and diabetes.

Effects of Cerebrovascular Accidents and Coronaries

Cerebrovascular accidents and coronaries are frequently followed by a decrease in sexual activity, for patients are fearful of having another stroke or heart attack. The findings in regard to death as a result of sexual activity are not yet conclusive. Butler gives a conservative estimate that 1 percent of sudden coronary deaths occur during intercourse.[10] Many men and women might not forgo sexual activity out of fear if they received counseling. Some men become impotent due to anxiety about consequences, if they do try to proceed.

Men and women who have had myocardial infarctions are usually encouraged by their physicians to continue sexual activity. They are often told that the amount of oxygen needed for sexual intercourse with partners of long standing is equivalent to the amount needed for climbing a flight of stairs or walking briskly; that heart rate averages 120 beats a minute, which is about the same as that incurred by light to moderate exercise.

Patients are usually warned that the heart is strained if there is a rapid heart and respiration rate that persists 20–30 minutes after intercourse, palpitations continuing 15 minutes after intercourse, or chest pain during or after intercourse, sleeplessness after sexual activity, or extreme fatigue the following day. Sexual relations are to be avoided immediately after a large meal or drinking alcohol; when environmental temperatures are extremely hot or cold; if the circumstances are stressful; or if there will be strenuous physical activity afterward.[11]

Stress can be reduced during coitus by using a side-lying position or by the patient assuming the on-bottom position during intercourse, with the partner kneeling, so the patient does not bear weight. Another recommended position is for the patient to sit in an armless chair with the partner on his lap. The chair must be low enough for both partners to touch the floor with their feet to avoid strain. The suggestion is also made to have sexual relations after a night's sleep and followed by a rest period.[12]

Directions given to postcoronary patients must be individualized by the physician. The patient's response to exercise must be assessed to determine whether the patient is physically able to resume sexual activity.

Although there is no conclusive research on incidence of sudden death during or after sexual intercourse, sudden death is unusual when sex is with a partner of many years.[13] It is important to note that the excitement engendered by a new partner or the anxiety produced by feelings of guilt may cause more stress, which could make greater demands on the heart than sex with a partner of long standing.

Prostatectomies

Prostatectomies are becoming more common, as there is a higher incidence of prostate hyperplasia (tissue buildup) with age. There appears to be a widespread but erroneous belief that *all* prostatectomies frequently result in impotency.

The most common types of prostatectomies are transurethral, suprapubic, retropubic, and radical perineal resection. The last, radical perineal resection, is frequently used in cases of malignancy. As the perineal nerves are severed, this type of procedure usually results in physiological impotence. The other kinds of procedures may cause psychological impotence in patients who believe or fear that impotency will occur.[14]

Another aspect of some prostatectomy procedures that may interfere with sexual functioning is a change in the subjective feeling of ejaculation which is experienced by some patients. Little or no ejaculation may be produced, due to retrograde ejaculation into the bladder. Although retrograde ejaculation is harmless and does not decrease sexual sensations, some men are alarmed by this change. Anxiety about the possibility of malignancy can also seriously interfere with sexual desire and potency.[15] When the individual micturates following retrograde ejaculation, urine may be whitish, thick, and mucousy. This may be alarming to the patient if there has not been forewarning.

Parkinson's Disease

Parkinson's disease is a progressive disease characterized by tremors, a masked expression, and depression. It is often treated by medication which enhances libido in some patients. Unfortunately, this is sometimes viewed as a laughable circumstance, and the patient is ridiculed. Enhanced libido requires sex counseling for patient and spouse. If the patient is institutionalized, privacy should be arranged for the couple.

Arthritis

In addition to the problems with sexual adjustment that may be caused by chronic illness and disability, arthritis interferes with sexual activity by presenting mechanical barriers, such as immobile or very painful hip joints. Arthritis patients may also be sexually disabled by their condition in that they must expend most of their energy on simply bathing, dressing, and meeting minimal needs. There is little energy remaining for sexual expression. Some of the medication used in the treatment of arthritis, particularly corticosteroids, diminish sexual desire. There are patients with deformities who believe they are unattractive to their sexual partners.[16]

Physicians who are sensitive to the sexual needs of arthritic patients may discuss with each patient, according to the severity of the condition, ways they can perform sexual activity without further damaging their joints. Some types of orthopedic surgery have the added benefit of enabling some arthritic patients to resume sexual intercourse. Patients need to be informed of this possibility.

Diabetes Mellitus

Diabetes mellitus does not cause sexual desire to disappear but can cause impotency in men. However, when the diabetes is well controlled, the impotence usually can be improved if the person has not had long-term impotence. The fear of becoming impotent may also interfere with potency.[17] The effects of diabetes on women in this respect are unknown.

AIDS (Acquired Immunodeficiency Syndrome)

Since the AIDS virus is commonly associated with sexually active individuals, there may be a lax attitude about providing information about AIDS to the elderly. However, the Centers for Disease Control, Atlanta reported that between 1981 and January, 1989, there had been 8,641 individuals over age 49 who were diagnosed as having AIDS. This amounts to 10 percent of the total AIDS population. Older people are affected both directly and indirectly by this new health crisis.[18]

Information on AIDS should be disseminated to older adults so that they may be correctly informed about the disease. It is important for people of all ages to understand how AIDS is transmitted from one person to another, what sexual precautions should be taken in the prevention of AIDS, and what precautions should be taken in the use of needles and syringes.

As the research on AIDS is ongoing and, at this time, much of it is inconclusive or controversial, only a brief summary of the Surgeon General's report is presented here.

AIDS was first reported in this country in 1981. AIDS is a deadly disease that is caused by the human immunodeficiency virus, HIV. The AIDS virus may live in the body for years before actual symptoms appear. Its primary effect is damage to the body's natural immune defenses against disease. Consequently, people with AIDS develop fatal diseases.

There are two major ways that AIDS can be transmitted: by having oral, anal, or vaginal sex with someone who is infected with the AIDS virus; or by sharing drug needles and syringes with an infected person. There is also a risk to infants born to mothers infected with the AIDS virus and to hemophiliacs and others who receive blood transfusions. However, the risk of getting AIDS from a blood transfusion has been greatly reduced.

AIDS cannot be transmitted through everyday contact, such as a kiss, saliva, sweat, tears, urine or a bowel movement, from clothes, a telephone, a toilet seat, or swimming in a pool, even if someone in the pool is infected with the AIDS virus.[19] More information can be obtained from local public health agencies or the local or national AIDS hot line.

Practice Applications

Social workers in health-care settings may need to focus attention on the desirability for more open discussions of sexuality between health-care professionals and patients. Ehrlich observes, in relation to sexuality as a legitimate area of inquiry in medical history taking, the following:

> For most of us, doctors and patients alike, it remains a very private area. In our society, it can be the subject of jokes, but it is rarely brought out into the open in clinical discussion. Reciprocal embarrassment prevents the physician from asking the proper questions and the patient from reciting his problems. The inhibiting effect of social mores leads us to circumlocutions. It is little wonder that there is practically nothing in medical writings dealing with arthritis, or even with chronic diseases in general, that refers to sexuality. A search of rheumatologic and orthopaedic textbooks uncovers little or no information.[20]

Mezey and others note:

> An often omitted area of the history is the sexual history. This may be a function of the discomfort of the practitioner rather than the reluctance of the client to discuss the topic.[21]

Although Ehrlich's observation was made over a decade ago, and Mezey and others' only a few years ago, the situation is probably about the same. The need to discuss sexual needs and to include the older person in these discussions still exists. One place to begin may be in requesting more information in the medical history as to the older patient's present physical capability and prognosis of capability for sexual expression. The social history could include the patient's past and present attitudes toward sexual expression. Identification of social and psychological problems that interfere with sexual expression are legitimate areas for social work intervention.

It is important to remember, when taking a sexual history, that some older men and women preferred members of the same sex for sexual partners when they were young, and these sexual preferences remain. They have endured the stress of concealment or "coming out" in addition to the other stresses that accompany aging. Older homosexual adults who are living in an institution may experience extreme anxiety over becoming ostracized by other residents or being embarrassed or mistreated by staff members. They may need counseling to help them deal with their fears and anxiety.

Dulaney and Kelly point out other problems homosexual individuals experience which may be helped by social work intervention. These problems include:

> ...having to deal with institutional policies, such as in nursing homes, that prevent homosexual individuals from sharing rooms; having to meet certain medical needs; and having to cope with the frequent lack of bereavement counseling, legal planning, and assistance with sexual dysfunction available to homosexuals.[22]

Women who are evaluated as in need of hormone replacement therapy but are too much at risk to make use of it may need counseling in regard to the effects this may have on their sexual activity. It may be helpful to include their spouses in any counseling sessions. The couple may also have questions they would like to ask the physician, if they feel comfortable enough to ask him or her. A conference including the couple, a physician, and the social worker may provide this opportunity.

When surgical procedures such as prostatectomies or some types of orthopedic surgery are being considered, social workers in health-care settings can ascertain whether the patient is fully informed as to the surgical procedures and their effects on sexual functioning. Surgeons sometimes explain a procedure in excellent, understandable detail, but do not refer to the effects of the procedure on the patient's sexual functioning. Physicians may not be aware of the patient's anxieties and fears, or they may believe that sexual activity is of little concern to the older patient. For example, the physician may omit explaining that retrograde ejaculation will cause a whitish, mucousy stream of urine.

A joint conference with the patient, the patient's sexual partner, social worker, and nurse or physician may also be necessary in this situation in order to answer questions fully. For the patient who may become physiologically impotent, a discussion of alternative methods of sexual expression may be helpful. This can be an extremely sensitive area in counseling older men and women, as most older adults of today have had a far different sexual orientation than the young of today. There may be strong negative feelings about any sexual activity other than sexual intercourse. The introduction of discussion about alternative sexual expression needs to be preceded by a careful evaluation of the clients' sexual attitudes. Some may be offended or shocked, but many clients may welcome such discussions and desire assurances that they will not be engaging in perverted or abnormal sexual activity.

There must also be recognition of the fact that some individuals are relieved to find that they have an acceptable reason for discontinuing sexual activity. There may be no desire to resume relations. Counseling of a different nature may be needed if the spouse or partner wishes to continue the previous sexual relationship.

Before attempting sexual counseling, there must be a careful examination by professional staff of their own attitudes and feelings about sex. All social workers are not skilled in sexual counseling and many may feel uncomfortable about offering this service. Physicians and nurses may be equally uncomfortable. In-service training may be needed for the social work staff and for other professionals before undertaking new policies regarding sexual counseling.

PROHIBITIVE INSTITUTIONAL POLICIES

Although social workers and other health-care professionals are working toward bringing about more awareness of the sexual aspect of older adults, institutional policies may interfere with social work intervention. Policies are seldom followed that take into consideration the sexual expression of older adults. The sexes may be totally segregated into different wards or even residential buildings. Little or no privacy is usually afforded residents during their daily routine and few arrangements made for conjugal privacy. When trying to bring about changes, a realistic assessment must be made of ways in which new policies can be instituted or old policies adapted to meet the needs of institutional residents.

In the zeal to correct past attitudes, a note of warning might be in order. Older men and women have dealt with being "sexless" for a great many years. Let us not provide a new image of highly charged sexuality that older adults may believe they must strive to emulate in order to be "normal."

When considering the sexual aspects of the later years, it is important to remember that sexual expression encompasses much more than the act of intercourse. Reedy makes the following observation:

The youthful fires of passion are quieter now....A smile, a nod of the head, a wink, a kiss, a hug, cuddling, and physical closeness take on added meaning in sexual expressions of love between older lovers. In addition to the immediate pleasure of physical intimacy, sexuality becomes an affirmation of a lifetime of shared experiences and memories.[23]

The following case example demonstrates some of the kinds of problems in regard to sexual activity that are experienced by older adults which may benefit from social work intervention.

CASE EXAMPLE: SEXUALITY AND AGE

Mrs. Jarvis is a 65-year-old widow who is attending an outpatient hypertensive clinic at City Hospital which serves the indigent. There is an open-ended patient education group meeting every week for hypertensive patients. The group is led once monthly by the same outpatient social worker.

The other meetings are led by a dietitian, a clinical nursing specialist, physical therapist, and on occasion, a physician. Each of these leaders presents patient education in regard to diet, medication, and exercise in relation to hypertension. The social worker discusses the effects of stress and tension and acts as facilitator in the group interaction that takes place in regard to their feelings and concerns about their illness. The social worker always stops by after meetings held by the other leaders and lets it be known that her time is available after the meeting for anyone who may need social work service.

The group is attended on a voluntary basis, but physicians frequently urge the patients to attend. Some are referred by their attending physicians, usually for noncompliance in regard to medication or diet.

The social worker receives a referral from one of the city hospital internists in regard to arranging transportation for Mrs. Jarvis to attend the group meetings. The physician is very concerned, for Mrs. Jarvis' blood pressure is elevated, and she doubts that Mrs. Jarvis is taking her prescribed medication on a regular basis. She believes that Mrs. Jarvis needs the patient education provided by the group leaders.

The social worker is surprised about the referral, for Mrs. Jarvis is one of the group's most faithful members. Mrs. Jarvis has been attending the group for four months, and the social worker doubts that she has missed more than one or two meetings. The social worker recalls that Mrs. Jarvis told the group that she has been widowed for less than a year and that her husband had cancer and died after a long, bedridden illness. She remembers, too, that Mrs. Jarvis lives with an arthritic son and his wife and children. The son is frequently hospitalized. Mrs. Jarvis receives Social Security and Supplemental Security income.

It is difficult for the social worker to believe that Mrs. Jarvis would be careless about her medication or unwilling to follow the directions given by the physician. She is one of the most attentive members of the group and seems to have a good understanding of the patient role in the management of hypertension.

During the group meeting, the social worker pays special attention to Mrs. Jarvis. She has the same interested expression she usually has. She is sitting next to a large man who appears to be about her age. The social worker recalls that this man is another of the regulars who nearly always attend the meetings. Mr. Franklin has been coming for about eight or nine weeks. He is a newly diagnosed hypertensive patient who suffered a light stroke which cleared in two weeks. The social worker remembers that he too is recently bereaved.

At the end of the meeting, the social worker asks those who would like to see her afterward, or at a later date, to stop by her office. Mrs. Jarvis is waiting in her office when she arrives a few minutes later. She tells the social worker that her doctor has told her to talk to her, but she doesn't know why.

The social worker explains the physician's concern. The patient appears uncomfortable and speaks so softly that the social worker can hardly hear her. She is apologetic about not taking her medication. She comments that she doesn't know why, but she simply cannot remember to take the "water pill" or the other medication. She thinks her forgetfulness may be due to her worries about her son.

Mrs. Jarvis then hesitantly tells the social worker that she is having a number of problems with her adult son and his family. However, she finds it difficult to express the reason for the distress. After much careful questioning, which the social worker makes as nonthreatening as possible, Mrs. Jarvis explains that there is a man that she would like to be with, but she knows that her children "would have a fit." She wishes now that she had not moved into her son's crowded home when her husband died. She has mentioned to her son and daughter-in-law that she might find her own place and they "won't hear of it." She wants to move and she could then have her friend come to her home. She is afraid her son will find out that she has a "beau."

She stops at this point and eyes the social worker warily. She adds that the social worker probably thinks she is terrible even to think of having a beau, for her husband has been "gone" for less than a year. The social worker assures her that she is not shocked. It is natural for Mrs. Jarvis to seek companionship, as she is probably very lonely.

At this point, Mrs. Jarvis bursts into tears and hides her face. The social worker mentally examines the statement that she has just made that provoked the tears. She quickly adds that Mrs. Jarvis may need more than companionship, that older men and women have a need for intimacy just as younger people do.

Mrs. Jarvis appears somewhat relieved and speaks of her loneliness and her needs. She explains that she met her boyfriend, Mr. Franklin, at the hypertensive group meeting and they immediately found they had a lot in common. They both feel a sense of urgency, having so recently experienced the loss of a loved one. She believes they may have "rushed things some" from the sense of not being sure of the future. She doesn't like "slipping around" and neither does Bob. He wants to get married right away, but she is not sure at this point whether she wants to marry anyone, although she likes to be with him. Bob receives Social Security benefits, but he also works part-time, so there would not be quite such a financial struggle. She thinks they should wait a while, and she would like to live in her own place somewhere while she thinks about it.

Mrs. Jarvis seems to be feeling very guilty about her new relationship. She also seems fearful over arousing her children's anger and ill will and depriving her arthritic son of the extra money that her Social Security checks bring into the home, if she should move.

The social worker believes that the client's feelings of guilt stem not only from the fact that the affair is extramarital, but from lying about her meetings with Bob and deceiving her son. She suspects that Mrs. Jarvis's "forgetfulness" about taking her medication is an unconscious self-punishment for lying, or perhaps an unconscious desire to remain "sick" so that there is a valid reason for attending every group meeting.

The social worker is also troubled by Mrs. Jarvis's statements about her son's poverty. She is concerned as to whether Mrs. Jarvis has the kind of low-salt diet that she needs. She wonders whether the nutritional needs of the client and the family are being met.

The social worker helps Mrs. Jarvis to explore the reasons for the feelings of anxiety she expresses. In a sense, the social worker gives "permission" to Mrs. Jarvis to continue the sexual relationship that is causing a mixture of joy, guilt, and anxiety. She assures the client that she is not "bad" or "abnormal." The social worker is supportive of the client's expressed wish to find a place of her own and of wanting to think things through instead of rushing into marriage. She understands the client's concern about her son's financial hardships and makes suggestions for the client to relay to the son and daughter-in-law in regard to resources for transportation to the clinic and to the city relief services for help with rent and food. The social worker also arranges a visit by a dietitian from the public health department to help both client and family.

The social worker continues to see Mrs. Jarvis weekly, following the group meeting. She learns that the client's daughter-in-law has followed through on the social worker's suggestions; it seems that the financial tension has eased a little.

Although Mrs. Jarvis says that "everything is better," she still makes references to feelings of guilt that seem out of proportion. Then, during one visit, she seems on the verge of speaking, and abruptly turns her head away. The social worker comments that she believes Mrs. Jarvis is still troubled about something that she has not yet discussed. Mrs. Jarvis nods, biting her lips, indecisively starts to speak, then stops, and finally speaks quickly. She reveals that she was pregnant when she was 15 and was sent to her aunt's home in a distant state to stay through her "confinement." She had a miscarriage at seven months and the baby died, which was "probably for the best." The father of the baby left town and nobody ever knew what became of him. She had tried to forget about all of it, although she had later told her husband, who had never "held it against" her. She thought she had succeeded in forgetting, but lately it is all that she can think about. She keeps remembering the shame she brought to her parents and sometimes she thinks she may be losing her mind to be so upset all over again. Mrs. Jarvis sighs heavily at the end of her story and looks away, visibly flushed and distressed.

The social worker helps Mrs. Jarvis to realize that the present relationship with Mr. Franklin is probably reminding her of the earlier event. The fear of her son's learning about it is a repetition of the fears she experienced in relation to her mother. She helps Mrs. Jarvis to differentiate between the two experiences so that she can recognize that she is making a mature, responsible decision at this time in her life. Not only has she changed, but the world around her, society's attitudes and beliefs, have undergone change.

Mrs. Jarvis appears to feel somewhat relieved when she leaves and very thoughtful. The social worker continues to see Mrs. Jarvis alone following the group meetings, and they review the earlier experience of unwed pregnancy and its effects on Mrs. Jarvis from several aspects. The client expresses more feelings of relief over "talking it through." She also mentions during one visit that she is not having as much trouble in remembering to take her blood pressure medication, now that she has "that bad feeling" off her mind.

A few visits later, Mrs. Jarvis suggests having Mr. Franklin accompany her. She comments that she believes she has her "head on straight" now and would like the social worker to help them in their planning for the future. From that time onward, they meet with the social worker together while they discuss where they should live, whether they should marry or have a common-law arrangement, how finances will be managed, and other concerns.

A few weeks later, Mrs. Jarvis reports that she has not only moved into her own place, but also told her son about Bob. He "put up a fuss" at first, but seems to be accepting it. She is still uncertain as to marriage, but Bob does not seem to mind since he is free to visit her whenever they both wish it. She believes her life has "settled down." Her doctor has told her that her blood pressure seems to be going down and she and Bob will probably not be attending every group meeting now. However, they will stop by to see the social worker from time to time as they want to "keep in touch."

In this case, the client has personal strengths that are temporarily weakened by a strong sense of guilt. The earlier conflicts she had experienced during adolescence were reactivated during the new relationship with her "beau." The social worker provides a supportive and reassuring relationship while helping Mrs. Jarvis gain insight as to the probable cause of her guilt and anxiety and work through her feelings. She is then able to accept herself and the new relationship. This may also have contributed to her improved physical condition. Had Mrs. Jarvis not received emotional support and help through counseling, she may have given up trying to leave her son's home and abandoned efforts to build a life of her own.

In addition to providing counseling, the social worker is cognizant of the client's physical health, home environment, socioeconomic requirements, and attends to these and other needs of the client and family.

NOTES

1. Harry L. Kozol, Murray I. Cohen, and Ralph F. Garofolo, "The Criminally Dangerous Sex Offender," *New England Journal of Medicine* 275, no. 2 (July 14, 1966): 81.

2. David Finkelhor, *Sexually Victimized Children* (New York: The Free Press, 1979), 74.

3. Frederick E. Whiskin, "The Geriatric Sex Offender," *Medical Aspects of Human Sexuality* 4, no. 4 (April 1970): 126.

4. Joyce Sutkamp Friedeman, "Development of a Sexual Knowledge Inventory for Elderly Persons," *Nursing Research* 28, no. 6 (Nov.–Dec. 1979): 373.

5. Ellen M. Berman and Harold I. Lief, "Sex and the Aging Process" in *Sex and the Life Cycle,* ed. Wilbur W. Oaks, Gerald A. Melchiode, and Ilda Ficher (New York: Grune & Stratton, 1976), 127.

6. William H. Masters and Virginia E. Johnson, *Human Sexual Inadequacy* (Boston: Little, Brown and Co., 1970), 326.

7. Ibid., 324.

8. Eric Pfeiffer, "Sexual Behavior in Old Age," in *Behavior and Adaptation in Late Life,* 2nd. ed., ed. Ewald W. Busse and Eric Pfeiffer (Boston: Little, Brown and Co., 1977), 135, 136.

9. Ibid.

10. Robert N. Butler and Myrna I. Lewis, *Aging and Mental Health: Positive Psychosocial and Biomedical Approaches,* 3rd ed. (St. Louis: C.V. Mosby Co., 1982), 144.

11. Nancy Sallese Puksta, "All About Sex...After A Coronary" *American Journal of Nursing* 77, no. 4 (April 77): 603.

12. Ibid., 605.

13. Ibid., 603.

14. Sheila Grossman, "Surgical Conditions," in *Sexuality, Human Needs and Nursing Practice,* Janie Spelton Weinberg with contributions by Sheila Grossman (Philadelphia: W.B. Saunders Co., 1982), 291.

15. Ibid., 292.

16. George E. Ehrlich, "Sexual Problems of the Arthritic Patient," in *Total Management of the Arthritic Patient,* ed. George E. Ehrlich (Philadelphia: J.B. Lippincott Co., 1973), 194.

17. Butler and Lewis, *Aging and Mental Health,* 144.

18. *AIDS Weekly Surveillance Report,* United States Aids Program, Centers for Disease Control, January 2, 1989, p. 5.

19. C. Everett Koop, *Understanding AIDS,* Centers for Disease Control, U.S. Public Health Service.

20. Ehrlich, "Sexual Problems," 193.

21. Mathy Doval Mezey, Louise Hartnett Rauckhorst, and Shirlee Ann Stokes, *Health Assessment of the Older Individual* (New York: Springer Publishing Co., 1980), 93.

22. Diana D. Dulaney and James Kelly, "Improving Services to Gay and Lesbian Clients", *Social Work,* 27, no. 2 (March 1982): 182.

23. Margaret Neiswender Reedy, "What Happens to Love? Love, Sexuality and Aging," in *Sexuality and Aging,* ed. Robert L. Solnick. (Monograph published by the Ethel Percy Andrus Gerontology Center, University of Southern California Press, 1978), 193.

11

IDENTIFICATION AND PREVENTION OF POTENTIAL PROBLEMS

This chapter presents the role of the social worker in relation to identifying potential problem areas and preventing their development. Many of the problems of older people stem from the losses incurred by bereavement and retirement. Both events are major life transitions. Bereavement of a spouse marks a transition from marriage to widowhood; retirement marks the leaving of employment and the beginning of leisure. Both events often bring about changes in income and include substantial losses. An event that may be disruptive in some families, the assumption of care of the older relative, may result in abusive or neglectful behavior, although there are other contributing causes. Each of these areas—bereavement, retirement, and abuse—is discussed in the following sections.

BEREAVEMENT

In this discussion of bereavement, widowhood is the reference point. The majority of studies on widowhood have focused on widows. The speculation in regard to widowers is that they probably deal with about the same problems as widows do and react in generally the same way. Further research is needed to test these speculations. Some sexual differences that have been noted in the literature on bereavement will be pointed out.

Grief

It is important to remember that grief is a normal process, not a psychiatric disorder. Bornstein and others concluded at the end of a follow-up study of 109 widows and widowers that while the normal depression of widowhood serves as an excellent model for depression as a result of a *clear-cut* loss, it is different from clinical affective illness and should be considered separately in studies of affective disorders in psychiatric patients.[1]

The majority of people are able to work through their grief and adjust to the loss without counseling. Most bereaved people receive the support they need from family members, the clergy, friends, or others who have experienced grief. However, many of them benefit from having reassurances that their emotions and behavior are normal manifestations of sorrow, and some may need additional emotional support.

The effects of bereavement on behavior and emotions usually last one to two years, but may last as long as three. Most people are able gradually to return to normal functioning within that time, although this does not mean that they have ceased experiencing pangs of grief. The loss of someone close and dear remains a loss throughout the survivor's life.

Caplan observes that most widows continue the psychological work of mourning for their husbands for the rest of their lives. However, during the first three years, they gradually learn how to segregate their mourning within their thoughts so that they can continue their usual activities. Although they may not actively mourn their loss, the loss remains a part of them. A resurgence of grief feelings is experienced from time to time, which gradually lessens but never ceases.[2]

Acute grief. There seems to be general agreement that acute grief lasts from two to six months, but then begins to subside. Acute grief has been described as producing the same feelings of panic and anxiety that are produced by fear or alarm. The bereaved individual is extremely tense; restlessness is a common symptom. It is almost impossible to relax so that sleep can be obtained. Although exercise might be helpful, the bereaved often feel too exhausted to try to exercise. Some widowed individuals avoid thinking about their pain and distress by exhausting themselves with activities or turn to their physicians for sedatives and tranquilizers to ameliorate their pain. As the person must deal with the emotions that accompany a grief reaction, continued avoidance may delay recovery and a return to normal functioning.

Loneliness is a feature of grief that remains long after acute grief subsides. The widowed spouse may be surrounded by family members, friends, and neighbors, yet still feel a wrenching loneliness. This may be the most difficult aspect of grief that is experienced.

Anticipatory grief. Anticipatory grieving has not been found to decrease the intensity of grief. Although older women may anticipate becoming widows, for they observe their friends in the role, and the survivors of a terminally ill person may be forewarned of the death, the grief *reaction* remains as great. However, the bereaved who have some time to "prepare themselves" for the event seem to have better coping skills over time in dealing with their loss.

This is borne out in the Harvard Bereavement Study of widows and widowers 45 years of age and under. There was a positive correlation between longer advance warning and eventual satisfactory adjustment to widowhood. Advance warning seemed to allow the widowed to prepare themselves emotionally for the loss.[3] Widows and widowers who were not forewarned were more likely to display symptoms of unresolved grief a year after the death.[4]

"Grief Work"

Coping with and resolving the feelings that occur as a result of the death of a person is often referred to as "grief work." Parkes observes that grief does not consist of several symptoms that are present for a while and then subside, but of a series of "clinical pictures which blend into and replace one another." The phases recur from time to time, with overlapping patterns. The stages of grief identified by Parkes are *numbness, pining, depression,* and *recovery.*[5] *Pining* is described as the "persistent and obtrusive wish for the person who is gone." Bereaved individuals are constantly searching for the person missing from their lives. Parkes attributes many of the actions of bereaved individuals, such as restlessness, anxiety, and preoccupation with thoughts of the dead person, as aspects of pining.[6] According to Parkes, widowed individuals must work through their feelings during these three phases until they reach the fourth stage, recovery.

The stages of dying described by Elizabeth Kubler Ross[7] also have been applied to grief. As it is difficult to fit every person's grief reaction into a set of phases, grief may be considered a process in which the various reactions and behaviors described by therapists and observers may appear repeatedly or at different intervals, according to the individual.

A factor that may interfere with grief work is the lack of a clearly defined "mourning role" for the bereaved person. When the very old of today were young, in the early part of this century, mourning customs were much more well-defined than they are today. The prevailing standard seems to be to return to usual activities a few weeks after the death. When the friends and relatives who helped the person through the crisis resume their normal lives, they seem to expect the widowed person to do the same. Expressions of grief that are necessary in order to work through the grief are often not encouraged.

Immediately after the death occurs, there are many tasks that demand attention and may temporarily occupy the widowed person; taking care of funeral arrangements, assessing financial resources, and handling legal matters. Other family members and friends are on hand, being supportive and helpful and protecting the widowed.

After the initial flurry of events, friends and less-affected relatives are back into their routine and the bereaved has fewer sources of support and assistance. Yet the widow or widower must learn to cope with the many changes that have occurred. Life must be restructured; substitutes for the roles that were a part of their former lives are needed. Older individuals who have outlived most of their relatives and have been isolated socially may be unable to find adequate replacements.

Several reactions that may occur at some point early in the grieving process have been identified by various clinicians. The initial reaction is usually one of disbelief or denial. There is an inability to realize that the person is dead. There may be feelings of anger and hostility toward God and toward the deceased, which may be followed by feelings of guilt for having felt such emotions. Anger may also be directed toward the physician or toward other relatives who are perceived as having done less than they should have. Guilty feelings related to quarrels, problems, imagined or real neglect, or failure to provide more love and understanding may be expressed.

There may also be a great feeling of relief. Relief occurs along with other feelings, such as emptiness and anger. This may come from being relieved of the caretaking responsibilities, perhaps of watching someone suffer for many months. There may also be a new sense of freedom, for any type of relationship involves some kind of restrictions. This may be mixed with feelings of guilt.[8]

Somatic symptoms occur, such as a loss of appetite, difficulty in sleeping, headaches, and digestive disturbances.[9] Episodes of severe depression may be provoked by special dates or events, such as birthdays and anniversaries.

Hallucinations in which the bereaved sees the deceased are not uncommon. Vivid dreams involving the deceased are frequently described.

Behavior During Grief

Many widowed people do not want to give up anything that belonged to their spouses. They appear comforted by the familiar belongings. They may speak of feeling the presence of the deceased when surrounded by personal objects that belonged to them. Others quickly divest their surroundings of all reminders of the person they are mourning. Their pain appears to be increased by the presence of personal objects associated with the person.

Some widows and widowers feel drawn to the grave and visit constantly. They may be very concerned about the weather, as if the deceased is aware of it. There may be a preoccupation with the condition of the grave, whether grass is growing, being properly mowed, and so on.

The widow may identify strongly with the deceased. Some widows observe that they seem to be thinking or speaking like their husbands and displaying the same preferences and dislikes. Identification may provide a means of holding onto the deceased person and feeling closer to him or her.

There may be difficulties in establishing new relationships due to idealization of the deceased. The negative aspects are forgotten. This is an attitude that is encouraged by other relatives and by society. However, idealization of the spouse may interfere with establishing new relationships.

Effects of Death on the Life-style
of the Survivor

There may be a tendency on the part of professional workers to stereo-type the reactions of older widows and widowers, for death after age 65 is more expected. Since the older person has lived "a rich, full life," the death should be readily accepted. It should be emphasized that even though the survivor may be very old, the feelings of loss and grief are deeply experienced. Older adults respond in individual ways to grief, according to the losses incurred by the death, their health, previous ability to cope, and for other reasons, just as younger persons do.

For many of today's older generation, if the husband dies, the wife must assume roles with which she may have little familiarity. She may be required for the first time to handle financial and legal matters. Maintenance of an automobile and house repairs that have traditionally been the male's responsi-bility now may become her responsibility. If the husband is the survivor, he may be required to assume homemaking roles that are unfamiliar. As older couples usually rely on each other for their major companionship, sexual needs, and emotional support, losses now exist that may be very difficult or impossible to replace.

If the bereaved individual is in poor health and has been dependent on the partner for personal care, or if income is sharply decreased, a drastic change in life-style may follow very quickly. Moving from a long-established home to an apartment, a relative's home, or a long-term-care institution may be inevita-ble.

In Lopata's investigation of Chicago-area widows, one-fifth of the respondents listed money as a major problem and another third listed money as the second problem.[10] Loneliness was listed as the most serious problem by almost half the women, with one-third listing it as the second most serious problem. Other difficulties given by this group of widows were child-rearing, making decisions, shortage of time, and self-pity.[11]

The age of the widowed person affects the way in which the life-style is restructured and the way others relate to the loss. Singles groups in the community may not receive older widows and widowers as readily.

In Lopata's study, each respondent was asked how her social life had changed since widowhood. Older women were most likely to report no change; for example, no change was reported by 60 percent of those 75 and over and by 56 percent of those between 70 and 74. The women who experienced a higher level of social involvement tended to have been in their sixties at the time of their husbands' deaths.[12] They possibly had good health and a number of widowed friends with whom they could socialize.

Men appear to be more subject to isolation when the wife dies. Women more often assume the responsibility for maintaining ties with family members and social relationships in the community. Some widowers may experience a deterioration in personal appearance which precedes withdrawal from socializing with others. Men are also reluctant to ask for help from others, as male autonomy and self-sufficiency are fostered by society.[13]

Practice Applications

The major aim of social work intervention with widows and widowers usually is to prevent the grief reaction from being inhibited or becoming prolonged. As discussed in Chapter 6, social workers need to be alert to the potentiality of suicide when working with bereaved clients. The suicide rate is highest among men between the ages of 80 and 84.[14]

Identifying whether the person is experiencing difficulties in coping with the loss and making certain that there are appropriate emotional supports are priorities. Social workers who are employed in senior citizen centers, housing developments, home health agencies, and other community agencies often come into contact with bereaved older adults in the course of their work.

It is unlikely that the widow or widower will request counseling for their grief. Many of the newly bereaved or those who are in the first year of bereavement introduce their feelings into conversations that are not initially concerned with grief or grief reactions. They may be implicitly requesting assurance that the reactions they are experiencing are normal. Hypnagogic hallucinations or the desire to frequent the grave site may be described, because of fears of insanity. The bereaved individual may feel frightened at the intensity of anger and hostility felt toward the deceased or others. Reassurances that these and other manifestations of grief are normal and that it takes time to work through the process of grief may be needed. Some bereaved men and women may need "permission" to express their grief and the assurance that to do so is healthy and normal.

Several discussion themes have been identified in group work with the recently bereaved: the appropriate duration of bereavement, which may include discussions of the importance of anniversaries and other special dates; the emotional state of members of the group; family problems; and the significance of social roles, including discussions of changes in the sense of identity.[15] Any of these areas could be a beginning point for helping a bereaved person.

Determining the quality and kind of relationship that existed prior to the death is helpful in planning strategies. Very dependent spouses may need much more assistance in coping with the changes brought about by the death. Some who appear to be independent and strong may need more help than is readily apparent.

Differentiating between the feelings of grief and the effects of death is necessary, for the bereaved person must cope with both but may only mention one facet. The widow may be able to deal with the feelings of loneliness and sadness but need assistance in working out financial or legal problems that are other effects of bereavement.

The widowed are often pressed to make decisions that have lasting effects on their lives. If at all possible, decisions that require drastic change, such as deciding to sell property or make a permanent move, should be postponed. If a vital decision cannot be postponed, the social worker may work with the bereaved and other relatives toward careful consideration of alternatives to avoid the disastrous results that may occur as a result of hasty decisions made during a time of stress.

Although bereavement may be accompanied by physical problems, symptoms of physical illness should not be treated as normal concomitants of grief that do not require attention. The client who complains of physical problems should be encouraged to seek a medical evaluation.

Social workers may initially feel helpless when confronted with the very old or ill widowed individual. Many older widows and widowers are too feeble, ill, or lacking in familial and community resources to build a new life, assume new roles, or replace the lost relationship. It is important at such times to realize that social work intervention may be in the form of assistance with practical matters. Determining eligibility for financial programs, locating appropriate housing, and finding a volunteer or neighbor to help the person for a time alleviates stress and additional anxiety. On a counseling level, the social worker may help these individuals to integrate the experience of loss into their lives.

Silverman points out that learning to cope with grief and integrating the grief experience into the approach to life indicate that an individual is living competently. Delegating all helping tasks to professionals encourages individual dependency and discourages creative solutions. She suggests that professionals need to reconsider their roles in relation to working with other helpers to provide assistance for the bereaved individuals who are coping with a normal life transition.[16]

In many communities, there is a widow-to-widow program in which widows volunteer their help to newly widowed men and women. The initial contact is made within a month of the bereavement. The helping widows are familiar with resources in the community and are able to offer alternatives to the loneliness and isolation that occurs.[17]

There is an organization called Naim for widowed Catholic men and women which has chapters in a number of dioceses. Other church groups and agencies also provide support groups for widows in the community.

If a similar group does not exist in a community, social workers may assist in forming one. There are also other avenues of assistance to the widowed population that social workers may explore in order to enlist their aid in supplying services, such as legal aid, investment programs, insurance information, and so on.

RETIREMENT

Fears are sometimes expressed about retiring in relation to becoming ill as a result of retiring. According to the Cornell Study of Occupational Retirement—a longitudinal study over approximately seven years of 1,486 urban males and

483 urban females born in 1887, 1888, and 1889, with widely divergent backgrounds from all over the country—the belief that retirement causes a decline in health is not supported.[18]

Most retirees adjust well to retirement. They know what they want to do and they are able to carry out their ideas, whether it means continuing in part-time employment or volunteer work, living in a retirement village, traveling around the country in a mobile home, taking educational courses, or pursuing other goals. If retirement does not live up to their expectations, the coping skills they have developed earlier in their lives assist them in working out the problem.

However, many working men and women anticipate retirement throughout their middle years without making any concrete plans as to what they will do once retirement is reached, or how they will manage financially on a decreased income. Some employees do not fully understand the retirement and insurance benefits provided by their companies. The benefits of government programs—for example, Medicare, Medicaid, Social Security, and Social Security Supplemental Income—are frequently overestimated.

Women Retirees

Very little research has been directed to the effects of retirement on women. More has been written about the effects of the husband's retirement on the wife's life-style. It seems to have been accepted that women invest more of their energy and interest in the home and in child-rearing and experience fewer negative effects of retirement. However, Streib found that women who retire report a sharper increase in feelings of uselessness than do men.[19]

In 1978 only 37 percent of women applying for Social Security benefits based on what they had earned had continuous earnings records since 1937. As a consequence of these and other factors, women were three times as likely to receive the *minimum* primary Social Security benefits.[20]

Statistics in regard to the continuity of employment in relation to possible effects in the future are needed. There is a large population of working women to provide subjects for study. During the period 1950 to 1975, women from ages 55 to 64 left their homes in generally increasing proportions to become employed outside the home. In 1950, 27 percent of women 55 to 64 were in the labor force. In 1975 this figure rose to 41 percent. In 1990 it is expected to climb to 43 percent.[21]

Retirement Expectations

Some research indicates that the attitude toward retirement is affected by the kind of retirement that is anticipated. Workers who can realistically expect a positive retirement experience in terms of finances, friends, social activity, and level of preparedness generally have a positive attitude toward retirement.[22]

Woodruff and Birren report four factors in retirement that make a positive experience more likely.

(1) Retirement is voluntary rather than forced; (2) one's income and health are good enough to live comfortably in retirement; (3) work is not the most important thing in one's life; and (4) some preparation and planning for retirement have occurred.[23]

Planning for the retirement years should start at least in early middle age. Although retirement planning programs are offered by some large companies, most employees do not have this opportunity. More programs should be implemented; existing ones should involve employees earlier than they now are doing. Maintaining health through exercise, nutrition, and keeping active are concepts that need to be included in retirement programs.

Phases of Retirement

Atchley separates the retirement role into various phases through which the retirement role is approached, taken, and relinquished: *preretirement*, in which fantasies of retirement are developed; *honeymoon*—a phase in which the individual tries to experience the retirement fantasies; *stability*—if the honeymoon period is successful, there is a stable period. If retirement is not successful, many people experience a letdown after the honeymoon period, which Atchley terms a *disenchanted* phase. This is followed by a *reorientation* phase, in which a more realistic view of alternatives is developed and new avenues of involvement are explored. The retirement role may be replaced by other roles, such as the disability role due to loss of financial support.[24]

Practice Applications

Retired older persons do not usually present themselves for retirement counseling. When social workers encounter retirees as clients, they may be expressing other complaints, such as depression or a dissatisfaction with their present home. They may be recovering from a myocardial infarction, surgery, or other disabling condition and retiring earlier than expected. The social worker instead of the client may identify retirement as a factor that needs to be explored.

If the retirement is earlier than had been anticipated because of illness, the retiree may need counseling in regard to self-image. An unexpected disabling condition, such as a disabling stroke, may be very difficult for a formerly healthy man or woman to accept. The plans that had been made for retirement may now seem impractical or impossible.

Social workers may find Atchley's phases helpful in "starting where the client is"; for example, retirees who are in the disenchantment phase may need counseling to reorient the individual as to viable alternatives. Whether the retirement was voluntary or forced, the amount of the change in income and the value placed on employment also may be explored.

The losses the person is experiencing must be determined. The losses may include loss of status, reduced income, loss of companionship with fellow employees, and a loss of purposeful activity. Counseling may also involve examination of the individual's values and determining how these values may have affected past goals and may affect goals during retirement. Preretirement fantasies may also be explored in order to evaluate the realism of the client's expectations.

Social workers often find that it is helpful to talk with the couple together when retirement presents problems in adjustment. The spouse of the retiree may need counseling as much or more than the retiree. The retiree may be making demands on the spouse that interfere with a life-style that the spouse has had for many years. They may need respite from each other.

It is important for social workers to keep in mind that retirement does not consist only of losses. Retirement provides the opportunity for a great many people to be relieved of boring, monotonous employment and stresses associated with working. Many retirees, for the first time in their lives, are no longer bound to a fixed schedule that they despised. Retirement offers a new kind of freedom that is welcomed. Social workers may help new retirees identify the positive aspects of retirement.

Many recent, able retirees want to find employment but need help in identifying the kind of work to seek and the availability of positions. Reeducation and retraining can often be encouraged, but older clients may need reassurance that they are able to learn something new. Some senior citizen centers operate a free employment service. The state employment offices usually have counselors who are designated to work with older citizens. The Area on Aging Office can supply information as to government programs that offer paid positions to older adults.

Older men and women who are unable to seek paid employment but have a great need to be doing something they perceive as worthwhile may meet this need through volunteer organizations. There are many kinds of telephone assistance that can be managed even by someone who is bedridden. As most people judge the value of any working activity by whether or not they are paid for it, the client must believe the contribution of time and effort is worthwhile and meaningful, even though unpaid.

Many volunteer activities are associated with building better community supports for older people, and are appealing to older volunteers for that reason. In 1980 federal programs administered by ACTION, the federal agency for volunteerism, made use of 270,000 Retired Senior Volunteer Program volunteers, 17,300 Foster Grandparents, and 3,800 senior companions.[25]

Many retirees want to explore educational opportunities for their leisure time. Fortunately, the resources are increasing in some areas. Many adult education classes are provided by public schools. Colleges offer bargain education in the summer through "elderhostel" programs that combine education with the opportunity to sightsee.

Some retirees have been acquainted with poverty all their lives. Trying to live on Social Security benefits represents one more struggle to stretch dollars to impossible limits. Ill health adds to the expense and to their problems. The social worker taps the available resources provided by the state and federal government and makes use of whatever resources the community may offer. Since many government programs have reduced budgets, more churches and private charities are possible resources, as they are placing emphasis on providing emergency assistance.

Since the effects of retirement may be lessened by adequate preparation, social workers may initiate or participate in programs in the community that emphasize retirement planning. A resource may be the retirement planning seminars sponsored by Action for Independent Maturity, an organization that is part of the American Association of Retired People (AARP).

Social workers may advocate for "part-time retirement," in which employees continue working past retirement age but reduce their hours. Advocacy for legislation pertaining to various aspects of retirement, such as allowing increased income from employment without cutting Social Security benefits, is another avenue for aiding older retired adults.

Social work advocacy in the area of reducing the inequities in Social Security is needed. The Older Woman's League (OWL), a nationwide organization, is a resource for obtaining educational materials and providing advocacy for programs that affect older women. One of the six key issues on the national agenda of OWL is to protect present Social Security benefits while pressing for changes to make the system fairer and more adequate for women. OWL is also working for changes that correct inequities in both private and public pensions; to combat age and sex discrimination in employment; to highlight the impact on older women of the cuts in human services and entitlement budgets; and has developed model state bills on health conversion rights and on respite services for caregivers of chronically ill spouses, parents, or children.

ABUSE AND NEGLECT

Medical and social research and some widely publicized instances of child abuse directed public attention to domestic violence in the 1960s. The span of interest increased during the 1970s to include wife abuse and, more recently, the abuse of older adults. The First National Conference on Abuse of Elder Persons was held in 1981. The discussion of abuse in this section is confined to abuse of elderly men and women who are living in the community. Abuse and neglect occur in institutions but constitute a different problem which must be addressed by the staff of the institution.

Definition of Abuse

There does not seem to be widespread agreement on the definition of elder abuse. The definition of abuse sometimes includes neglect, but may be restricted to physical abuse only. It may be comprehensively defined to include physical abuse, sexual abuse, neglect, self-neglect, psychological abuse, abandonment, financial abuse, medical abuse, and incidences of fraud against the elderly.

Incidence of Abuse

The number of abused older men and women is unknown. Estimates of abuse vary, according to the definition used in the studies. In a review of several studies, Callahan observes that elder abuse affects a relatively small percentage of the elderly, by any measures, even in states with mandatory reporting laws.[26] An investigation undertaken by the Subcommittee on Health and Long Term Care estimated the national incidence of elderly abuse at about 4 percent, approximately one million, of the nation's elderly population.[27]

The actual incidence of abuse may be higher than studies indicate for abuse of the elderly may be under-reported. The victims may be reluctant to accuse or place charges against the perpetrator. Fear of reprisal may be the major deterrent. The effect of the threat of being sent to a nursing home, if a complaint is made, is a powerful deterrent to reporting abuse. If the perpetrator is a relative, the older person may feel ashamed to admit that relatives are being abusive or neglectful. There may also be an inability to report because of physical or mental limitations, or as a result of feelings of helplessness and powerlessness.

Legislation

National legislation has been proposed to remedy elder abuse. The Prevention, Identification and Treatment of Elder Abuse Act did not pass in 1981 or in 1983, when it was reintroduced. However, national legislation may not be an effective response to the need to remedy elder abuse. If the focus is placed on the identification and punishment of abusers, the funds for programs to help the elderly in other ways, such as helping them remain in the community, providing day care, and the like may be diminished or diverted into legislative channels. Meeting needs of the elderly in ways which reduce pressures on caregivers may be a more effective deterrent to elder abuse.

Types of Abuse

The kinds of physical abuse that have been reported include assault, actual battering of the person, burning, shaking, and shoving. Bone fractures, cuts, bruises, dislocations, and even death have resulted. Mild physical abuse, such as shaking, can be very damaging to a frail older person with osteoporosis, arthritis, and other conditions.

Abuse may consist of forcible confinement. The older person may be tied into a chair or locked in a room while the caregiver attends to household chores or leaves the house. Physical constraints are also used unnecessarily.

Abandonment of an older adult is a form of abuse. The older person who is unable to care for himself may be knowingly left by a spouse, or other relatives, to survive alone.

Overmedicating an older person is another type of abuse. This may be done in an effort to keep the person quiet and out of the way.

Verbal abuse is probably the most common form of abuse. It may be intimidating, consisting of outright or implied threats. Verbal abuse may also be demeaning, mocking, and belittling.

Neglect may be willful neglect in which caregivers deliberately withhold nourishment or medication, or fail to provide other needed care. It may consist of instances in which the caregiver does not purposely neglect the individual but is unable to provide, for varying reasons, the appropriate care. The question arises as to whether the latter instances should be termed neglect. Failing memory, confusion, depression, lack of money, transportation, or other resources may be major causes of neglect.

Types of exploitation and fraud are more clearly and easily defined. These include work-at-home schemes, sale of phony securities, franchises introduced by con men, funeral abuses, medical quackery and sale of unproven medical remedies, promotion of valueless land, and home-improvement rackets.[28] Older individuals are victimized not only by strangers perpetuating some type of fraud, but by their children and other relatives. They are persuaded or threatened into signing over their homes, insurance, Social Security checks, or other property and assets.

Why are older men and women so frequently victimized by fraudulent practices? There are many possible reasons, including the following: Older adults grew up in a more trusting environment and are more gullible; they have more leisure and are more easily approached in public places and willing to engage in long conversations; they are targeted by con artists because many of them have savings; because of shame and embarrassment, they may be reluctant to report being deceived; and their limited income makes "get rich quick" schemes appear attractive.

Social work intervention is important in the area of prevention of fraudulent practices. Raising the awareness of the older population to the likelihood of being approached by con artists and the necessity of reporting suspicious requests or "business schemes" may reduce some types of fraud. Public programs in regard to false advertising claims and medical quackery are educational measures that may prevent some older people from responding to misleading advertisements.

Characteristics of the Abused

Douglass describes the population at risk of domestic violence, in relation to several studies, as follows:

> ...those elderly who are most vulnerable due to advanced age, frailty, chronic disease, or physical or mental impairment. Victims of abuse and

neglect are those who are least capable of independent living and thus most dependent on others. They are generally less aware of alternative living arrangements or means of support than others in their age cohort, and they are more likely to be aged women than men. On the average, victims will have two or more ongoing physical disabilities. All research has found these conclusions.[29]

Douglass adds that although most victims will be highly vulnerable individuals, older people without impairment are also victims of abuse.

Characteristics of Informal Caregivers

Studies have shown that caregivers may be children of the older person, siblings or other relatives, the spouse, and friends or neighbors. The person may be cared for at home or in a relative's home.

In a study of 111 older adults with informal caregivers in New York City, 33 percent of primary caregivers were spouses. Most were at least 60 years of age; almost half were 75 or over. Slightly over half the caregivers were males. Thirty-six percent of the caregivers were children, mainly married women with families. They tended to be middle-aged; more than half were between 40 and 59, with 10 percent over 60. Sixty percent of the children who provided care were employed.[30]

Factors in Abuse and Neglect. The increase in the number of frail older adults, the lack of preparation by society for addressing their needs, societal prejudice and discrimination toward the older segment of the population, devaluation of older people, and the cultural acceptance of violence in our society are considered some of the social factors in the perpetration of abuse and neglect.

The stress of providing care for an older relative appears to be a major factor. The material presented in earlier chapters in regard to mental and physical disabilities should help in understanding the stresses experienced by many caregivers: incontinence, catastrophic reactions and other delirious and demented behavior, paranoid ideation, wandering behavior, and the like. In addition, many family members are trying to care for individuals with complicated medical conditions such as aphasia as a result of stroke, chronic obstructive pulmonary disease, Parkinson's disease, and other conditions. They have the added stress of uncertainty as to whether they are caring properly for the patient.

As discussed in earlier chapters, the dependency needs of an ill older person and the familial responses may create a great deal of strain on family relationships. The middle-aged or older child is burdened with resolving those conflicts in addition to meeting the needs of a frail older person.

Some caregivers are attempting to maintain full-time employment, meet the responsibilities of homemaker, and provide care to an aged parent or even two older adults. The caregiver, at whatever age, may have physical problems that interfere with providing appropriate care. Marital discord, disruptions in relationships with children who may feel displaced by another person in the home, lack of sufficient financial resources, and inadequate housing space are among the possible factors in abuse and neglect. As a result of deinstitutionalization, there are also many former mental patients living at home with elderly parents. They may respond to stressful situations with abusive behavior.

The caregiver may be the spouse of the older ill person and may be only slightly less feeble. One or both may be suffering from chronic physical disorders, as well as any of the several reversible or irreversible brain disorders discussed in Chapters 5 and 6. The caregiver also is under the stress of observing the decline of the older person.

The use of drugs and alcohol, with the latter much more often mentioned, has frequently been identified as a factor. The older person, the abusive person, or both may be more volatile as a result of intoxication.

Practice Applications

Social workers and other professionals who provide services to older people must teach themselves to be aware of the possibility of abuse and neglect, just as school social workers and others who work with children had to learn to be alert to signs of child abuse. It may be very difficult to discern whether the bruises on the face and arm of an older person are the result of physical abuse by the spouse, who is a "sweet elderly person"; or to look for bruises on the wrists of the mildly demented old lady as indicators of being tied to a chair, when the pleasant-faced, bustling middle-aged daughter describes the amount of shopping trips and errand running she accomplishes without a sitter.

It is very important not to consider incidents of abuse in terms of "perpetrator" and "victim." Even with the small amount of research that has been undertaken, the results indicate that the causes of abuse are extremely complex, embracing a great deal more than even the complicated interrelationships of family dynamics.

Reports of abuse are often made to protective services in the local department of human services, although another agency may be designated. Abused individuals may be referred to shelters for victims of domestic violence, which have increased over the past decade in some areas. Housing for battered elderly people may also be obtained through missions operated by churches. Crisis intervention centers can supply information as to available resources in their areas.

Strategies that are used to prevent abuse and neglect depend on the evaluation of each situation. Some families may need education in regard to care and assistance in providing it, such as homemaker services, visits by the public health nurse, and other therapeutic services. Most caregivers will need resources to provide respite from the demands of care. Some of the caregivers are not emotionally and/or physically able to handle the problems involved in caring for an older person; some other arrangement must be worked out to protect both the caregiver and the older individual.

Family counseling may be needed. Social workers in protective services and in other agencies may not be able to assume full counseling responsibilities. They may focus on the older person and the caregiver, referring the entire family to other clinical resources for family therapy.

POLICIES AFFECTING SOCIAL WORK INTERVENTION

Social workers must work within the framework of the existing legislation. Most states require the older person's permission to intervene. Fears of retaliation may prevent the granting of permission. The older adults who present mental problems are also the most difficult to have in the home and may be more likely targets for aggression; yet they are unable to make the required decision.

Social workers in protective services often have case loads that are too large for them to provide adequate services. Gentry and Nelson point out that intervenors in family abuse or neglect often have little training. They may identify with the aggressor or the victim and place blame on one or the other. They suggest the intervenors be desensitized to abuse and neglect so that they can deal with their own hostile and sexual impulses and fear of losing control. Avoiding the rescue syndrome is emphasized.[31]

Rathbone-McCuan points out several barriers to intervention that are present in many human service agencies. They include:

1. Reluctance to identify the problem
2. Lack of agency and staff awareness of the problem
3. Agency concerns about confidentiality
4. Constraints on data accessibility
5. Manpower and resource drains on the agency[32]

It is important for social workers to identify and attempt to remove such barriers in the agencies in which they are employed. This may involve conducting in-service training for the agency and for the community at large, as well as assessing the need for changing existing policies.

Social workers or others who investigate reports of elder abuse may need special training so that they will be able to distinguish between an environment that can be made safe and one which requires removal of the older person. Although counseling of some kind may be needed, identifying other needs and locating and providing services, such as day care, respite care, home health aides, and the like may be more helpful or equally helpful to the family.

Nearly every older individual, if asked to make the choice, will prefer staying in the home instead of being removed to a long term care facility. The present emphasis on case management as a means to help keep the elderly out of institutions may also exert pressure on those who are investigating abuse to keep the victim in the home. However, it is not always possible to maintain a safe home. Keeping older relatives in homes of family members *even with extra financial assistance and community supports* may not be the best arrangement for a number of families.

Professionals may need to guard against unwittingly pressuring families into accepting older members that they cannot maintain without sacrificing other relationships that are vital to maintain the family system. If financial assistance and home health services are increased, some families may feel even more pressured, believing that they do not have a legitimate excuse to refuse to take the person into the household. Social workers must also be alert to the possibility that families with marginal incomes may agree to provide care that they know they cannot give, in order to receive reimbursement.

Each of these issues—strengthened legislation to protect older adults, smaller case loads and better preparation for protective services workers, removing barriers that exist in agencies, the provision of more adequate resources, and more attention to the identification of at-risk families—needs to be addressed. Otherwise, even the best social work efforts may accomplish very little in the area of abuse of older adults.

NOTES

1. Philipp E. Bornstein et al, "The Depression of Widowhood After Thirteen Months," *British Journal of Psychiatry* 122, no. 570 (May 1973): 566.

2. Gerald Caplan, Foreword to Ira O. Glick, Robert S. Weiss, and C. Murray Parkes, *The First Year of Bereavement* (New York: John Wiley & Sons, 1974), viii.

3. Glick, Weiss, and Parkes, *The First Year*, 32.

4. Ibid., 33.

5. Colin Murray Parkes, *Bereavement: Studies of Grief in Adult Life* (New York: International Universities Press, Inc., 1972), 7.

6. Ibid., 46.

7. Elizabeth Kubler Ross, *On Death and Dying* (New York: Macmillan, 1969).

8. Richard A. Kalish, *Death, Grief and Caring Relationships*, (Monterey, Calif.: Brooks/Cole Publishing Co., 1981), 223.

9. Parkes, *Bereavement*, 34.

10. Helena Znaniecki Lopata, *Widowhood in an American City* (Cambridge, Mass.: Schenkman Publishing Co., Inc., 1973), 72.

11. Ibid., 70.

12. Ibid., 188.

13. Kathleen McConnell, "The Aged Widow," *Social Work* 27, no. 2 (March 1982): 188.

14. Ibid.

15. Philip F. Roy and Helen Sumpter, "Group Support for the Recently Bereaved" *Health and Social Work* 8, no. 3 (Summer 1983): 231.

16. Phyllis R. Silverman, "Bereavement as a Normal Life Transition", in *Social Work with the Dying Patient and the Family*, ed. Elizabeth R. Prichard et al. (New York: Columbia University Press, 1977), 272.

17. Ibid., 270.

18. Gordon F. Streib and Clement J. Schneider, *Retirement in American Society* (Ithaca, N.Y.: Cornell University Press, 1971), 160.

19. Ibid., 161.

20. *The Older Woman: Continuities and Discontinuities*, Report of the National Institute on Aging and the National Institute of Mental Health Workshop (September 14–16, 1978), 47.

21. "Demographic Aspects of Aging and the Older Population of the United States," in *Sourcebook on Aging*, 2nd. ed. (Chicago: Marquis Academic Media, 1979), 249.

22. Francis D. Glamser, "Determinants of a Positive Attitude Toward Retirement," *Journal of Gerontology*, 31, no. 1 (March 1976): 104.

23. *Aging: Scientific Perspectives and Social Issues*, ed. Diana S. Woodruff and James E. Birren (Monterey, Calif.: Brooks/Cole Publishing Co., 1983), 340.

24. Robert C. Atchley, *The Social Forces in Later Life* 2nd. ed., (Belmont, Calif.: Wadsworth Publishing Co., 1972), 165, 166.

25. Carole Allen and Herman Brotman, comps., *Chartbook on Aging in America: The 1981 White House Conference on Aging*, (Washington, D.C.: Superintendent of Documents, n.d.), 132.

26. James J. Callahan, "Elder Abuse: Some Questions for Policymakers?" *The Gerontologist*, 28, no. 4 (August 1988): 454.

27. *Elder Abuse: A National Disgrace, A Briefing by the Chairman of the Subcommittee on Health and Long Term Care of the Select Committee on Aging, U. S. House of Representatives*, Introduction and Executive Summary, Ninety-Ninth Congress, First Session, May 10, 1985. (Washington: U.S. Government Printing Office, 1985), 1.

28. Claude D. Pepper, "Frauds Against the Elderly," in Kosberg, ed., *Abuse and Maltreatment of the Elderly*, 68–83.

29. Richard L. Douglass, "The Etiology of Neglect and Abuse of Older Persons." in *The Abuse of Older Persons*, ed. David F. Holden and Peggie L. Care. Papers presented at The Tennessee Conference on Abuse of Older Persons, Knoxville, Tenn. (December 3–4, 1980). Copyright 1981 by the University of Tennessee School of Social Work.

30. Marjorie H. Cantor, "Strain Among Caregivers: A Study of Experience in the United States," *The Gerontologist* 23, no. 6 (Dec. 1983): 599.

31. Charles E. Gentry and Barbara D. Nelson, "Developmental Patterns for Abuse Programs: Application to the Aging," *Abuse of Older Persons*, 80.

32. Eloise Rathbone-McCuan, "Elderly Victims of Family Violence and Neglect," *Social Casework* 61, no. 5 (May 1980): 302.

12

MAINTAINING COMMUNITY RESOURCES AND SUPPORTS FOR OLDER PEOPLE

A viable system of community supports is needed in order to maintain older people in the community and avoid unnecessary institutionalization. Most communities have resources that are being used to help older men and women, but they are often fragmented and cannot serve all who need them. Before discussing existing services, it may be helpful to consider some major legislation which has influenced the kinds of resources available to older people and the way that services are delivered.

THE OLDER AMERICANS ACT

The Older Americans Act (OAA) in 1965 set forth a series of goals and objectives for older people. In addition, the Administration on Aging (AoA) was created as the principal agency to carry out the provisions of the act. This was the first time that a central administrative office concerned with the aged was created within the federal government.

The Older Americans Act emphasizes coordination and planning services and helping older people to make use of existing services. Areawide Agencies on Aging (AAA) were established in each state and received federal funds for coordination and planning of services.

The Act specifies ten national objectives for older people: an adequate income; the best possible physical and mental health; suitable housing; full restorative services; opportunity for employment; retirement in health, honor, and dignity; civic, cultural, and recreational opportunities; efficient community services; benefits from research; and the free exercise of individual initiatives in planning and managing their own lives.

AoA is empowered to serve as the advocate for the elderly within other agencies of the government and to evaluate and coordinate programs related to older people, as well as to work with public and private agencies to improve the lives of older men and women.

Title III is the most comprehensive of the titles. Title IV of the Act authorizes transportation, recreation, and demonstration projects. Title V defines the Community Service Empowerment program, and Title VI specifies programs for Indian tribes.

Funds from Title III of OAA are specifically designated to help older men and women avoid institutionalization. A number of supportive services can be included, such as homemaking, home health, shopping, and escort services. The sole eligibility requirement is age; the recipient must be 60 or older. In a 1982 sample survey, 25 percent of Title III expenditures by Area Agencies on Aging were found to be for in-home services, with 12 percent for home-delivered meals, and 13 percent for other kinds of services. According to AoA's program records, all states support in-home services to some degree with their Older American Act funds.[1]

The Areawide Agencies on Aging constitute the important program structure under Title III. The area agency is responsible for assessing needs of the older people in the area, setting priorities for services, awarding grants and contracting for services to older people with the greatest need, planning and coordinating existing services, acting as advocate of the older population in that service area, and designing "focal points" for service delivery. The area agency cannot provide direct services without documentation of the inability to obtain the service through contracting.

The main purpose of the AAAs is to develop an area plan which carries out the details of Title III. In practice, judgments are made as to which agencies and organizations in the area will receive funds for services that are provided for by the Act. The planner must consider the alternatives before making a decision as to which organization will maximize the use of services for older people better than the others. The plan that is submitted to the state must show how the funds will be used by the selected organizations in order to obtain the greatest value for the older people in the area.

Each planning area has its own array of services because the resources vary from one area to the next, and the way that choices of agencies are made also vary. Social workers need to be familiar with the AAA in the regions in which they work in order to learn which services are available in that community and in what ways they are patterned.

Although the Older Americans Act has had an impact on the lives of older men and women, it has been limited. There are many criticisms of the OAA in relation to the fragmentation and variability of services in different areas of the country.

TITLE XX OF THE SOCIAL SECURITY ACT

In 1974 Title XX was included in the Social Service Amendments to the Social Security Act. The funds were distributed to the states according to the population size. Although Title XX funds were not specified as being for older people, many of the services are targeted primarily to older adults. In 1982, Title XX funds were replaced by the Social Services block grant. Under this program, states may determine which services they want to fund. A public hearing must be held and an explanation given to the federal government as to how the block grant money will be given to the needy.

EXISTING COMMUNITY SUPPORTS

This chapter is primarily concerned with the programs and services that are presently available. These include housing and financial assistance programs, day-care centers, home health services, mental health services, senior citizen centers, employment services, transportation services, support groups, social services provided by churches, and legal services. As will be seen, services are limited in many ways. The same kinds of services are not offered in every community. Some services are being duplicated; others are inadequately provided. It becomes apparent that case management skills are needed to avoid duplication, to make certain that the client does not become entangled with intake procedures, or become "lost" in the system.

It seems appropriate to start the discussion with a problem that often confronts older people: housing needs. The social worker may try to avoid relocating the client by helping the client make changes in the present living arrangements, or by adding supports. If this cannot be done, then alternative housing is considered.

HOUSING: THE MICROENVIRONMENT OF OLDER ADULTS

The majority of older people live in their own homes and, almost without exception, want to remain in their own homes as long as they possibly can. An apartment, rented home, mobile home, or a rented room may comprise home. "Home" is familiar, a symbol of stability in an ever-changing world. Remaining at home means remaining in the community and living outside of an institution. Many older people have lived in the same home for 50 or more years. More than 36 percent of older occupant-owners moved into their homes before 1940.[2] For some older people, home ownership is an asset. For others, who cannot afford the cost of home repairs or are unable to make mortgage payments, home ownership is a serious burden.

Home Repairs

Housing costs are extremely variable, depending on home ownership status and age. In 1983, older householders spent 4 or 5 percent more of their income on housing, depending on whether they were owners or renters and excluding maintenance and repairs, than younger householders.[3]

Funds for repairs are available in some communities. Title III of the Older Americans Act funds local services through state and local allotments. Although every state uses some of the money from Title III for home repairs and maintenance, these services are not mandated. They are elective services at local option, and many communities do not opt to provide these services. If they are unavailable in a given community, social workers may advocate for obtaining them.

Rent Subsidy Programs

The 1965 and the 1974 Housing Acts established rent-subsidy programs in which funds are provided to state or local housing authorities or to individuals to pay the difference between the local market rental and a percentage of the eligible person's income. Admission priority is given to persons who have been displaced because of government action and to older, disabled, and handicapped individuals.

When individuals must move from their homes, alternative choices of varying suitability are suggested, when available. It must be emphasized that there are waiting lists for most public housing and moderately priced housing, and some types of alternative housing are not found in every community. However, housing concerns are receiving more attention, with many communities devising plans to provide more resources for older people. Alternative choices that exist in most communities include public housing, congregate housing which may be publicly or privately funded, boarding homes, resident and "SRO" hotels, and shared homes. Each of these will be discussed briefly in the following sections.

Public Housing

Public housing began in 1937 to replace substandard housing occupied by people with low incomes. The Housing Act of 1956 provided legislation related specifically to older adults. The financing for public housing is administered by the U.S. Department of Housing and Urban Development (HUD). Information on public housing may be obtained by calling the local office of this department.

To be eligible for public housing designed for older people, the applicant must be 62, or the spouse of a person aged 62. Handicapped individuals, regardless of age, are also eligible. There are limitations on the amount of income that the person may have. Rent is figured on a sliding scale according to limits provided by HUD which are periodically adjusted.

Congregate Housing

Congregate housing refers to housing that provides a central kitchen and a common dining area for all residents. However, complete or partial kitchens are provided in some apartments. Congregate housing may be government funded, privately or commercially sponsored, or on a profit or nonprofit basis. The buildings may be high-rise towers or one-story, multiple-unit dwellings.

The kinds of living arrangements and services that are offered vary widely. Congregate housing established by commercial investors may be very lavish compared to more modest establishments operated for nonprofit. The buildings are designed for older people and handicapped individuals. Congregate housing offers an alternative to older adults who need a more protected environment. This type of housing makes it possible for the marginal person to remain in the community.

Some facilities offered by churches or other private investors contain three types of living arrangements: independent, intermediate care, and skilled nursing care. A single person or couple may reside in the facility while independent and able-bodied and have access to the nursing-care facilities when needed.

Financial arrangements for nonsubsidized housing of the type just described are variable. Some offer a refundable "life right." In this arrangement, the tenant is initially required to pay a large lump sum. This fee may be refundable or partially refundable if the tenant dies or decides to move. A monthly maintenance fee, usually adjusted on an annual basis, is required, which may include one meal a day. Nursing home-care is not included in the initial and monthly payment but is paid by Medicare, Medicaid, or other insurance and financial resources of the tenant.

Role of Social Worker.   Social workers are employed in government-subsidized housing and in some nursing-home components of privately subsidized establishments offering independent and dependent levels of care. In 1983, over one-third, 36 percent, of elderly homeowners lived alone. Nearly two-thirds, 65 percent, of elderly renters lived alone.[4] The large number of single older people living alone implies that the older tenant may have no one at hand to be of assistance in the event that illness occurs. Social work services with older residents are largely involved with case management services related to their health-care needs. This usually includes contacting and making use of a variety of community agencies and providing follow-up. Appointments must be made, transportation arranged, including escort service, medication obtained, relatives notified, home-care services sought, applications for services filled out, and so on.

Social workers in public and privately sponsored housing visit tenants, supply supportive counseling, and refer them to community resources, as needed. Many older residents come to the social worker's office to seek assistance in filling out forms, such as applications for Medicare and Medicaid, and to have mail read or interpreted.

Boarding Homes

The term *congregate care* is sometimes loosely applied to boarding homes. If the older person can no longer function independently, discharge to a relative's home is not feasible, and no government housing is immediately available, boarding homes are sometimes more acceptable to the person than an institution. Some boarding homes accept only older adults who have mild mental or physical impairment that prevents their living alone. Others accept individuals who have much greater needs than the boarding home can adequately meet.

Boarding homes are not required to have federal licensure. Some states require licensing, but the requirements vary widely. Social workers are often reluctant to relocate an older person to a boarding home, as it is so difficult to determine the quality of care. However, there are clients who prefer this style of living over any other living arrangement. Clients and family members are often advised to visit and assess the boarding home. Unfortunately, there is sometimes little time to seek a place, little money, and few options.

Foster Homes

Foster homes are provided in some communities for impaired older people, including deinstitutionalized mental patients. Foster homes usually house less than five residents and provide care on a twenty-four-hour basis. Payment to caregivers amounts to about $200–400 per resident per month, although total program costs are from about $500–900 per month. The Veterans Administration, local Departments of Human Services, and State Departments of Mental Hygiene support foster home programs. Demonstration foster care programs have been begun by several hospitals for patients being discharged who would otherwise have to go into nursing homes.[5]

Resident and SRO Hotels

Some older people live in single rooms in resident hotels or in hotels called "SRO" hotels, single-room-occupancy hotels, which have a more transient clientele. Resident hotels have middle-class tenants and usually provide telephones, television, and private baths. They are located in better urban areas than SRO hotels, which are located in deteriorating downtown areas and offer few amenities. Many discharged mental patients and other marginal people live in SRO hotels.

In a study designed to explore the health utilization patterns of older people residing in downtown hotels, the findings suggest that residents of SRO hotels seek medical care in facilities in which they can retain their anonymity. Older men and women turn to other hotel residents when they are ill and need help. Social workers may find that the informal support system of the hotel provides the access route for provision of social work services.[6]

Home Sharing

Home sharing, or small-group home, is a concept that is rapidly taking hold in many areas of the country. Shared housing is an arrangement in which two or more unrelated people share a home. Homeowners may wish to share their homes and not know how to locate suitable tenants. Some agencies are conducting "matching programs" to help those who wish to participate in such an arrangement. Another type of shared housing is offered by some organizations which lease or purchase homes to accommodate small groups or groups as large as 10 or 15 people.

Social workers and others who are interested in exploring the house sharing concept may obtain information in regard to local efforts from their local commission on aging or council of community services. There are not-for-profit organizations which provide information and workshops on shared housing, including the following: Home Care Research, Inc., 30 East Patrick Street, Frederick, Md. 21701, and Shared Housing Resource Center, 8344 Greene Street, Philadelphia, Pa. 19144.

One of the problems in relocating older adults is that they often do not make the decision to move until a crisis occurs. Even if the person or couple has financial resources, there are waiting lists for almost every kind of housing.

FINANCIAL ASSISTANCE

The resources for financial assistance that can be obtained for older people are limited. Supplemental Security Income, veterans' benefits, food stamp programs, and the nutritional program discussed in Chapter 11 are the primary resources used by social workers to alleviate financial problems of older or disabled people. Many older people are aware of some of the programs but do not know how and where to apply for them. Some believe they are not eligible, and others are ashamed to ask about the availability or eligibility requirements, considering the programs "welfare."

Individuals who are not eligible for Social Security or who receive a very small income from Social Security should be encouraged to apply for Supplemental Security Insurance (SSI). SSI is based on financial need, not the work history or past earnings of the applicant. Eligibility requirements in regard to need vary from state to state. It is important to note that the SSI payment may be only a small amount of money, but other benefits are available to SSI recipients, such as Medicaid (and possibly some other services), which make it worthwhile for the person to apply.

Depending on the need and the amount of income received from Social Security, the older individual may be eligible for food stamps. Eligibility is based on the size and income of the family.

Veterans' Benefits

Veterans' benefits are another possible source of financial assistance, as well as other kinds of benefits. Widows of veterans are occasionally unaware that they may be eligible for a widow's pension. Veterans who were injured during service may apply for a service-connected disability pension. Wartime veterans over 65 years old with a limited income may be eligible for a nonservice-connected pension. Outpatient or inpatient medical care, alcohol and drug dependence treatment, nursing-home services, domiciliary services, and other aids to medical care are also available to veterans meeting certain eligibility requirements. A veteran who is a patient in a nursing home or permanently housebound may be entitled to higher income limitations or additional benefits, depending on the type of pension received.

Relatives who are concerned about burial expenses may consider burial of the veteran in a national cemetery, as this is available to any deceased veteran of wartime or peacetime service (other than for training) who was discharged under conditions other than dishonorable. Burial is also available to an eligible veteran's wife or husband, minor children, and, under certain conditions, to unmarried adult children, but applications for burial space for family members must be made prior to the veteran's burial. Headstones and markers are provided for the gravesites of those interred in national cemeteries.[7]

Although most veterans and their families are familiar with veterans' benefits and have explored the possibilities, there yet remain some who, for one reason or another, are eligible and have not applied. There may be disabled veterans who applied at an earlier time and found they were not eligible for veterans' benefits but who may now be eligible. When encountering an aged veteran or veteran's spouse in need, social workers refer the client to the Veterans' Administration for determination of eligibility for benefits. Toll-free telephone calls may be made to benefits counselors at Veterans' Administration regional offices.

DAY-CARE CENTERS

Adult day care is a term that embraces a wide variety of programs, ranging from drop-in centers where older adults stay for a few hours and may engage in crafts or other activities to day hospital care that resembles in-hospital care. Day-care centers are often associated with mental health centers, senior citizens centers, and other community agencies and institutions.

There is an increasing demand for day-care centers in communities to provide respite for caregivers, or a place to leave older adults when the caregiver is employed. Social workers are often involved in planning and administering day-care programs. Although day-care centers appear to be a simple and practical solution to a complex situation, there are more problems involved in providing day care than is often realized. This is especially apparent in relation to the provision of day-care centers outside of an institutional setting. It is beyond the scope of this book to discuss each area of concern, but a brief description of some prominent problem areas follows.

1. *Management problems.* Earlier chapters of this text have presented discussions of various disorders and conditions that would be very difficult to manage in an agency-based day-care center; for example, dealing with the catastrophic reactions of demented individuals, communication with aphasic stroke patients and individuals with severely impaired sight and hearing, and preparing appropriate meals for widely differing dietary needs.
2. *Incontinence.* Even the more mobile older adults may be incontinent, which is embarrassing to the individual who requires a change of clothing, cleaning, and so on.
3. *Program planning.* Meaningful programs for vastly different levels of mental and physical accomplishment are very difficult to provide.
4. *Administering medication.* Some types of medication, such as insulin injections, may require extra staff to provide this service.
5. *Medical crises.* Some arrangement must be made by the center for handling emergency health situations, such as the occurrence of coronaries and cerebrovascular accidents.
6. *Liability.* The cost of insurance, if the center is held responsible for results of a fall or other injury sustained in the center, must be covered.
7. *Difficulties in planning costs and payment.* Irregular attendance due to chronic illnesses interferes with financial planning.
8. *Resistance of older adults.* In addition to the internal problems, the resistance of the older population to attending day-care centers must be overcome. Some older people are understandably reluctant to leave familiar surroundings to be with a group of strangers in a new environment.
9. *Neighborhood resistance.* Residents of some neighborhoods do not want a day-care center located near their homes and are voluble in their objections.

Because of these and other problems, many existing day-care centers in the community are meeting the needs of only a small number of individuals. Many day-care centers are open only a few hours a day or a few days a week. In addition, most day-care centers have restrictions, such as refusing incontinent or nonambulatory individuals.

Some hospitals and nursing homes are adding day-care programs located within, or adjacent to, the institutions. With trained health-care workers and medical facilities available, the medical problems that are presented can be managed. Since hospitals are looking for new sources of revenue, it is possible that adult day-care centers established as extensions of hospitals and long-term-care facilities will soon become far more numerous. This should relieve some of the pressure on community agencies that are trying to provide care for the more physically and mentally disabled older men and women.

In addition, the National Institute on Adult Day Care, a program of the National Council on Aging, has been established to provide a means for communication and action for all who work in day care. One of its purposes is to provide assistance and guidance to adult day-care programs and to those seeking to establish new programs, through consultation and other services.

HOME HEALTH SERVICES

Home health services are sometimes erroneously believed to be an innovation that was created with the advent of Medicare. However, in the late 1800s, lay persons organized and administered home nursing services. They taught home care to the ill and their family members, in addition to providing nursing care. In the 1870s and 1880s voluntary agencies provided home nursing care, with the first graduate nurse employed to care for the sick at home in 1877. In the first quarter of the twentieth century, insurance companies added home nursing care to their benefits. By the 1940s, governmental agencies, voluntary health associations, and private insurance companies were providing home care.[8]

The social welfare system has also offered in-home services since the turn of the century. Homemakers have traditionally been provided to families in crisis by private family agencies.[9]

The advent of Medicare and Medicaid regulations for home care certification in 1966 supplied a major impetus toward growth of home health agencies. As their coverage for home health services was discussed in Chapter 7, these two programs will not be reviewed here.

It is important to note that most home health-care agencies, prior to the passage of Medicare, offered only nursing services. The home health nurse often made use of community resources and provided whatever counseling the patients received. However, in order to be certified under Medicare, home-care agencies had to have at least one additional service besides nursing services. Social services began to be added, but are defined in Medicare regulations as *secondary* services, thus requiring a referral in order to provide services, by a *primary* service provider: physician, nurse, or physical, speech, or occupational therapist. Since the social worker is a secondary provider of service and nurses have traditionally been the home-care provider, the nurse usually assumes responsibility for case management.

The major goal of home health care is to maintain patients at home by providing medical care and related health services that are needed. Home health services are provided under the primary physician's orders by community agencies, such as the public health department or Visiting Nurses Association, independent local agencies, and by some hospitals.

The kinds of services provided and the number of professionals employed by home health agencies vary widely. Some agencies offer only a few services, such as nursing care and physical rehabilitation, but many agencies offer a wide range of services that approximate hospital care. These include nursing care and supervision; social work services; physical, occupational, and speech therapy; homemaker services; kidney dialysis; intravenous and intramuscular drug therapy; laboratory and radiology services; and a great number of other kinds of skilled medical and technical services.

Only one or two services are needed by some older people; others need a vast array. The amount of assistance that individuals receive depends on the coverage by Medicaid, Medicare, private insurance, and their other financial resources. This is severely limiting for patients with no private insurance in the states that have inadequate Medicaid coverage for homecare services.

At this time Medicare may provide for rehabilitative or restorative care or care of the chronically ill, as long as the skilled need is identifiable. Many of the patients who need restorative care also need ongoing care in order to continue to maintain themselves in the community. Beallor points out that social workers often find themselves in an untenable ethical position when they identify needs that require attention but which cannot be met under Medicare regulations or with the assistance of Medicaid and other resources.[10]

Social Worker's Role

Social workers in some health-care agencies use their skills in ways similar to social workers on interdisciplinary teams in nursing homes and hospitals. When the agency is initially contacted by the family, the social worker may make a home visit with the nurse and assess the family situation. If the patient has been discharged from a hospital, a social service evaluation may have been made and sent to the social worker before the agency visit. The social worker's responsibilities include performing a full psychosocial evaluation and evaluation of the home in terms of both the emotional and physical environment of the patient. A major service provided by social workers in health care is making use of their knowledge of community resources.

A factor that may enhance the social worker role is the proximity of the family. Interaction between patient and family is more often observable, which may enable social workers to make identification of problem areas more readily. There is the opportunity for counseling of family members. The social worker may work with the patient and family to resolve the many kinds of problems and crises that may occur as a result of illness: financial, housing, and living arrangements; adjustment to changes in bodily functioning and life-style; interfamily relations; concerns in regard to terminal illness; and other related problems.

MENTAL HEALTH SERVICES

Older people appear to comprise the large majority of long term hospitalizations in mental health hospitals. This is thought to be due to the lack of availability of appropriate living arrangements and support services instead of a reflection of serious mental illness of these older patients.[11]

The emphasis on deinstitutionalization that has prevailed in mental hospitals for several years has resulted in pushing out many older people. As they often have few resources in terms of family or community support, they eventually become residents of nursing homes. The process of deinstitutionalization for many older people discharged from mental hospitals has only resulted in a change of institutions.

As the vast majority of older people are living in the community, there is a need for available out-patient mental health services. Federally funded community mental health agencies have been mandated to provide services to older people; however, all older men and women do not have access to these agencies. Research indicates that older people have been underserved by community mental health agencies in the past.[12]

It is likely that members of the future older population who are more attuned to psychology and psychiatry will be less reluctant to seek help for mental health problems and will make more use of out-patient community mental health programs. In addition, some centers are making more effort to publicize services for older people and are assigning trained workers to the geriatric population. With the emphasis on increasing supports in the community for older people, community mental health centers will likely become even more responsive to the needs of this population.

It is important for social workers to be aware that Medicare pays for outpatient treatment of mental illness under a special payment rule. The maximum amount, at this time, that medical insurance can pay for these services is $250 in a year. If charges for these services are used to meet part or all of the $75 deductible payment, the Medicare payment would be less than $250.

When hospitalization for mental health reasons is being considered, the patient and family should know that total expenses for mental health care which is provided in public or private hospitals are not met by Medicare. Private insurance often does not pay in full for such services. Hospitalization, whether public or private, is not totally free.

Some hospitals are opening geriatric units to provide care to older people with physical and mental health problems. As mentioned earlier, adult day-care centers are also being provided by some hospitals which may provide care to patients with mental disorders.

In addition to the traditional providers of mental health care in private practice, there are also social workers in full- or part-time private practice who have had experience in working with older people. They are working with older clients and their families in relation to mental health problems and locating resources.

SENIOR CITIZEN CENTERS

Senior citizen centers offer supportive services of various kinds, as well as a number of programs designed to keep older men and women active, both mentally and physically.

Senior citizen centers are private, nonprofit organizations which may be located in their own buildings or in locations provided by churches, community recreation centers, public housing projects, and other community settings. Group activities, adult education, recreation, referral information, employment services, health education and counseling, day care, and sheltered groups for the physically disabled may be offered. In addition, some of the centers provide meals at reasonable prices, as well as home-delivered meals.

According to a national survey, one-half of the participants are between the ages of 65 and 74 and slightly more than a quarter are ages 75 to 84. The large majority are unmarried women and report incomes of less than $10,000 a year.[13]

Some of the kinds of referrals that are made to senior citizen centers have been discussed in earlier chapters. In addition to responding to referrals and working in the various programs of the center, social workers in senior citizen centers are in a location amenable to identifying potential problems. A number of men and women initially join the centers when they are bereaved or following retirement. Since the members are at the time of life when deaths of relatives and friends occur, this is a constantly recurring event. Members of the center die, sometimes very suddenly, and their deaths may greatly affect other members. Social workers provide supportive counseling, help the members adjust to the losses, and refer clinically depressed individuals for psychotherapy.

Much of the interaction of social workers with the members of the centers is informal. Members seek help for each other by mentioning to the social workers the difficult situations or problems other members are having. Because of the social nature of the setting, social workers are involved with peer group relationships as much as or more so than with family relationships. Some members are rejected or feel rejected by certain groups; jealousy occurs in relation to male–female relationships; friction may occur when women depart from traditional roles; power struggles divide the group. These and other peer-group problems are part of the social worker's concerns.

It should be noted that senior citizen centers vary in the kinds of counseling, health, and activity services that are provided. It is necessary for social workers to become familiar with the centers in their area in order to make appropriate referrals.

EMPLOYMENT

The Title V Senior Community Service Employment Program (SCSEP) authorized under the OAA has three primary objectives: to provide part-time employment for low-income individuals, age 55 and over; to enhance the general welfare of a community by bolstering its human service capacity; and to encourage the transition of older workers to the unsubsidized job market through training, job-finding support, and counseling. This is now a program supporting about 62,500 jobs. In addition, Title V has provided the impetus for many states to become more actively involved with the private sector in helping older men and women to continue or resume employment.[14]

Another impact on employment of older people has been brought about by the Job Training Partnership Act (JTPA), which expresses a federal commitment to help people who have serious employment barriers to become productive members of society. JTPA differs from CETA in that it makes use of program funds for job training instead of for salaries and wages. It also redirects the overall thrust from public service jobs toward the creation of jobs in the private sector.[15]

Social workers who are trying to help older individuals to locate employment should contact their State Unit on Aging for information on older worker training programs. Many states are undertaking innovative programs as a result of the JTPA and the SCSEP.

THE FOSTER GRANDPARENT PROGRAM

The Foster Grandparent Program is open to people 60 years old or over who have low incomes. A modest tax-free stipend, a transportation allowance to visit the child, hot meals while in service, accident insurance, and annual physical examinations are all provided.

A child with special needs is assigned to the foster grandparent who maintains a relationship with the child. Physically disabled, mentally retarded, and disturbed children in institutions receive visits, but in some instances, noninstitutionalized children also have foster grandparents. There is a pilot project involving abused and neglected children which makes use of the Foster Grandparent Program. Another new program involves the use of foster grandparent visits to young prisoners in a training institute.

This program appears to meet the needs of many older people. It is something they feel comfortable doing, providing a needed service to children, and they receive a few benefits which help to increase feelings of self-esteem.

Information for persons who are interested in applying for the Foster Grandparent Program can be obtained from the ACTION regional office or the toll-free number for ACTION.

TRANSPORTATION

Transportation for the elderly is a need that is inadequately met in most communities. Without transportation the elderly person may be unable to carry out everyday chores such as grocery shopping. There may be complete isolation from the larger community, so that the older individual is unable to attend clinics or take advantage of health fairs, attend group meetings in out-patient clinics, or make use of whatever resources the community may offer the elderly.

Many community and voluntary organizations are attempting to address this need. Some senior centers provide buses to transport members to and from the centers, on afternoon excursions, or on longer trips. Other organizations sponsor special buses for needed trips, such as the YMCA in Chicago, which organized a Senior Citizens Mobile Service, offering free transportation to welfare agencies as well as transportation for other outings. Volunteers from churches and civic organizations often provide transportation for trips to hospitals, clinics, and physicians' offices.

A great many cities offer lower rates for public transportation to older people during nonrush hours and on Saturdays and Sundays. This is helpful to the poorer segment of the older population who have no other way to travel. Transportation for older people remains an area that needs to be addressed.

THE ESTABLISHMENT OF GROUPS AS A SUPPORTIVE MEASURE

Group work in hospitals and nursing homes, and some types of self-help groups, have been discussed in earlier chapters. Among the many purposes that groups involving older people in the community may have is that of being a supportive measure to maintain older men and women in the community. An example of this kind of group is the group for families of patients with Alzheimer's disease. The group members exchange ideas and suggestions while being emotionally supportive. One result may be that the patient can be maintained at home a week, month, year, or more longer.

Group work with older individuals may be conducted in a variety of community agencies: mental health clinics, YMCA and YWCA, charitable organizations associated with certain churches, American Red Cross, family and children's services, hospice organizations, day-care centers, and other settings.

It is important for social workers not to overlook referring clients to groups that are not necessarily led by social workers and that do not exclude younger members. There are a great many interest groups that may help the newly widowed person, the recent retiree, and the older individual who has just moved to the community to become involved with others. There are educational groups which may be related to second careers, legal matters, development of community resources, eligibility for programs, politics, and so on. National organizations that are geared to meeting needs of older individuals have a specific appeal. These include The Older Women's League, the Grey Panthers, the National Council of Senior Citizens, the National Caucus of the Black Aged American, and the American Association for Retired People (AARP).

Self-help Groups

As mentioned in an earlier chapter, helping individuals to organize self-help groups is another means that social workers use to enhance mental health and prevent institutionalization. A major difficulty in organizing self-help groups seems to lie in the avoidance of the social worker dominating the group. There may be feelings of ambivalence toward the professional worker. The group feels both grateful and resentful.[16] If the social worker takes the role of facilitator and involves the members during the process of setting up the group, then the members may be better able to plan and direct the course of the group with little further assistance.

The professional worker may play different roles at different points in the life cycle of the group. In the initial stages, professional help may be needed in helping members to leave or come into the group. A disruptive or disturbed member may require referral to more appropriate help. Without such guidance, the group may disband.[17] Other ways the social worker may assist self-help groups is by aiding in the maintenance of the group by having the agency provide clerical services or a place to meet in the community, and by informing other professionals about the existence and effectiveness of the group.[18] Groups are an effective means to provide the socialization that so many older men and women need in order to remain intellectually stimulated and socially involved.

THE CHURCH AND CHURCH-RELATED ORGANIZATIONS AS RESOURCES

There are more than 500,000 churches and synagogues in the United States with a total membership exceeding 140 million. Men and women 65 and older constitute nearly one-fourth of their total membership. Religious organizations are the largest single network of voluntary community organizations which serve the needs of older people.[19]

Many community leaders have turned to the churches for assistance in response to the changes in federal fiscal policies placing responsibility for the needy on local governments. Although churches have traditionally provided recreation and fellowship, and collected money, clothing, and basic food items for distribution to the needy, many of them are broadening existing services and increasing services to the aged. A number of programs reflect the increased awareness of church leaders of the material and supportive needs, as well as the spiritual needs, of older people. Services are often fragmented and vary widely in different areas but are usually provided to members of the community, whether they are members of the church or not.

Most cities have a "Rescue Mission" or "Union Mission," which is largely supported by interdenominational churches in the community, to help the poor, the homeless, or the abused who need food and/or shelter. This resource may be located in the telephone directory under the name of the city or community agencies.

A few churches employ social workers to oversee social services, but most of the Protestant churches depend on a minister, assistant minister, or other person or committee designated by the church to accept referrals of people needing some kind of assistance.

Social workers find that flexibility is a major advantage offered by the informal arrangement of church social services. Individual circumstances can receive more consideration. When a specific situation is described and individual needs are identified, the members of the church are free to respond, in accordance with their available financial and manpower resources. They are not deterred or obstructed by institutionalized rules requiring the client to fit into a certain category before receiving assistance.

In many rural areas which have few formal resources for assisting older people, churches are often a major resource for filling the void. Social workers who are planning hospital discharges call on churches to arrange telephone calls or visits to isolated older people following discharge, to provide transportation to the doctor, "meals on wheels," or other kinds of home assistance.

The church is also a resource when additional space is needed for a specific kind of service. Many kinds of group meetings and activities, such as Alzheimer support groups, are held in churches.

The increasing involvement of churches in meeting the needs of older people is reflected in the literature on aging prepared by churches. Booklets and articles describe the needs of the aging population and discuss ways that programs can be initiated by church members to meet those needs. One such publication, *Aging Persons in the Community of Faith*, by Donald F. Clingan, is in its seventh printing.

Protestant and Catholic churches and synagogues are also working together to meet the needs of older people. In 1972 the National Interfaith Coalition on Aging (NICA) was established. The Coalition involves a national staff from the national religious bodies of the Roman Catholic, Protestant, and Jewish traditions. In addition, there are staff members representing public and private organizations with special expertise in the field of aging who are associate or reciprocal members of the Coalition.

The NICA has been committed to the following primary objectives:

1. To develop an awareness of and to vitalize the role of the church and synagogue with respect to their responsibilities in improving the quality of life for the aging.
2. To identify and give priority to those programs and services for the aging which best may be implemented through the resources of the nation's religious sector.

3. To stimulate cooperative and coordinated action between the nation's religious sector and national private and public organizations and agencies whose programs and services relate to the welfare and dignity of aging people.

4. To encourage the aging to continue giving to society from the wealth of their experiences and to remain active participants in community life.[20]

One of the best known joint efforts of churches in relation to meeting needs of the aged is possibly the Shepherd's Center Concept. Other outstanding charitable organizations which provide assistance to the aged are Catholic Charities and Jewish Family Services. Each of these is discussed briefly in the following paragraphs.

The Shepherd's Center

The Shepherd's Center is not a single place but a concept of services. The original Center in Kansas City has served as a model for the development of over sixty Shepherd's Centers located in inner cities and rural areas throughout the country. In this concept, churches and synagogues work together, using existing space in their facilities for various programs.

The Shepherd's Center concept embodies the idea that older people should have the major responsibility for caring for each other; that they should control the planning and implement the program; and that they should own the organization by contributing to its cost. The prevention of premature and inappropriate institutionalization is central to the concept.[21] It provides a method of empowering older people so that they can assist one another. It is also an expression of the ways that churches and synagogues can work together in a given community so that they can accomplish things that could not be done by individual churches.

Focusing on a limited service area, Shepherd's Centers work with other public and private agencies, but avoid competition and duplication. Informal support systems are strengthened. As older volunteers are essential components, recruiting and training volunteers is a vital part of the program. Volunteers are given the authority to make decisions and take action.

Services that may be provided by Shepherd's Centers include transportation, meals on wheels, handyman services, friendly visitors, sitters for those who cannot stay alone, crisis call service, preventive illness programs, life enrichment classes, support groups, peer counseling, and hospice services for the terminally ill. Although the delivery of home services is limited to a target area, the programs which take place at the Centers are open to anyone living in any area.

Older clients who are interested in organizing this program can obtain information from Shepherd's Centers, International, located in Kansas City. Workshops, seminars, and consultation in relation to starting a Shepherd's Center or conducting programs for older people are offered by this group.

Catholic Charities

Catholic Charities coordinates the charitable social services and social action programs of the Catholic Church. Each diocese provides services in keeping with the needs of that area. Catholic Social Services include the following services: child placement services; family, marriage, individual, and geriatrics counselling; refugee resettlement programs, including recruitment and training of sponsors for refugee families. Short-term emergency assistance is also available.

Volunteers of the Catholic Church operate the Ladies of Charity organization and provide emergency, medical, and material help, such as food and clothing, to the indigent and ill. Services for older men and women that are provided by Catholic Charities in some areas include day-care centers, congregate living, nursing home care, and emergency shelters.

Jewish Family Services

The major emphasis of Jewish Family Services is on counseling. In addition to offering services to children and families, counseling services to older people and their relatives are also provided in such areas as social/health problems, financial and health-care planning, adjustment and family problems. A homemaker/health aid program is available in some areas to assist older people who are able to function at home. Emergency assistance for the indigent may also be obtained from this agency.

The National Council of Jewish Women has been active in developing programs for the older population. In all of their programs for the aged, the emphasis is on older people to remain productive members of the community. Day-care centers and housing for the elderly, Golden Age Clubs, enrichment programs, volunteer placement programs, sheltered employment, nutrition and transportation services, multipurpose centers, and nursing homes are among the projects available in some areas.

Salvation Army

The Salvation Army is both a church and a ministry that is responsive to needs of the community. This denomination has approximately 1100 core community centers throughout the country which provide food and shelter to the homeless, emergency protective care, after-school day care, rehabilitation services to alcoholics, and other services.

LEGAL SERVICES

Most states have legal care programs that are located throughout the state to aid older men and women. If affordable legal aid is difficult to find, the ombudsman for the area may be contacted for assistance in locating legal resources for the client.

There are several legal issues that older people or their families ask about or that arise repeatedly in social work practice. Nearly every older person has questions about wills. Some couples wonder about the legality of common-law marriages. A newly disabled individual may ask the social worker's opinion in regard to adding an apartment to a child's house or signing over property to children in exchange for lifetime care. Others who are beginning to experience memory loss or have impaired vision may inquire about having a relative pay bills. Family members who are concerned about the mental status of their older relative have a number of decisions to make in relation to guardianship, conservatorship, and related concerns. Questions in regard to refusing life supports in terminal conditions are also asked frequently. Social workers may provide general information, and refer clients to lawyers. They often discuss with the client the possible ramifications of actions the client is contemplating, in order to help the individual to understand the need for obtaining professional legal help.

Wills

A will is needed, for if none exists, the estate is disposed of in accordance to the laws of the state, which may be contrary to the wishes of the individual. Social workers urge the client to have a will legally drawn so that there will be no question as to inheritance when the client dies.

Some clients are adamant about refusing to have a lawyer draw up the will. The social worker may find that the refusal stems from fear that witnesses who sign it will be required to know the contents of the will. Witnesses do not have to read the will in order to sign as witnesses; they are testifying to the fact that the person signing the will is actually that individual. If individuals refuse to seek legal counsel, they should be warned that it is difficult to supply the appropriate legal language to carry out the wishes of the person.

There are several other issues related to wills that clients may need to know, including the following:

- Individuals who are adamant about refusing to obtain professional legal assistance should be warned that the will must be written by hand by the person making it, as typing the will makes it invalid.
- If a will has been made in another state, it should be reviewed by a competent attorney, as laws vary from state to state.
- Wills may need revision following divorce, the death of a spouse, death of a child or children, or other change.

As stated earlier, the only way to make certain that the will is legal and expresses the wishes of the client is to have the assistance of a competent attorney in drawing up the will.

Common-Law Marriage

Social workers encounter older couples who have not married but have been living together as man and wife. The couple may have preferred to marry but did not want to have their Social Security checks decreased or alimony payments stopped.

Unfortunately, the couple may believe that if one of them dies, the common-law marriage will entitle the survivor to the same benefits that accompany death of a spouse. Only about 13 states and the District of Columbia recognize common-law marriages. The states that do give recognition have stringent requirements.

The common-law marriage depends primarily on the duration and kind of relationship between the man and woman. It is tested on the basis of whether the couple has "put themselves forward" as man and wife.[22]

Social workers need to know the requirements of the state in which they work and to make certain that this information is communicated to the older community. Older clients who raise questions about entering into a common-law marriage should be referred to an attorney for advice.

Additions to a Relative's Property

Clder couples become concerned about becoming frail and disabled as a result of advancing age or illness and want to plan for the future while they are reasonably well. They begin to consider ways to ensure the welfare of the mate if one should die. They may turn to their children or closest relative to try to work out some kind of living arrangement that will endure until their death. Adding an apartment or building a small cottage adjacent to the relative's home is frequently considered.

The children are agreeable, often enthusiastic and relieved, as they also have been concerned about their parents' becoming disabled or needing temporary or permanent care. Having the couple close to them means that they will be able to monitor the health of their parents. As the move being considered may not involve a few blocks but hundreds or thousands of miles, they are relieved that they will not have to cope with traveling.

Social workers may be consulted when the older couple is considering this change in their lives. The social worker may know the relatives and feel confident that there is genuine warmth and caring on the part of the future caregivers. However, the possible ramifications must be considered. Some of the questions that may be examined include the following: What will happen to the property if the homeowners, or even the older couple, divorce? Will the property then be sold? How will the older couple obtain the money they have invested in the property if it should be sold for any reason? What happens to the total property if the younger couple should die before the older? When the older couple dies, will other relatives feel entitled to a return of the investment?

Legal consultation is necessary so that the couple and the relatives fully understand the legal implications. A legal document should be prepared by a competent attorney so that rights of all involved will be protected.

Signing Over All Property

Some event, such as a sudden disability, usually precedes the decision to sign over a house or farm to a son or daughter in return for the husband and wife having the privilege of living on the place until death. The older parents may feel very grateful to a son or daughter for help that has been given and trust that child so wholeheartedly that the agreement seems very reasonable and sensible.

A son or daughter of the older person may initiate the plan. The suggestion may be made that the home be turned over to them upon the person's death. The parents may be unable to pay the taxes and maintain repairs on the house. If the child must assume the costs of these items, perhaps for years, it seems reasonable that the child be assured that the house will become theirs when the parents die. This suggestion may be made without any intention on the part of the adult child to take advantage of the parent in any way, but in some instances it may be proposed as an unscrupulous effort to gain control of the property.

Problems similar to those involved in adding an apartment to existing property may arise, such as the possibility of divorce or death of the homeowners or the older couple, or a disruption in the relationship. Legal advice is necessary, in order to protect the rights of all parties.

In addition to legal problems, other issues arise, such as the ego effect that the loss of control of the property may have on the older couple. Owning a home, however modest it may be, still endows the owner with an asset which may be a means to exercise control when some kind of control is desired. If everything has already been given, the older person has nothing to negotiate. Much of the care that is provided by children to their parents may be made more bearable by the knowledge or hope that there will be some substantive gain, however small, when the care is ended. If the "gain" took place 10 or 20 years earlier, it may no longer be taken into consideration.

It is also important for the older couple to know the value of the property that they are considering signing over to the relative. In some areas in which older people live, the land may now be worth a great deal more than when it was purchased. The house itself may appear to be worth little, but may now be in a neighborhood that has been designated as "historical," so that it has high restorative value.

Legal issues and the other kinds of issues related to ownership of property are appropriate topics for many groups to discuss. It is important to help older men and women to be aware of the possible results of actions that may seem on the surface relatively simple and reasonable.

Power of Attorney

A power of attorney is a relationship of trust. Creating a power of attorney usually does not require any kind of court procedure or court costs, but requires an attorney's fee. It may be simple, amounting to a notarized statement drawn up by an attorney, or it can be much more complicated and more expensive.

A *limited* power of attorney may be given to a relative or friend which empowers that person to take care of business affairs for a specified length of time. A *general* power of attorney gives the person the right to do anything with the property and possessions that the person has without any restrictions.

In some states a *durable* power of attorney to manage business and other affairs can be arranged which takes effect only after a person becomes disabled. This should be done with great care as it may be difficult to revoke, after the person becomes disabled. "Disabled" should be described specifically in the terms the person wants to have recognized.

A limited or general power of attorney becomes void when the maker is no longer competent. In cases of Alzheimer's disease in which the patient is capable of executing a contract, a durable power of attorney that is specifically designed to continue in effect despite a mental or physical breakdown should be obtained. In some states it can be drawn up in such a way that it becomes effective only when the individual becomes disabled, and it can contain the definition of disability.[23]

Conservatorship and Guardianship

Confusion sometimes exists in regard to the differences between a conservator and a guardian. Guardians are appointed for minors and for *mentally incompetent* adults. The guardian has custody of the individual. A conservator, as the name implies, manages the business affairs of an individual who is unable to look after his or her own business affairs. This person may or may not be physically and (or) mentally incompetent. Older individuals for whom conservators are appointed are often mentally able but are physically too feeble and too weak to manage their affairs. The older person may not be physically disabled or demented but may be easily swayed or persuaded by unscrupulous people to turn over anything of value to them. An unprincipled person who appears very kind and friendly and is helpful in some way may gain control of everything the person owns.

Social workers in hospitals and mental health clinics are frequently approached by relatives about procedures for applying for a guardian or conservator for their older family member. It is vital for professionals who work with older people to identify the extent and kind of mental impairment that may exist. A distinction must be made between the incapacity to write a check, because of arthritis or poor vision, and the incapacity to manage business affairs. The person who is too feeble to attend to personal grooming needs and has abandoned efforts at housekeeping may still be able to keep track of the money that is spent and to make appropriate decisions regarding finances. The utmost care should be taken to examine very closely as many aspects of a situation as possible before stripping an older person of the right to exercise control over his or her affairs. There are countless stories of instances in which older people have lost the right to manage their affairs as a result of an inaccurate appraisal of their abilities.

The legislation governing the appointment of a guardian or conservator varies slightly from state to state. In Tennessee a petition for a conservatorship is filed in the chancery, probate, or county court by the older person, or a friend or relative, for a conservator to be appointed. The petition requests the appointment of a conservator and a guardian ad litem, a person who is usually an attorney, to protect the best interests of the individual needing a conservator. Medical reports from at least two physicians are usually required to substantiate the older person's disabling condition.[24]

The older person is served the petition. The guardian ad litem must call on the individual, explain the petition, and inform the person that he or she has a legal right to contest it. The individual may not object to having a conservator but not wish to accept the person designated. This also can be contested. If the individual wants the conservator appointed and is agreeable to the selection of the person who is the guardian ad litem, it is unnecessary to do anything except leave it to the court.

It is very important for the person who is contesting the petition to be represented by an attorney. Protesting to the guardian ad litem may be of no help, as that person is designated to see that the person's best interests are served and the guardian ad litem's views may differ from those of the older person.

If for some reason it is impossible to have a lawyer represent the person, then that individual should appear in court and explain the objections to the judge. The judge makes the decision as to whether the person needs a conservator or guardian and will make the appointment. If someone is appointed, this person must make an annual accounting of what has been spent for the person, as required by the court.

If the individual becomes able to take care of his affairs, a petition for the restoration of rights can be filed. The judge may restore all rights. If a change in guardianship is requested, the judge may appoint another individual to assume this responsibility.

The procedures for establishing a limited guardianship in Tennessee are very similar to those for conservator, with a few important differences: a jury trial is permitted when requested, the court may give the guardian custody of the person, and the court is required to appoint adversary counsel (an attorney to oppose the appointment, if this seems to be needed). As guardian procedures are more time-consuming and more protective of the person against whom the petition is filed, more cases are filed for appointment of conservators.[25]

If a person with Alzheimer's disease can no longer execute a contract and a durable power of attorney has not been obtained, a petition for limited guardianship or conservatorship must be made. The conservator or limited guardian may make decisions and sign the consent papers necessary for treatment or placement.[26]

It is important to note that obtaining the signature of a relative as the "responsible party" for the patient is not legally sufficient, for this person does not have legal authority to authorize treatment or the withholding of treatment, or the right to sign the patient's name on legal documents. The patient's rights may be violated unless a truly legal representative is involved.[27]

It is important to note that all court costs, including attorney fees, are paid out of the disabled person's funds, if there is an attorney, unless the court decides that no guardian or conservator is needed. In that case, the person who filed the petition is responsible for paying the costs.

As stated at the beginning of this section on guardianship and conservatorship, the procedures vary among states. Social workers should have some understanding of the procedures in the states in which they work, or be able to readily provide an informational resource for the client.

Representative Payee

Many older people are able to manage their business affairs and only need someone to receive and cash their Social Security or other pension checks and pay their bills for them. Application can be made to Social Security for the person specified to receive and cash the check. This may be revoked at any time. As a safeguard against mismanagement, the person designated as representative payee must meet certain reporting requirements. A complete report of how funds have been spent may be required at any time by the Social Security Administration and, if not deemed satisfactory, the person may be removed as payee.[28]

Deciding to Forgo Life-Sustaining Treatment

In 1968 a Harvard Medical School Report on irreversible coma set standards for determining brain death which are now accepted by the majority of medical professionals. In 1983, 31 states and the District of Columbia had brain-death statutes.[29]

Although current laws allow rational individuals to make their own decisions in regard to their health care, physicians, due to fear of malpractice suits, are wary of violating relatives' wishes. The patient's competency to make such decisions may also be questioned.

Several states have legalized the use of "living wills" which instruct the physician attending the person to discontinue artificial efforts to save life, if the person is dying. However, there is no guarantee that this document will prevail when the decision must be made, as there are so many circumstances that cannot be predicted.

Living wills may be a choice for Alzheimer's patients, if they are able to execute this document while they are capable of making rational decisions. A few states allow the appointment of a proxy to be named within the living will. Decisions about the continuation of life supports can be made by the proxy when the patient is incompetent or too ill to make the decision.

Development of a Legal Assistance Program

The need for legal assistance programs for the elderly has been met in one area by the combined efforts of the Southwest Georgia Council on Aging (SOWEGA), the Area Agency on Aging for the region, and a local bar association. Although legal services had been provided through a subcontractor, the services were limited; consequently, a full-time paralegal was employed to organize comprehensive legal services for the older people in the state.

Upon researching the kinds of legal problems the elderly were having, the paralegal found that she could resolve some of the problems, such as applications for Social Security, Supplemental Security Income, veterans' benefits, Medicare, Medicaid, and food stamp applications. There were other needs that required the services of an attorney. She then recruited 14 volunteer lawyers, one for each of the counties served by SOWEGA, to provide legal services to the elderly on a pro bono (reduced fee) basis.

In order to increase lawyer participation, several months later all members of the bar association of the program were informed about the program, invited to participate, to specify their preferred areas of the law, and to name the counties from which they would take referrals. The response was gratifying, more than doubling the number of participating lawyers.

One of the county bar associations has formed its own Elderly Legal Assistance Referral Panel. The impetus for the panel was supplied by the paralegal who assured them that someone would coordinate and maintain the referral system.

The older population is made aware of the availability of legal services through posters listing the paralegal's telephone number and describing the lawyer referral program. These posters are placed in senior centers; the offices of community agencies, such as mental health and family and children's services; and nursing homes and county courthouses. In addition, periodic contacts and monthly visits are made by the paralegal to all the senior centers and nursing homes in the area.

The initial contact with the individual requesting assistance is made by the paralegal. An assessment is made and clients whose needs cannot be met by the paralegal are referred to an attorney who has requested cases in that specific area of law. The paralegal also sets up the initial appointment and advises the attorney that the client is being referred by the Legal Assistance Referral Program. The initial consultation is free. If the case is accepted, a fee is negotiated with the client. Once the legal matter is settled, the attorney fills out a card giving follow-up information so that the progress of the referral panel can be monitored.[30]

The successful organization of this program seems to have depended largely on the efforts of the paralegal and the support of the Council on Aging, the Area Agency on Aging, and the local bar association. It seems possible that other areas could use the organization of this referral panel as a model to obtain legal services for clients.

In addition to working toward locating service for older clients, social workers may exercise their citizen prerogatives. Social workers who provide services to older men and women are aware, as possibly few other professionals may be, of the many unmet needs of the older population. Older clients are often too frail or weak or disabled to pursue their rights vigorously. Advocacy for the provision of adequate health care, nutrition, and a mentally and physically nourishing environment for every older person is a major responsibility of social workers, as well as other caring individuals.

NOTES

1. Julianne S. Oktay, "Maintaining Independent Living: The Role of Community Support Groups," *Aging* no. 349 (1985): 17.

2. *Aging America: Trends and Projections*, 1987–88 edition. Prepared by the U.S. Senate Special Committee on Aging in conjunction with the American Association of Retired Persons, the Federal Council on the Aging, and the U.S. Administration on Aging, 145.

3. Ibid., 144.

4. Ibid., 145.

5. Oktay, "Maintaining Independent Living...," 17.

6. Ruth E. Dunkle and J. Evin Eckert, "Use of Health Services Among Elderly Single-room Occupants," *Health and Social Work* 7, no. 2 (May 1982): 128.

7. *Federal Benefits for Veterans and Dependents*, (Washington, D.C.: Superintendent of Documents, January, 1984).

8. Allen D. Spiegel, *Home Health Care: Home Birthing to Hospice Care* (Owings Mills, Md: National Health Publishing, 1983), 2, 3.

9. Oktay, "Maintaining Independent Living", 16.

10. Gerald Beallor, "Social Work in Home Health Care," Statement to the Health Care Financing Administration on behalf of the National Association of Social Workers, Inc., H.C.F.A. Baltimore, Md. (January 26, 1984), 2.

11. Andrew W. Dobelstein, *Serving Older Adults: Policy, Programs, and Professional Activities*, (Englewood Cliffs, New Jersey: Prentice-Hall, Inc., 1985), 142.

12. Gene D. Cohen, "Prospects for Mental Health and Aging" in *Handbook of Mental Health and Aging*, ed. James E. Birren and R. Bruce Sloan (Englewood Cliffs, N.J.; Prentice-Hall, Inc., 1980), 974.

13. *The Organization, Operation, and Programming of Senior Centers: A National Survey*, John A. Krout, Project Director. Final Report to the AARP Andrus Foundation (June 1983), p. ii.

14. Susan Coombs-Ficke and Ann Lordeman, "State Units Launch Employment Initiatives", *Aging* (February–March, 1984), 19.

15. Ibid., 20.

16. Jennifer Coplon and Judith Strull, "Roles of the Professional in Mutual Aid Groups" in *Social Casework*, (May 1983), p. 262.

17. Ibid., p. 261.

18. Ronald W. Toseland and Lynda Hacker, "Self-help Groups and Professional Involvement", *Social Work*, 27, no. 4 (July 1982): p. 342.

19. Carole Allan and Herman Brotman, comps., *Chartbook on Aging in America: the 1981 White House Conference on Aging*, (Washington, D.C.: Superintendent of Government Documents, n.d.), 140.

20. Donald F. Clingan, *Aging Persons in the Community of Faith*. New revised edition. Published in cooperation with the Institute on Religion and Aging and the Indiana Commission on the Aging and the Aged, 1983, p. xi.

21. *The Shepherd's Center Movement: A Decade of Development.* Speech given by Paul B. Maves at the meeting of Professionals in Aging, September, 1983, Kansas City, Missouri.

22. Donald Breiland and John Lemmon, *Social Work and the Law* (St. Paul, Minn.: West Publishing Co., 1977), 302, 303.

23. William M. Stephens, "Legal Problems of Alzheimer's Victims and Their Families." Abstract of Presentation at Alzheimer's Conference, Nashville, Tenn., (Dec. 3, 1984).

24. William M. Stephens, "Need a Guardian—or Just a Little Help from a Friend?", in *Tennessee Legal Care, Guardianship Issue*, Tennessee Commission on Aging, Nashville, Tenn., pp. 7, 8.

25. Ibid., 8.

26. William M. Stephens, "Problems of Alzheimer's Victims," 6.

27. Ibid.

28. "Need Help In Managing Your Affairs?" in *Legal Problems, Rights & Benefits*, ed. William M. Stephens, (Nashville: Tennessee Commission on Aging, 1981), 25.

29. "Law: Debate on the Boundary of Life," *Time*, (April 11, 1983): 69.

30. "Experience Exchange: What a Paralegal Can Do for an Area Agency on Aging," *Aging* no. 347, (1984): 25–30.

APPENDIX

The helping agencies, organizations, and government services that were presented as resources in *Social Work for Older People* are listed below. The index provides the page number for each resource.

National Citizens' Coalition of Nursing Home Reform

National Council on Aging

National Council of Jewish Women

National Council of Senior Citizens

National Energy and Aging Consortium (NEAC)

National Interfaith Coalition on Aging

National Institute on Adult Day Care

Nutritional Program for Older Americans (NPOA)

Older Woman's League (OWL)

Ostomy Quarterly

Ostomy Rehabilitation Program

Presidents' Council on Fitness and Sports

Reach to Recovery Program

Rescue Mission

Retired Seniors' Volunteer Program

Salvation Army

Senior Citizen Centers

Senior Community Service Employment Program (SCSEP)

Senior Olympics

Shared Housing Resource

Shepherd's Centers, International

Social Services block grants

State Department of Human Services

State Legal Aid, Legal Assistance, or Legal Care Program

State Mental Health and Mental Retardation Department

State Ombudsman for the Elderly

State Public Health Department

Supplemental Security Insurance (SSI)

The 1984 Guide to the Nation's Hospices

The 36-Hour Day

Union Mission

United Ostomy Association

United States Department of Housing and Urban Development (HUD)

United States Social Security Administration

Veterans' Administration

Visiting Nurses' Association

Weatherization Assistance Program

Young Men's Christian Association (YMCA)

Young Women's Christian Association (YWCA)

INDEX